NEGOTIATING
THE
WORLD
ECONOMY

J O H N S . O D E L L

CORNELL UNIVERSITY PRESS ITHACA AND LONDON

First published 2000 by Cornell University Press
First printing, Cornell Paperbacks, 2000

Printed in the United States of America

Library of Congress Cataloging-in-Publication Data

Odell, John S., 1945–
    Negotiating the world economy / John S. Odell.
       p.   cm. — (Cornell studies in political economy)
    Includes bibliographical references and index.
    ISBN 0-8014-3743-1 (cloth) — ISBN 0-8014-8646-7 (pbk.)
    1. International economic relations. 2. Negotiation in business. 3. Commercial treaties.
    I. Title. II. Series.

    HF1359.O3 2000
    341.7'5026—dc21

                             99-055906

Cornell University Press strives to use environmentally responsible suppliers and materials to the fullest extent possible in the publishing of its books. Such materials include vegetable-based, low-VOC inks and acid-free papers that are recycled, totally chlorine-free, or partly composed of nonwood fibers. Books that bear the logo of the FSC (Forest Stewardship Council) use paper taken from forests that have been inspected and certified as meeting the highest standards for environmental and social responsibility. For further information, visit our website at www.cornellpress.cornell.edu.

Cloth printing   10 9 8 7 6 5 4 3 2 1
Paperback printing 10 9 8 7 6 5 4 3 2 1

To my parents

Earl Todd Odell and Jeraldine Busby Odell

Contents

Contents

Figures and Tables

Figures

Tables

Acknowledgments

Diverse projects over the years have added to my understanding of international economic negotiations, even though not all were designed exactly for that purpose, and it is a pleasure to record my gratitude to those who made those projects possible or aided their progress. My first large study concerned international monetary policies and the International Monetary Fund and benefited from support from the Carnegie Endowment for International Peace. A grant from the Ford Foundation in 1979–81 sent me to Brazil, Mexico, Hong Kong, South Korea, and U.S. cities to study trade conflicts between these countries and the United States. In each country I interviewed many former negotiators and industry representatives, who taught an academic much about the real economic bargaining process. During those years I enjoyed faculty support from the Harvard Center for International Affairs, directed by Samuel Huntington.

An International Affairs Fellowship from the Council on Foreign Relations permitted me to spend a year in Washington in 1984–85. For nine months I was attached to the office of the U.S. Trade Representative, where I observed the process from the inside and learned more from experienced practitioners. I came to know the GATT in Geneva for the first time, and that year I also began a fruitful period as a Visiting Fellow at the Institute for International Economics, directed by C. Fred Bergsten. The main product was *Anti-Protection: Changing Forces in United States Trade Politics,* co-authored by I. M. Destler.

The Social Science Research Council honored me with its Fellowship in Foreign Policy Studies in 1987–88. During this time I built a much larger set of cases from which to select and began comparing cases. Some of the results appeared in articles along the way. This fellowship also allowed me to spend more time with finance and trade negotiators in Japan and Korea.

A grant from the Pew Charitable Trusts to the University of Southern California encouraged me to write cases for teaching purposes and to launch my first course on economic bargaining, where I have further refined my ideas. Pew enabled me to conduct field research in Brazil, Belgium, France, the United Kingdom, and Washington on two negotiations covered by this book. Training I conducted in Mexico City for the Mexican Foreign Ministry in 1992 further encouraged me to think these ideas might have practical value.

In 1994–95 I was privileged to spend a sabbatical year at Stanford University, thanks especially to the warm hospitality of Walter Falcon and Coit Blacker of the Institute for International Studies. David Holloway and Michael May of the Center for International Security and Arms Control, Daniel Okimoto of the Asia-

Pacific Research Center, Henry Rowen of the world economic growth project, and Stephen Krasner of the sovereignty project also sponsored and encouraged my work. The Stanford community shared valuable suggestions and helped me make substantial headway drafting this book. That year William Zartman at Johns Hopkins University invited me to join a related project of the Processes of International Negotiation group at the International Institute for Applied Systems Analysis near Vienna. And not least, the University of Southern California Center for International Studies has, since its founding in 1986, provided a stimulating intellectual environment as well as much research assistance. I am deeply grateful for all this generous encouragement and support.

Co-authors and publishers have given permission to incorporate material from earlier papers: Anne Dibble, Margit Matzinger-Tchakerian, and the University of California Press for material in chapter 6, reprinted from Peter Evans et al., *Double-Edged Diplomacy: International Bargaining and Domestic Politics.* Copyright © 1993 by the Regents of the University of California; and Barry Eichengreen and the University of Chicago Press for chapter 8, which appeared in an earlier form as "The United States, The ITO, and the WTO" in *The WTO as an International Organization.* Copyright © 1998 by the University of Chicago. All rights reserved. Parts of chapter 4 appeared in Japanese in *Leviathan.*

I am pleased to acknowledge the fine help of research assistants John Beer, Richard Burkholder, Alberto Cimadamore, Surupa Gupta, Thomas Jacobsen, Gautam Jaggi, Nisha Mody, Jill Obery, Mark Oliver, Silja Bara Omarsdottir, Anna Ponder, Lavone Seetal, Paul Steenhausen, and Tracey Tierney.

For thoughtful comments on chapters or related papers over the years, I am most grateful to David Baldwin, Robert Biller, Vivian Castro, Benjamin Cohen, Eileen Crumm, David Dessler, Marc Dillard, George Downs, Geza Feketekuty, Alexander George, Judith Goldstein, Joanne Gowa, Jana Harrison, Thomas Heller, Robert Jervis, Sung-jun Jo, Saori Katada, Robert Keohane, Jonathan Kirshner, Stephen Krasner, Andrew Kydd, Jeffrey Legro, Scot Macdonald, Andrew Manning, David Mares, Stephen Marks, Lisa Martin, Walter Mattli, Frederick Mayer, Timothy McKeown, Jonathan Mercer, John Meyer, Ronald Mitchell, Robert Mnookin, Ben More, James Morrow, Elayna Mosley, Vai-Lam Mui, Emerson Niou, Robert Neugeboren, Henry Nau, Sharyn O'Halloran, Susan Peterson, Robert Powell, David Priess, Carolyn Rhodes, Peter Rosendorff, Wayne Sandholtz, Leonard Schoppa, George Shultz, Murat Somer, Beth Simmons, Michael B. Smith, Richard Smoke, Debora Spar, Pamela Starr, Shibley Telhami, Alexander Thompson, Gilbert Winham, and Feng Xu.

Hayward Alker, Michaela Dabringhausen, Randall Henning, Gary Hufbauer, Robert Paarlberg, Paul Steenhausen, Andrei Tsygankov, and Virginia Walsh were good enough to work over more than one chapter for me. Several friends made the ultimate sacrifice—laboring through the entire manuscript page by page with painstaking care. I am supremely grateful to Jonathan Aronson, I. M. Destler, Robert Friedheim, Joseph Grieco, Peter Katzenstein, J. P. Singh, Etel Solingen, Roger Tooze, and anonymous referees for sharing their expertise so generously.

All these friends and associates suggested ideas I have incorporated and saved me from some problems.

Editor Roger Haydon of Cornell University Press has long been a superb guide and critic. He also improved this book, like so many others. Finally, a special acknowledgment to my friends Robert Putnam, Robert Keohane, and particularly Peter Katzenstein for their inspiring intellectual leadership. After all this help, the only credible explanation for remaining shortcomings must be the author's limitations.

JOHN S. ODELL

NEGOTIATING THE WORLD ECONOMY

Introduction

Hidero Maki and Michael B. Smith sit across the table from each other, staring in silence, for nearly an hour. Meeting in Tokyo in June 1988, Maki represents Japan; Smith, the United States. Their two governments are embroiled in a long-running dispute over Japanese quotas that limit imports of beef and citrus products. Producers in each country are well organized and vocal, and their preferences are diametrically opposed. Each industry enjoys substantial political support in the national legislature. One deadline has already passed, and the chief executives, Prime Minister Takeshita and President Reagan, are scheduled to meet a few days hence. The delegations are at an impasse.

Suits around a table: the image has become commonplace in our understanding of the contemporary world. Normally we expect a soundtrack as well, and indeed Ambassadors Maki and Smith did eventually resume their exchanges. At the eleventh hour they managed to fashion an agreement that no observer had expected: an end to Japanese beef and citrus quotas.

The image may be commonplace, but the outcomes are often surprising. Currently we work with much less than full understanding as we contemplate the international economic negotiations that shape and reshape our world. What do government negotiators do when bargaining with one another over trade and finance? Why do some talks yield agreements but others end in impasses or ratification failures? What difference does the process make? Can they do better?

Since the end of the Cold War many have said that economics has become as important as security in international relations. Yet even though we embrace the cliché, we still have no general book devoted to the experience of the United States, the most influential player of all, in international economic negotiations.

We are told that world affairs become ever more complex. Yet governments have been conducting economic negotiations ever since sovereign states came into being. To be sure, many Americans, and probably many Chinese and Russians as well, paid less attention before 1989, and especially before 1970, but people in less-gigantic countries took notice long before. If Americans believed during the Cold War that international relations were nothing more than a matter of war and peace between East and West, their thinking was oversimplified. Much of this book's evidence comes, in fact, from the Cold War era, and it shows that that era was certainly not as simple as some would have us believe. If its propositions were valid even then, they ought to be just as relevant, perhaps more so, for periods of lower security threat.

In the future, reliance on negotiation surely will not decline. The much-noted opening of nation-states to integration with regional and world markets has also opened them to new forms of friction and conflict. Considering the depth and speed with which their policies penetrate each other's societies, governments' negotiations may cover more aspects of world society today than at any previous time. With this liberalizing policy trend, governments have constrained their abilities to decree economic and political outcomes and empowered other actors: commercial firms, banks, international agencies, and nongovernmental organizations concerned with the environment, human rights, and peace. All these actors seem destined to be thrown together repeatedly in multiple, overlapping processes of conflict and bargaining. Whatever institutions may prevail in future world affairs, negotiation will determine what they mean in practice for states, firms, and people.

We cannot understand international economic conflict and cooperation without a better grasp of the process of economic negotiation. The central idea of this book, in a nutshell, is that variations in this process make a significant difference to outcomes, and that we can understand the process and practice it better than we do. Current political-economy knowledge emphasizes structures. Sounder understanding of the process would be valuable to any citizen or nation affected by it.

The book expands this main idea into a set of specific causal propositions. It is organized around two core questions: (1) What strategies do international economic negotiators use and why do their strategies vary from case to case? (2) Why do negotiators gain more in some cases and less in others, even when using the same strategy? I concentrate on ten negotiations involving the United States, all from the last half of the twentieth century.

Here is a preview of these specific conclusions. Trade and finance ministers use different negotiating strategies in different cases, and the options are not limited to defecting or cooperating, as other theories have assumed. What negotiators do varies along a theoretical spectrum (spelled out in chap. 2) from a pure distributive strategy on one end to a pure integrative strategy on the other, or from what I call "value claiming" through mixed strategies to "value creating." In many episodes since 1985, for example, Washington's trade negotiators have employed strict value claiming, demanding unrequited concessions from another country and threatening penalties otherwise (chap. 6 develops two cases). In other cases, though, U.S. negotiators have chosen a mixed strategy dominated by distributive tactics but including some integrative moves (chap. 7). On many other occasions the Americans bargained with a roughly-balanced mixed strategy (chap. 5), and in still others with a mixed strategy dominated by tactics from the value-creating end (chaps. 4 and 9). Purely integrative behavior is rarely observed.

The economic negotiator's choice of strategy will vary, among other things, with objective market conditions (chap. 3). Unlike diplomats working for the same government on other issues, the finance or trade official is embedded in interactions with markets as well as with other states. Often, for example, reliance on markets as they stand represents an alternative to creation of a new governmental agreement. The better that market alternative looks to the negotiator, the more she is likely to demand inside the official negotiation, and the less she will concede to get the agreement, other things equal. Should her market alternative worsen during the talks, she is likely to soften her bargaining position (chaps. 3 and 5).

Actual strategy variations may not necessarily track objective conditions perfectly. The real economic diplomat must act with less than complete information. In a hazy atmosphere, her ideas also influence her behavior. Negotiator A's belief about how B will respond to possible strategies—a belief based on more than objective conditions—will also shape A's strategy choice (chap. 4). If the real world is one of bounded rationality, identifying such key beliefs and their effects becomes a productive way to advance knowledge about, and the practice of, economic bargaining.

Strategies in turn shape outcomes. In 1942–44, for example, had either Washington or London used a strict distributive strategy during their financial bargaining, they probably would not have produced the Bretton Woods agreements as we know them (chap. 9). In 1967 Brazil stirred an integrative element into what was an otherwise purely distributive strategy responding to U.S. demands concerning coffee trade, and almost certainly lost less than it would have had it stuck to strict value claiming. In 1988, agreement was out of reach for Ambassador Michael Smith, who was attempting to claim value from Japan on beef trade, until he too added an element of value creation to the mix (chap. 7).

External strategies are not alone in shaping outcomes. Along the way the average negotiator will be subject to common judgment biases, just like the rest of us, and those biases will affect the values that the negotiator places on alternatives to agreement and proposed deals, and how she responds to negative feedback. For example, the more A uses tactics to offset biases on her own side, the more she will gain in the end on average, even without a change in strategy or the broad power structure (chap. 5).

Finance and trade ministers also are embedded in complex two-level political games. While they are doing business with each other on one level, constituents and other officials at home are trying to influence their dealings. Thus, for example, the gains achieved abroad by a threatening distributive strategy will diminish to the extent that domestic politics at home undermines the threatening negotiator's credibility in a foreign capital (chap. 6). Domestic politics also affects the minister's perception of her alternative to international agreement.

Domestic political institutions structure the process of negotiation and ratification after the signing ceremony. These institutions may not change often, but when they do the alterations can improve or worsen outcomes. Chapter 8 shows that requiring the agent to consult with principals more intensively during the negotiation reduces the odds of ratification failure. This chapter also extends earlier analysis to multiparty regime bargaining.

All these propositions focus on the process of international economic bargaining in some way. They emphasize market conditions, negotiators' beliefs, and domestic politics as three key influences on strategies and outcomes. Some claims are specific to economic negotiations whereas others may apply more generally. Chapter 3 highlights what most clearly makes economic negotiations distinct from those confined to political-military issues.

This book's primary audience is scholars interested in the world's political economy. Most of them are not specialists in negotiation, though that is changing. Most of all I write for those who wish to learn in depth about international economic negotiations and to improve theories about them. Simultaneously the book reflects dissatisfaction with the gap between academic theory and real-world policy making—a frustration shared by many academics. It aspires to contribute to theory that will be more useful. Thus I hope the book will also intrigue readers outside the academy—all those in any country who wish to understand the world political economy or negotiation at any level.

This volume grapples with two enduring intellectual challenges in the study of international relations. The first is the phenomenon of negotiation, which is recurrent, widespread, and important. It is far more pervasive than war, fortunately, yet far less studied.

Briefly, *negotiation* and *bargaining* refer to a sequence of actions in which two or more parties address demands and proposals to each other for the ostensible purposes of reaching an agreement and changing the behavior of at least one actor. Concretely, the process of international economic negotiation refers to what finance and trade ministers and diplomats as a group, joined sometimes by others, do with one another. The process includes which strategies negotiators choose, how markets and negotiators influence each other, whether they add tactics to unearth possibilities for joint gains, how much they use tactics to guard against their own biases, and how they go about forming and splitting coalitions. This process includes how the negotiator's moves shift domestic politics in her own and other countries and the odds of subsequent ratification. The *outcome* refers to the terms of a government agreement or implicit settlement (or an impasse), and not the effects official settlements may have later in markets or politics. The *context* involves the surrounding conditions that monetary and trade diplomats normally inherit and cannot influence much in the short run—cultures, international security conditions, international institutions, or domestic political institutions.

Despite substantial good research, social science still does not understand the international economic negotiation process nearly well enough. This shortfall has left vivid marks on public debates about particular negotiations. For example, debates about other areas of public policy—early childhood development programs, pollution regulations, or even trade policy—often show at least some signs of exposure to relevant scientific findings. But when it comes to bargaining, the foundation is often no deeper than common sense homilies. Opinions are expressed with great confidence—"Our diplomats must be tougher with those foreigners"; "Don't damage our long-term political relationships"; "Agriculture must have higher priority this time"—but rarely is an argument for a particular bargaining strategy based on empirical findings of any kind. Many economic negotiators themselves, at least in the United States, are making do with improvisation—based on briefing papers on technical issues and intuitions from personal trial and error, but precious little systematic framework grounded in wider evidence—to guide the bargaining itself.

The second perennial challenge to which this book speaks is methodological: How can analysts of international relations develop theories that will prove valid and empirically more useful? This ultimate purpose—theory that is valid empirically—gets short shrift in too much theoretical writing about international relations (IR). With phenomena like negotiation, where practice poses obvious barriers to the outside observer, what empirical research methods are capable of uncovering relevant facts about real negotiations while simultaneously strengthening generalizations and inferences across cases? This book responds to this challenge primarily by proposing explicit hypotheses and supporting several with focused contrasts between pairs of case studies selected to provide variation on the causal variable but matched with respect to other possible causes.

The resulting book is, I believe, unusual, both empirically and theoretically. Empirically, most work on IR bargaining and conflict resolution is based on observation of only military crises, peace settlements, arms control talks, or the like. This is one of only a handful of books to concentrate on conflict and bargaining over economic issues in general, rather than on one or two cases. It is also the first general analysis, to my knowledge, of the experience of the United States in both monetary and trade bargaining. It reports the inside back-and-forth among diplomats, markets, and constituent organizations. These case studies are not limited to Washington's behavior; each analyzes the experience of at least two governments seen from each side. Readers interested in how agents for Brazil, the European Union, Japan, or Mexico behave in economic bargaining and in how to influence them, will find interesting material here.

Much of our concrete knowledge about monetary and trade negotiations comes from case studies that have not been conducted primarily to develop negotiation theory. This book's cases are selected for theoretical purposes, its main method is comparative, and its main points are relevant beyond the events studied. This volume illustrates a promising method for additional comparative studies on other countries, issues, and times.

Theoretically, this book departs from the most popular meaning of bargaining, as only a devious, manipulative business. Many commentators impose the metaphor of warfare or an athletic contest to interpret examples. Journalists try to evaluate outcomes by asking which side won. Even some specialists define the parties as "opponents," loading conclusions into the language itself. Yet many bargaining outcomes are not like those of wars or most games—they have positive sums. Not all moments in the process look like the eyeball-to-eyeball standoff in the snapshot of Mr. Maki pitted against Mr. Smith.

On the other hand, some negotiation and cooperation studies concentrate on behavior and arrangements that might help everyone win, but neglect distributive behavior. Many actual agreements are not "win-win," despite soothing rhetoric at the end. Some mean gain for one party and loss for the other, relative to the prior status quo. Risks of exploitation are genuine and common, and lasting alternatives to costly conflict will need to include protections against such risks. A win-win bias can also obscure vital aspects even of episodes that do end with joint gains. Here negotiation is defined so as to anticipate both distributive and integrative behavior.

Many cooperation studies (and even some bargaining studies) abstract from what actual negotiators do, or have only a partial conception of what goes into the bargaining process. Concentrating on background conditions, many leave the impression that process does not make much difference. One specific innovation here replaces the binary distinction between defecting and cooperating with the spectrum of strategy options. This concept helps to recognize much more accurately how actual negotiators' strategies vary, while still keeping the range of possibilities simple and ordered. Cooperation studies have also seriously underrepresented two-party cooperation and conflict, which can have large consequences and are emphasized here.

This book assumes negotiators and others make decisions using bounded rationality, setting it apart from works that assume unbounded optimization as well as those that reject rationality. Nor will it fit easily into familiar IR molds such as realism or liberalism or constructivism. Horse-races between their partisans have distracted us, I believe, from the development of useful middle range theory. The evidence in books such as this one compels us to go beyond grand "isms" and toward something else—negotiation theory.

Part 4 highlights the main implications for future research and practice. Scholars can make economic negotiation theory still better and more useful over the long term, chapter 9 argues. Chapter 10 closes with suggestions for improving negotiation performance today.

PART ONE

ELEMENTS OF
ECONOMIC NEGOTIATION

CHAPTER 1

Purposes and Present Knowledge

Every month, national governments negotiate over economic issues with each other and with international organizations and corporations. Why do these governments act as they do during their financial or trade bargaining, and what difference does it all make? How good is our knowledge of this process, and can it be improved? This chapter explains briefly why we need a new study and makes clear what this book aims to do.

A VALID AND USEFUL THEORY

My ultimate aim is a theory of economic negotiation that is better-grounded empirically and more useful than what we have today—useful both inside and outside the United States and outside as well as inside governments. A theory is useful when it helps one to understand the past and present accurately, to reduce the future's apparent uncertainty, or to choose courses of action that are not fundamentally contradicted by events.

Some may doubt that a theory is necessary, or that such a thing is feasible in the case of international negotiation. The most elementary response is that no one can think without theory at some level. Stanley Hoffmann gives us a helpful distinction between theory as a set of questions and theory as a set of answers.[1] In the first sense, theory is a set of concepts telling us how to carve reality into parts, about which we can then gather evidence and draw conclusions. Even observation of a single negotiation and reflection on it requires a theory in this modest sense, and every observer employs some sort of taxonomy or conceptual framework, whether the observer knows it or not. Theory-as-answers is a set of general propositions that connect cause and effect, designed to help us understand why the social world behaves as it does, and how it will probably respond if we attempt to change it.

A second response to the skeptic is that one who must approach every new event like a child—with concepts perhaps, but without any causal generalizations to guide—will be intellectually impoverished and socially ineffective.[2] Every day, adults make personal decisions that reflect at least primitive theoretical knowledge in this second sense. We use general propositions: smoking cigarettes in-

---

[1] Hoffmann 1960.

[2] I avoid "he" and "she" and their forms when possible. When the only alternative is awkward, I use one of the two consistently and they alternate by chapters.

creases the risk of lung cancer; the faster one drives a vehicle, the greater the distance one needs to come to a safe stop; the more hostile my speech to another person, the less friendly the response is likely to be. The manager of a baseball team knows that every pitch will be unique, yet baseball managers often replace a right-handed pitcher with a left-hander when a left-handed batter approaches the plate, for everyone knows that on average the latter combination produces more outs. Likewise, when we consider a past or current international conflict or negotiation, we often reach for patterns to help us classify the events. The effort to improve negotiation theory is an effort to strengthen the general ideas we have available at such times.

Generalizations are never sufficient for understanding any particular event. Theory is not everything but it is essential, and empirical validity is just as important inside the academy as outside. In fact, users of theory are surely more numerous inside the academy than outside. At least some of the time, we should fix our eyes on the prize: What is the best-grounded theory available today? How can it be improved?

BARGAINING AND NEGOTIATION

When developing answers, this book observes several conventions and scope limits. The terms *bargaining* and *negotiation* are used interchangeably. Some have suggested reserving a specialized meaning for each, but the added complexity turns out to be more trouble than it is worth. The *negotiation process* refers broadly to the sequence of actions in which two or more parties address demands and proposals to each other, whatever particular steps it may include in a given case.

Negotiation is not limited to manipulative behavior designed to take advantage of an opponent. Social psychologists have confirmed in laboratory experiments that many people bring a strong initial assumption that negotiation only divides a fixed pie. More striking still, deliberate efforts to train subjects to think otherwise have persistently failed to eliminate this zero-sum mentality, even when interests permit mutual gain.[3] Business professors who teach skills that go beyond the purely distributive find that prolonged and intensive training is necessary before experienced U.S. sales personnel become confident in their ability to negotiate with customers toward mutual gain.[4] Most of this evidence comes from North Americans, but some suggests the bias may be more general.[5] We should discard the war and sports analogies because they fundamentally confuse us. Scope for joint gain is a matter for investigation.

Neither is negotiation only accommodation, conflict resolution, and win-win agreement. Zartman has defined negotiation as nothing but a positive-sum exer-

---

[3] Thompson 1995 and works cited.
[4] Lewicki 1997, 264–65.
[5] Cohen 1996.

cise,[6] one that begins with a shift from a winning mentality to a conciliatory one.[7] Others differentiate between negotiation and coercion or imposition,[8] implying that negotiations are encounters where imposition is absent. Insisting on this meaning, though, would reduce bargaining to virtually an empty set in practice. Coercion and influence are matters of degree and are present in almost every encounter of cooperation or conflict. Put differently, coercion is to negotiation as all is to some. *Coercion* and *all* are extreme end points on continua, and almost the entire continuum is occupied by *negotiation* and *some* respectively. Whenever party A's best alternative to agreement is superior to that of party B and the parties perceive them so, B will feel it is facing unequal influence and A can impose terms less desirable than B would prefer, even when both feel they are gaining from agreement. Only in the theoretical case where parties happened to have equally attractive alternatives to agreement would imposition be balanced. In practice, even bilateral encounters between the largest players, such as the European Union and the United States, are often imbalanced, as we will see. Balance is even less likely in multiparty encounters, with so many more opportunities for pairwise inequality. It is difficult to find any historical international negotiation in which unequal influence and distributional struggle were not at work. It is easy to find bargaining outcomes that benefit one party at the expense of another.

This book is not about all bargaining, only bargaining that is both international and economic. *International* means that at least one party is a national government and at least one other party is based outside that country.

Economic negotiations are those in which parties' demands, offers, and related actions refer to the production, movement or exchange of goods, services, investments (including official development loans), money, information, or their regulation. This book concentrates on trade and finance, but economic bargaining includes other issues such as transportation, communication, and investment. All such episodes share a crucial property that is absent from typical security negotiations: they are sensitive to concrete markets. This market sensitivity is found in many cases that are otherwise diverse. Economic episodes are important enough and distinctive enough for study and yet they have not been viewed together in this light.

Note that *economic* refers to the issues that parties discuss explicitly with each other, not necessarily to the goals that negotiators might have in mind. Suppose government A offered government B a trade or financial concession, and suppose one unstated objective was to make B heavily dependent on A in wartime. I would call this episode an economic—not a military—negotiation in which a secret security objective was heavily weighted. We already have substantial scholarship on

---

[6] Zartman 1987, 6. "By its very nature, it is not a process of winning and losing, so that success must be evaluated against the problem, not against the adversary" (10). Actually, the author's own evidence shows that real parties try very much to win from adversaries and not to lose. A win-win bias also characterizes Fisher and Ury 1981, the world's best-selling negotiation book.

[7] Zartman 1989, 9–10.

[8] Milner 1992; Hopmann 1996, 29.

economic sanctions and statecraft driven primarily by security and other noneconomic purposes.[9] This book instead aims to illuminate the great bulk of economic negotiations—those whose negotiating objectives are economic and domestic-political. Here, where most of the action in economic bargaining probably takes place, received knowledge is much less well developed. Eventually a valid single theory covering both types of economic bargaining would be even more useful.

A third set of negotiations mixes economic with military, human rights, or other issues. For example, the Philippines and the United States bargain over military base rights and foreign aid; Ukraine and Germany negotiate over initial diplomatic recognition and establishment of relations. This book also sets aside such mixed episodes in order to concentrate on those limited to explicit economic issues.[10] There are already many studies of bargaining over military-political issues.[11] It seems sensible to clarify purely economic negotiations next, before investigating whether mixed cases require additional analysis.

PRESENT KNOWLEDGE

We already have many good studies that are relevant in some way, but our knowledge at the moment (including my own previous efforts) is fragmented, disparate in form, and full of gaps. Consider four relevant bodies of knowledge.

Cooperation

International cooperation studies have achieved much and continue to deepen and expand.[12] For present purposes there are also four significant opportunities for further improvement. First and foremost, many empirical investigations have paid little specific attention to negotiators, even though they define cooperation as involving negotiation[13] and most investigations select cases where cooperation resulted from explicit bargaining. Many assume state preferences are fixed by background conditions such as hegemony, interdependence, or domestic institutions. Or they point the spotlight on an international organization and report only thin evidence, if any, about what negotiating strategies the diplomats used and what difference they made.[14] True, international cooperation extends beyond negotia-

---

[9] On this interesting adjacent subject see Baldwin 1985, Hufbauer, Schott, and Elliott 1990, Martin 1992, Kirshner 1995, Morgan and Schwebach 1997, Pape 1997, Elliott 1998, and other works cited there.

[10] Mixed episodes are analyzed in Thompson 1975, Stein 1993, and other sources cited below.

[11] For a sample and additional references see Schelling 1960, Schelling 1966, Snyder and Diesing 1977, Downs and Rocke 1990, Bueno de Mesquita 1990, Weber 1991, Bunn 1992, Leng 1993, George and Simons 1994, Zartman 1995, Bennett 1996, Hopmann 1996, Peterson 1996, and Walter 1997.

[12] These achievements and remaining challenges are well detailed by Haggard and Simmons 1987, Milner 1992, Hasenclever, Mayer, and Rittberger 1997, and Martin and Simmons 1998. The present discussion concentrates on studies of cooperation on economic issues, especially empirical studies.

[13] See definitions in Keohane 1984, 51–52, and Milner 1992.

[14] E.g., Keohane 1984, Webb 1991, Yarbrough and Yarbrough 1992, Simmons 1994, Weber 1994, Suzuki 1994, Iida 1995, Raustiala 1997, Oatley and Nabors 1998, and Remmer 1998. Greater evidence about the external negotiation process can be found in Putnam and Bayne 1987, Jönsson 1987, Iida 1993, and Milner 1997. Related points have been made by Sebenius 1992a and Fearon 1998.

tion to include the institutionalization of rules and the degree to which governments implement and comply with them. But negotiator behavior is not fully determined by international structures. We will better understand cooperation failures and successes if we improve our understanding of the bargaining process.

Second, the empirical literature, as distinct from cooperation theory, tends to restrict cooperation to multilateral institution-building,[15] which is certainly important but only part of the domain. Generally neglected are the many bilateral economic negotiations between governments and others, some producing agreements and others stalemates. Examples include the talks between Britain's Cobden and France's Chevalier in 1860 that propelled European trade liberalization in the mid-nineteenth century; bargaining during the Great Depression that produced discriminatory bilateral agreements between Britain and Denmark, Norway and Argentina;[16] unsuccessful discussions between Norway and Sweden toward a common market during the 1950s; India's and Exxon's 1959 process establishing a joint petroleum refinery; and many bilateral talks over the years between a poorer and a richer state concerning development aid and military aid.[17]

In fact, action in the bilateral talks may be the most consequential—both directly and indirectly via its influence on multiparty processes. According to one veteran diplomat, "what becomes apparent at the [multilateral] negotiation session is often less a product of that meeting than a result of the painstaking groundwork that has occurred, on a bilateral basis, in the weeks or months preceding."[18] If we overlook bilateral cooperation, we deny ourselves many possible observations for studying propositions that apply in both two-party and multiparty cases, and thus risk biased conclusions. Moreover, we cannot isolate the degree to which cooperation is impeded by the number of parties, as distinguished from other conditions that appear in dyadic encounters, regardless of the number of parties.

A third feature of prominent cooperation studies is the suggestion that regimes can be explained using transaction-cost economics. Governments ought to be concerned, when they negotiate to form regimes, about high transaction costs of operating without institutions; regimes should help governments reach negotiated agreements by providing them information or focal points that they would not discover otherwise. While these conjectures seem worthy of investigation, little close empirical research has demonstrated that concerns over prospective transaction costs, rather than other concerns or conditions, really have been significant reasons why governments formed or modified international institutions. Nor is

[15] E.g., Keohane 1984, Young 1989, Grieco 1990, Garrett 1992, Raustiala 1997, and Milner 1997. This is not true of the evidence reported in Oye 1986. A few recent works have applied the term *cooperation* to phenomena other than multilateral regime-building: Martin 1992 on imposition of economic sanctions, Suzuki 1994 on monetary policy, Ross 1995 on China-U.S. relations, Legro 1996 and Goldstein and Pevehouse 1997 on restraint in war fighting, and Remmer 1998 on bilateral treaties.

[16] Oye 1992 develops two-level reasons why discriminatory practices might promote openness in other countries inadvertently, and why even states seeking trade liberalization might engage in bilateral ad hoc bargaining toward discriminatory agreements rather than multiparty bargaining toward rules against discrimination.

[17] Aid negotiations have been analyzed from different angles by Lipson 1976, Thompson 1975, and Mosely 1987.

[18] Benedick 1993, 234.

there much evidence that creating multilaterals has reduced subsequent transaction costs significantly. How much *have* these costs been reduced? How much bilateral negotiation has been displaced? Certainly a great deal of it continues. What about transaction costs that the multilateral adds? Even if institutions do change the process of negotiation among member-governments, the institution is only one possible influence on that process, and it might not be the most important. We can best understand its relative importance, and how it interacts with other variables, if we set it within a fuller conception of bargaining.

The most seminal example of these first three points is Robert Keohane's *After Hegemony* (1984). Keohane used the multilateral negotiation of the International Energy Agency (IEA) in the 1970s as the primary illustration for his theory, which effectively limited cooperation to international institution-building. The book made an eminent theoretical contribution, but it did make clear that the Agency's practical consequences were quite limited.[19] Meanwhile, the book did not examine bilateral bargaining in roughly the same period between Algeria and France. This bargaining led to an agreement on higher gas prices and the movement of billions of cubic meters of gas as well as improved political relations between the two states.[20] The book also does not help us understand why bilateral bargaining between Mexico and the United States failed to make a significant difference in international gas markets and damaged their political relationship. Bilaterals were not its chosen subject. Finally, the book was not intended to report enough of the back-and-forth of negotiating the IEA to show whether the main explanatory variable proposed—the desire to reduce transaction costs of future relations—actually influenced any government's behavior, or how important it was relative to other features of the negotiation.[21] These remain opportunities for further investigation.

Fourth, cooperation research also has generally overlooked agreements that make some parties worse off than they were before negotiation started. An international financial market or a government can worsen another's alternative to agreement. In that situation, all too common in recent years, an unhappy but rational agent may well sign a win-lose deal in which he accepts a loss relative to his prior status quo (though probably not a loss relative to his best alternative available now). Chapter 6 shows that this possibility is hardly trivial for economic diplomats. Now, theorists could choose to define win-lose agreements as outside the boundaries of cooperation. But then a world depicted by cooperation theory would look truncated to the observer and the diplomat,[22] especially one in a disadvantaged country that knows all too well the potential for others to worsen the

---

[19]   Keohane 1984, 224–40.

[20]   Zartman and Bassani 1988.

[21]   Martin and Simmons 1998 reports that more recent work has provided additional evidence that international institutions affect state behavior, but also calls for greater attention to how those effects are achieved.

[22]   In this book the term *negotiator* is occasionally replaced by *diplomat* for relief. Since the latter is meant as a synonym for the former, both refer not only to foreign ministry personnel but to any economic negotiator.

alternatives as a means of squeezing out concessions. Acting on a theory that conceals this type of outcome could be risky. It would be more useful to identify the differences between two cases—where disadvantaged parties achieved beneficial concessions and where they received none. A fuller sampling from the strategies that real diplomats use—their distributive tactics as well as behavior that expands the pie—also would give us better knowledge of how governments produce cooperation failures and successes and how the gains are split. Cooperation studies would be more useful if developed in these four ways.

Formal models

A second relevant body of knowledge consists of mathematical models of international bargaining (a few of which are framed in terms of cooperation). Over the last two decades, game theorists have made their products increasingly realistic and appealing. Deductive theorizing can generate interesting original ideas, sometimes can reveal unsuspected commonalities among particular events, and can uncover inconsistencies in less formal writings. A prominent class of models tackles aspects of the negotiation process by representing rational players with incomplete information, and by thinking about signaling and changes in beliefs during bargaining.[23] Another class has begun to model two-level games.[24]

Most formal IR bargaining models, however, are designed to represent military encounters, not trade or monetary negotiations. Hypotheses from security models might be valid for the latter as well but we have little evidence showing that they are.[25] Furthermore, each method achieves its gains at some cost, of course. The tight integration of the formal model is attained by omitting many ideas that might prove useful but would make the model mathematically intractable. Many models leave no space for decisions or actions that could vary from those predicted by background conditions, and many models still assume an extremely simple set of strategy options, not the range of different things that actual diplomats use. The fundamental assumption that actors maximize their utility often rules out ideas that promise to make theory more useful (more on this later). And many formal articles claim to show that Y depends on X without presenting any evidence at all—neither showing that the conjecture explains a single actual case nor acknowledging that anything is missing.[26] In sum, today's best formal bargaining models have made substantial advances over those of two decades ago, theoretically and empirically on military-political issues. They provide us with interesting analytical ideas, but more can be done in the future. They leave much

[23] See Iida 1993 on monetary bargaining, Fearon 1994, Bueno de Mesquita, Morrow, and Zorick 1997, and the many earlier works cited there.

[24] See Milner and Rosendorff 1997 on trade and other articles in the same issue.

[25] Some case studies of economic conflict or bargaining have, however, applied game theoretic models constructed for the economic issue in question. See Conybeare 1987, Lake 1988, Martin 1992, Aggarwal 1996, and Milner 1997. Another exception is Suzuki 1994 on monetary issues. The international negotiation process gets only thin scrutiny in most of these studies, however.

[26] E.g., Powell 1988, Ward 1990, Snidal 1991, Mo 1994, Iida 1996, Schultz 1998.

uncertainty about which variables have the greatest influence on financial and trade negotiations between governments.[27]

Atheoretical case studies

A third body of knowledge is atheoretical case studies of trade and monetary negotiations. Thorough case studies by historians and others[28] provide evidence on the give-and-take in selected instances and sometimes imply a general hypothesis. But the coverage seems haphazard. And when a case study takes few explicit steps to encourage cumulation with others, its findings tend to remain isolated or even overlooked. Future case studies will be more valuable for generalization if they use and help improve a common theory.

Verbal negotiation theory and case studies

A fourth body is verbal negotiation theory—a diverse set of concepts and hypotheses about negotiation—developed originally in business, law, political science, psychology, and sociology, and applied in selected international cases.[29] This body of work attempts to develop general knowledge about the negotiation process and prizes empirical validity. A few projects have proposed typologies of components, stages, or influences and have described multiple cases in the same language. These, however, sometimes stop short of hypotheses linking cause to specified effects.[30] One set of studies analyzes negotiations between multinational firms and governments.[31] Apart from these business studies, though, most projects in this category also have neglected economic bargaining. Most international relations applications of psychology have been limited to security affairs.[32] Few conflict resolution studies have analyzed financial or trade conflicts. A number of case studies of international economic bargaining have deployed theories in their interpretations or offered general contributions of some type.[33] A few multiple-case studies of economic bargaining have supported causal hypotheses about as-

[27] Outside game theory, Hudson 1991 shows how artificial intelligence modelers attack related problems. Alker 1988 and Duffy, Frederking, and Tucker 1998 illustrate formal dialogical analysis applied to security negotiations.

[28] E.g., Glenny 1970, Clarke 1973, Varg 1976, T. Cohn 1978–1980, Varg 1976, Ravenhill 1979–1980, Sissons 1981, Keeley 1983, Urban 1983, Rooth 1984, Hart, Dymond, and Robertson 1994, and many other case studies written for teaching purposes.

[29] The pioneers of verbal theory were Schelling 1960, Iklé 1964, Walton and McKersie 1965, Fisher and Ury 1981, Raiffa 1982, and Zartman and Berman 1982. Also see Lax and Sebenius 1986 and the review and synthesis in Sebenius 1991 or Sebenius 1992c.

[30] E.g., Zartman and Berman 1982 and Sjöstedt 1993.

[31] Moran 1974, Smith and Wells 1975, Stoever 1981, Encarnation and Wells 1985, Kobrin 1987, Bartlett and Seleny 1998.

[32] E.g., Jervis 1976, Larson 1985, Levy 1994, and Levy 1997. Stein and Pauly 1992 includes unusual attention to economic bargaining.

[33] E.g., Zartman 1971, Odell 1979, Odell 1982, Winham 1986, Hampson and Hart 1994, Kapstein 1994, Mayer 1998.

pects of the process.[34] Overall, however, less-formal negotiation research has also neglected economics, and it could benefit from greater theoretical development and integration. In chapter 2 and later, ideas from this body of literature will be extended to economic negotiation and developed further.[35]

CHOICES AND CAVEATS

We have various fragments of quality knowledge on which to build, but we do not yet have a valid theory of economic negotiation. Where, then, does this book fit in? Most directly, it builds on and contributes to verbal negotiation analysis. It also reflects three deeper choices or premises that can be made explicit, though not defended at length. I contribute an IR theory of the middle range, an eclectic theory, and one that assumes bounded rationality.

Robert Merton, writing for sociologists in 1949, defined middle range theories as those "that lie between the minor but necessary working hypotheses that evolve in abundance during day to day research and the all-inclusive systematic efforts to develop a unified theory that will explain all the observed uniformities of social behavior, social organization, and social change."[36] Theories of the middle range are common in international relations, too.

That is, this is not a polemic for or against any of the grand "isms" of international relations. These all-inclusive theories are used to organize university courses and adversarial debates fancied especially in the United States. Debates between partisans may sharpen arguments and focus attention on research needs, but they also have costs. Most important, decades of empirical research have shown conclusively that none of these grand approaches is adequate by itself. I believe the most lasting advances come from research that concentrates on an important empirical phenomenon, shifts attention toward formulating clear causal hypotheses, rejects an overriding commitment to any single "ism," and combines hypotheses as indicated by the evidence.[37]

Second, my aim is a better-grounded and more-useful theory above all, not necessarily the simplest or most tightly integrated one. Naturally any theory simplifies in some way, and any research program must limit itself in the short run in

---

[34] Odell 1980, Odell 1985, Krauss and Reich 1992; some chapters in Evans, Jacobson, and Putnam 1993; Bayard and Elliott 1994; Ryan 1995; Milner 1997.

[35] A review such as this could reach still farther out into surrounding neighborhoods. E.g., some European Union studies have chronicled its members' special bargaining to establish a common market and build regional political institutions. See Moravcsik 1998 and earlier works cited. Diverse case studies of international environmental negotiations have also generated interesting analytical ideas. Their accomplishments and shortcomings are similar to those on monetary and trade negotiations, according to Parson 1997. Also see Sebenius 1984, Haas 1992, Friedheim 1993, and Young 1994.

[36] Merton 1968, 39. Merton traces this tradition to Mill and Bacon, who cited Plato.

[37] Exemplary in this respect, for example, are Snyder and Diesing 1977 in international security studies, and in political economy, Keohane and Nye 1977. The latter book acknowledges limitations of two "isms" and attempts to show how they might complement each other in an integrated, comparative empirical analysis.

order to make headway. This book aims to contribute greater order in several ways. It is organized around two main dependent variables and concentrates on a few influences on them, deliberately omitting many other possible aspects. It proposes hypotheses that might make sense of other cases too, and chapter 9 shows how negotiation theory might help integrate a wider range of empirical studies over the long term.

The book does not, however, promise an extremely simple theory. In particular, its ideas are not restricted to a set that can be deduced from a single set of axioms. Its propositions benefit heavily from inductive as well as deductive thinking, and they are linked together more loosely, as is the bulk of social science. Simpler is better if there is no loss from simplifying, but the loss from extreme simplification is usually large. Alluring parsimony almost always turns out to be an optical illusion; the partial model fails to account for significant evidence. In fact, international relations has no genuinely parsimonious theories, as George Downs has noted,[38] but only various underdeveloped ones that, as their advocates hope, may become fully developed some day. Facing this trade-off, many of us prefer not to obsess over a loss of tidiness. Simplification is not an end in itself, and over the long term, it is not more important than empirical validity.

Third, in this spirit let us assume that negotiators and others will make decisions using bounded rationality. This premise stands between two better-known positions—unbounded utility maximization and antirationality. Rational choice in its most influential variant assumes the actor has coherent and stable preferences; that he has a fixed set of alternative courses of action; that he knows the probability distribution of outcomes for each alternative; and that he chooses the one he expects to maximize his utility subject to constraints. This agent suffers from no limits on his capacity to make complex calculations. Unbounded rational choice will surely generate valuable new contributions, but it will not be found in this book. I do not assume fixed preferences or maximization. But this need not imply that decision-making is irrational or nonrational. Freudians were perhaps the most extreme partisans for that position, but they decamped from international studies years ago.[39] More recently postmodernists and many others have rejected rational choice analysis.

Bounded rationality, in Herbert Simon's words, means "rational choice that takes into account the cognitive limitations of the decision maker—limitations of both knowledge and computational capacity."[40] The actor "wishes to attain goals and uses his or her mind as well as possible to that end,"[41] but the postulate of ra-

---

[38] Downs 1989.

[39] The authors of one of the most convincing empirical studies drawing on this tradition, George and George 1964, dropped it in subsequent work. As exceptions, Adler, Rosen, and Silverstein 1998 and Kowert and Hermann 1997 explore the effects of emotions and personality types, respectively, in bargaining.

[40] Simon 1997, 291.

[41] Simon 1997, 293. See Simon's seminal 1955 article "A Behavioral Model of Rational Choice," Simon 1982, vol. 2, 239–58. Decision-making studies were influential in international relations during the 1950s and 1960s, but then intellectual fashion mostly moved elsewhere.

tional choice is modified to fit voluminous empirical findings about these systematic limits of the human mind.[42] Briefly, effective preferences are not necessarily
fixed; they can be influenced by such things as the way issues are framed, which
can change as a result of the negotiation process. Rather than consider all conceivable alternative courses of action, the actor conducts a limited search for a
few alternative courses, often following standard operating procedures or social
norms. Instead of maximizing, which is also beyond his computational capacity,
he satisfices. He chooses "an alternative that meets or exceeds specified criteria,
but that is not guaranteed to be either unique or in any sense the best."[43]

This conception of bounded rationality entails the premise that the international negotiator will lack theoretically complete information about the situation—such as how markets will trend in the future, the other side's true reservation value, what deals the other might be persuaded to consider a gain, or how
moves will affect markets and domestic politics both abroad and at home. Imagine, for instance, a trade minister deciding whether to negotiate international
agreements bilaterally or multilaterally. His cabinet expects him to aim at goals
such as improving his nation's living standards while simultaneously protecting
political relationships with other governments and his party's hold on power. Science is plainly inadequate to forecast, with precision and confidence, how a given
strategy or proposal will affect so many complex things, no matter how powerful
the computer. Thus our decision-maker necessarily substitutes simplified rules of
thumb for estimating consequences and putting rough values on alternative
courses of action. These subjective heuristics can in principle be studied, and
some may prove to be widespread and predictable rather than idiosyncratic.

If our bargainer necessarily relies on beliefs about these causal chains, one way
to improve our knowledge of the negotiation process is to study negotiator beliefs: to conjecture which types will make the most difference, gather evidence
about them, and generalize about their sources and effects. A surprising number
of political economists still bend over backward to avoid conceding that what
people think makes any independent difference—an odd position for an intellectual working to influence readers' thinking. A purely objective theory blinds us to
useful insights. After all, one of the things negotiators do is try to change other
parties' beliefs—about whether we can be trusted, how they will benefit from a
proposal, or what will happen to them if they refuse. A much better approach, in
my view, is to replace interests with a combination of concepts, such as market
and political conditions defined objectively plus negotiator beliefs, and to collect
evidence about each. Appendix A presents further responses to common doubts
about international relations theories that incorporate cultures, ideas, and psychology.[44]

---

[42] For introductions and references to these many findings, see chapter 5 as well as Neale and Bazerman 1991, Levy 1997, and Rabin 1998.

[43] Simon 1997, 295.

[44] Note that when it comes to concrete situations, the line between "information" and "rationality"
can be drawn in more than one place. Presumably the unboundedly rational actor seeks out whatever

This book, therefore, embraces both objective and subjective causes in the negotiation process. Chapter 3 concentrates on market conditions defined objectively such as prices of goods and imbalances of payments. Imagine a monetary negotiator estimating likely reactions to a proposal to increase global credit. One objective rule of thumb might tell him to expect support from deficit countries and resistance from surplus countries. Then chapter 4 proposes that A's bargaining strategy will also vary with A's belief about how negotiator B will respond to a given strategy—which could deviate from what B's payments balance seems to indicate. Chapter 5 introduces consideration of subjective biases on A's part, biases of which he may be unaware. In short, once we acknowledge that all rational decision requires cognitive shortcuts, we can consistently treat negotiator beliefs about material causes as hypothetical candidates in the negotiator's mind along with other beliefs or biases. Evidence can shed light on whether any of these hypotheses is valid.[45]

Rationality need not entail other assumptions that often come packaged with it. Rational economic diplomats care about political as well as commercial values and about the long term. This book does emphasize commercial objectives and does not isolate political relationship goals, for instance, as influences on economic bargaining, but it would be interesting to do so. This analytical focus is not inherent in this theory. Rational decision-making also need not mean the state is unitary. On the contrary, each government negotiator is an agent for principals in his country and divisions among principals are common. Some of this book's propositions illuminate how domestic politics complicates what economic negotiators do.

METHOD

This book stems from the inductive case study tradition but also uses general hypotheses and comparison to link its findings to a wider enterprise. Scientific investigation of international negotiation faces daunting methodological challenges, though not unique ones. Official secrecy makes direct, uniform observation of the negotiators' interaction virtually impossible. Then again, uniform observation of war is hardly a simple endeavor either, yet substantial, careful sets of data on that subject have been assembled. That work, though not free of con-

---

information he needs. If a particular diplomat does not have all possible information, this could be modeled either as imperfect information in the hands of an unboundedly rational maximizer, or as incomplete search by a satisficer. Most mathematical theorists have preferred to blame behavioral anomalies on imperfections in information in the hands of presumed maximizers, rather than attempting to model satisficing. This is a modeler's choice, and a few, following Simon, are working to formalize the second approach. In economics see Conlisk 1996; in political science see Bendor 1995.

[45] Operating rules of thumb and policy beliefs can be supplied by social norms, local or international, for the boundedly rational actor is not an atom isolated from socialization. Bounded rationality at the individual level is consistent with some variants of IR constructivism. For an argument that IR constructivists need not and do not reject rationality, see Finnemore and Sikkink 1998 and discussions elsewhere in the same issue.

troversy, has contributed to useful theory on military conflict and its management. In contrast, we have no uniform descriptions of a representative sample of real-world negotiating strategies, for instance, or of governments' bargaining outcomes on trade or monetary issues. We have not even begun to discuss what representativeness would mean. Uniform data on international negotiation by many countries would require research studies in many countries over a long time. Data collection would need to rely partly on indirect measures, such as archives, memoirs, the media, and interviews after the fact. But large efforts have been undertaken for many other subjects of scientific research, from medicine to economic development to mass public opinion to global warming to astronomy. We have not invested proportionate resources in negotiation.

Faced with this lack of uniform data, parts 2 and 3 (except chap. 7) develop and substantiate each major idea by contrasting two negotiations. The pair of observations is chosen to illustrate variation in the cause of interest and the effect while holding other possible causes constant.[46]

Research and analysis entail three steps that overlap in practice and blend inductive and deductive thinking.[47] Step 1 generates hypotheses about strategy choices or outcomes by whatever means prove productive—previous research, deduction, or preliminary study of particular episodes. Step 2 identifies and provisionally selects pairs of strategies or outcomes as candidates for deeper analysis. One chooses some set of countries and some period of time, and within that population, the sampling of negotiations is purposive, not random. The analyst seeks a pair of cases that seem likely to show variation in the causal variable and the effect—the strategy or outcome—but also rules out at least three significant rival hypotheses regarding that same effect. For many of the hypotheses generated in step 1, no such pair of observations has yet been found. Step 2 is also an important time for generating new hypotheses.

In step 3 further research is conducted on candidate pairs, ideas are refined, and inferences are drawn. (Sometimes additional evidence indicates that a possible pair must be rejected because preliminary expectations about the facts are not borne out. If so, work returns to step 2.) Parts 2 and 3 present paired case studies that satisfied these requirements. The purpose in each case is to provide not a comprehensive history but information relevant for the proposition under study.

This two-case method of difference offers four appealing advantages. First, each contrast between two strategies or outcomes poses an interesting puzzle, a sharply posed empirical question whose answer is not obvious. Second, exposure to case studies generates hypotheses about the process that may prove valid. Closer contact with the people whose behavior is under study sharpens intuition and turns up innumerable leads for further investigation. Surely it is vital to learn about the negotiation process in concrete detail in some historical episodes if we

---

[46] This is a variant of Mill's method of difference, using historical evidence. Mill 1843, book 3, VIII, "of the four methods of experimental inquiry."

[47] What follows is a simplification of the process I followed, which though not radically different, was complicated by more tours of box canyons than can well be admitted in public.

are to generalize about it successfully. Of course interesting conjectures can be generated in other ways too, but the further we move away from evidence about the experience to be analyzed, the greater the risk that the conjecture will prove off base.

Third, the method offers strong empirical grounding for a causal hypothesis, compared with the more common single-case study or the set of case studies selected without regard to such threats to inference. Explicit, disciplined comparison gives greater impetus to causal generalization in the first place and over time enhances cumulation. This method also allows much fuller confidence that the hypothesis is valid for the episodes observed than is possible with a statistical method that observes a larger number of cases but measures only a few variables, and then often using proxies. Without conducting a case study, the analyst is simply unable to know about the many aspects of the process that are not observed—which could change interpretation. Even the most comprehensive regression analysis is subject to bias due to measurement error and omitted variables.

Fourth, case studies report much more information about the negotiators' beliefs, tactics, context, and outcomes than would be reported if these dimensions were reduced to statistical variables. The rich case evidence may stimulate others to formulate alternative ideas, to compare and reanalyze diverse published cases, and perhaps to use them as raw material for constructing negotiation variables. Especially now, when we have little general knowledge about economic negotiation confirmed by empirical comparisons even in qualitative form, it seems valuable to report as much information as possible.

Every method has inherent drawbacks as well. Developing two case studies for each major hypothesis necessarily limits the number of propositions one book can cover. This book stops short of presenting a complete analytical picture of the process. It does zero in on critical features, and chapters 3 and 7 supplement the primary method by adding points with lesser empirical support. Chapter 9 shows a way to enhance the picture. Even the most exhaustive research on real history will probably never find two negotiations that are matched perfectly with respect to every possible rival hypothesis; perfection is not a realistic expectation. Even when a pair eliminates many important threats to inference, some remaining differences could be related to the effect. Also we cannot be certain these observations, selected purposively, are representative of a larger population or that the hypothesis is valid generally until research is conducted in other domains. There is no obvious reason why these propositions are likely to be disconfirmed in other instances, but the task of testing them elsewhere remains. Finally, qualitative contrasts deny us statistical techniques that would support more precise claims about the relative magnitudes of different causes.

The product of this method, then, is intermediate—more than rich description but less comprehensive than a true test. Since the ideas were generated in part by looking at the reported cases, the analysis does not constitute a test in the statistical sense. Yet the case pair is not just any two cases. Thorough contrasting case studies that rule out three or more rival causes provide deeper and more rigorous empirical grounding for hypotheses than can be found in many earlier economic bargaining studies.[48] No previous work, to my knowledge, has provided equivalent grounding in economic negotiations for any of the propositions supported here by this method. Such results establish a warrant for more extensive and costly testing. Appendix B provides preliminary operational definitions for some key variables. Only by using multiple, complementary methods can researchers collectively transcend the limits of each.

In part 2 I attempt to use two-party interactions whenever bilateral episodes fit the other requirements. Multiparty negotiations introduce greater complexity and additional threats to inference. Thus the book supplements the picture of international cooperation painted by most empirical political economy. Parts 3 and 4 suggest how these ideas can illuminate multilateral institution-building in new ways.

This theory is designed for any government's negotiations on any economic issue. This book, however, concentrates empirically on the United States and the countries that have accounted for most of its economic bargaining experience since 1945: those of Western Europe, Latin America, and East Asia. I emphasize the United States because my expertise is greatest with respect to its bargaining experience and because no county in the world is more important to more countries or companies. No matter how much one approves or disapproves of how Washington bargains, one must understand it to influence Washington's behavior, to take advantage of it, or to mitigate its consequences. Attention is not limited to Washington's behavior, however. Each case study analyses the experience of at least two governments.

In sum, current knowledge about international economic bargaining is substantial but still disjointed, full of gaps, and greatly in need of improvement. Much of our knowledge of what negotiators do comes from single-case studies that have not generated causal hypotheses and that need to be better integrated into other scholarship. Many empirical studies of international economic cooperation and institutions have concentrated on structure and background factors and neglected processes. Scholars can do much better, and doing better might have some value in practice. This book assumes bounded rationality and works toward a middle-range theory that is well grounded in case study evidence. Chapter 2 operates within these premises to offer a basic set of concepts that may help generate valid hypotheses and integrate related scholarship.

---

[48] Some of the following might be regarded as exceptions: Lieber 1970, Conybeare 1987, Putnam and Bayne 1987, Lake 1988, Evans, Jacobson, and Putnam 1993, Hudec 1993, Bayard and Elliott 1994, Aggarwal 1996, and Milner 1997.

CHAPTER 2

Strategies and Outcomes

The process of negotiation begins with the negotiators' opening moves and strategies and ends with some outcome. As they choose strategies, economic diplomats face a wider range of options than just cooperating or defecting. This chapter introduces a way to classify observed strategies that captures more of this range, while still simplifying. It also clarifies what counts as an outcome, and defines six other concepts that have proved useful in negotiation analysis on other issues and in the classroom. Answers to the eight implied questions describe key dimensions of any negotiation. Subsequent chapters use these building blocks as they develop specific analyses. That is, rather than thinking of the negotiation process in terms of a single overarching concept, let us break it into several variables and explore possible links between them.

The spectrum of strategies, as defined here, is original to this book. The other concepts will be familiar to bargaining specialists,[1] but most international relations scholars and negotiators do not use them in this way. Future case studies that use standardized concepts like these could help us accumulate broader knowledge. This set of concepts also identifies basic information to collect in planning for a negotiation.

BASIC BUILDING BLOCKS

Three key building blocks are *parties*, *issues*, and *objectives*. The first question, "which *parties*?" sometimes raises a crucial practical decision. Should countries negotiate and write rules bilaterally or multilaterally on nuclear proliferation, human rights, and trade issues?

This book concentrates on bargaining among governments, for an adequate analysis of even these predominant parties is still lacking. Each government is represented by individuals, of course, and this book's initial propositions are stated in reference to an individual negotiator. This simplification puts the focus on what negotiators do and helps isolate key causal relationships by temporarily setting aside many complexities. In practice, an economic diplomat typically is limited to some degree by instructions and politics in his country. Later propositions add to the picture by introducing some of those variable constraints.

Non-state players such as multinational firms and environmental groups have

---

[1] Walton and McKersie 1965, Raiffa 1982, Lax and Sebenius 1986, and Walton, Cutcher-Gershenfeld, and McKersie 1994 have been especially influential for my thinking.

become more important over the decades. I hope many of their effects will be captured by defining the process as a two-level political game involving markets. Non-state actors operate through markets or at level 2 and influence official agents interacting at level 1. If non-state actors in some cases are best viewed as parties in their own right, some propositions that explain governments' negotiating behavior may prove valid for them as well.

To make this discussion more concrete, imagine fictional talks to occur next year between two hypothetical parties called "China" and "Russia." Suppose China's people produce a small pump that is especially useful for irrigating farmland, and they have produced a surplus. Suppose Russia's people have a pump deficit. Other countries also export and import comparable farm pumps, but both China and Russia are large players in the world market. Ministers Wang and Pushkin will be agents for the two governments and their countries. China has asked us to analyze the prospects for agreement, considering only a bilateral deal for now, and ignoring internal divisions in both countries.

Suppose for now that the price of the pumps is the only *issue*, and that all pumps are equivalent in quality and other respects. Here *issues* means subjects discussed explicitly and not underlying purposes or objectives. Such subjects appear as points covered by agreements when explicit agreements are reached. Selecting issues to include and exclude is another critical strategic and tactical question.

Suppose every official trade or monetary negotiator will have three types of *objectives*:

- *economic*—to realize commercial or financial gain for my country or avoid loss;
- *relational*—to maintain or increase my country's future influence with the other parties, and hence to avoid worsening their attitudes toward us if possible; and
- *domestic political*—to maintain or increase the popularity of our chief executive or ruling party with constituents.

This last objective is not necessarily irrelevant in authoritarian polities.

These goals may not be fully consistent with one another. Furthermore, the negotiator's priorities may vary. In one case she may place 70 percent of the weight on commercial gain, 25 percent on pleasing voters, and 5 percent on preserving political relationships; in another, the same negotiator may assign 80 percent priority to restoring a damaged relationship. Negotiators for a given country may vary their priorities according to the issue, environmental conditions, or experience. Average weights can vary from one negotiating country to another uniformly, regardless of the issue. The use of percentages to represent weights is only illustrative, naturally. A rough judgment is the most a negotiator will have.[2] Goals will be difficult to observe directly; indirect evidence or proxies may be

---

[2] For a rare effort to assign numbers based on rigorous observation see Friedheim 1993.

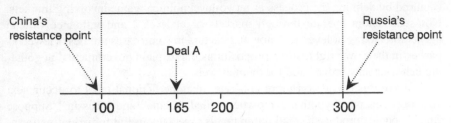

Fig. 1. Resistance points and the zone of agreement

necessary. The negotiator's main objectives and priorities need not be idiosyncratic. Many bargaining goals, determined through a domestic process, are shared effectively by many officials in a government.

The negotiating process itself may shift priorities. One of Pushkin's tactical goals, for instance, may be to raise the salience of the bilateral relationship for Beijing as a way of blunting demands for a painful commercial sacrifice. A theory that recognizes this possibility will be more useful than one that assumes such elements are fixed. For now, however, let us suppose that China wishes only to sell pumps for an attractive price and Russia wishes only to buy pumps at an attractive price. The parties have no other goals.

The resistance point and the zone of agreement

We need additional key concepts to account for parties' behavior and "bargaining power." Suppose each party has some maximum or minimum outcome, such that a hypothetical settlement beyond that point would seem worse than no agreement with the other party at all. *The resistance point* (or reservation value) is the value of the worst deal a party will accept.[3] Suppose that for China, the seller, any deal at a price of 100 or more creates a gain; at any price below 100, Wang would prefer no deal with Russia. For Pushkin, a deal for any price higher than 300 will be worse than no deal at all. The notion of the resistance point applies in all bargaining. For two governments fighting a war and negotiating armistice terms, the resistance point describes the worst armistice terms the party prefers to accept. Offered anything less, it prefers to continue fighting.

The set of possible outcomes between the two resistance points, if any, is known as *the zone of agreement* or contract zone[4] or bargaining range. To estimate the promise of a possible negotiation, we may ask, "do these parties have a

---

[3] Strictly speaking, I should not say "best" or "worst" alternative since I do not assume parties maximize. This usage is widespread, however, and the alternatives are cumbersome. I follow common usage but only after stipulating that here "the best alternative" always means "the approximately best" or the best that will be found by average effort.

[4] Pen 1952.

positive zone of agreement?" Or "can one be opened?" The situation pictured in figure 1 is one in which the potential seller's minimum happens to be lower than the potential buyer's maximum, creating a positive agreement zone. Outside that range no agreement is feasible, and inside more than one is feasible. In choosing among those alternatives, the two parties can set a price only by bargaining. The illustrated agreement at 165 gives Russia the lion's share of the joint gain, but China too is better off than it would be with no Russian agreement.

Nothing guarantees that parties will settle at the midpoint, or that every actual bargaining situation will have a positive zone. As we shall see, conflicts erupt when parties' objectives are opposed and their resistance points create a negative zone at that time. Distributive tactics such as threats are used to move the other party's resistance point and open a positive zone. Recall that the zone of agreement is defined not by the parties' opening positions or highest aspirations but by the *worst* deal each will accept.

The location of the resistance point depends on the party's *best alternative to negotiated agreement* (widely known by the acronym *batna*):[5] the worse the alternative, the lower the resistance point. The batna refers to a course of action outside the negotiation—what the party will do if negotiation ends in stalemate. "Best" means the most satisfactory in the negotiator's eyes. Suppose other countries also offer to buy the same Chinese pumps, and suppose the highest alternative bid is Pakistan's at 100 currency units per pump. Wang's batna would be to sell to Pakistan for 100 per pump judging from these objective data. This alternative would set Wang's resistance point within the China-Russia talks at 100. If Pushkin offers 95, Wang would prefer no deal with Pushkin. If China's alternative improves after the talks begin (say Pakistan increases its bid to 125), we expect Wang's negotiating behavior toward Pushkin to become more demanding, and vice versa. Similarly Pushkin will presumably walk away from the talks if Wang's final asking price is higher than that for equivalent pumps offered by another supplier.[6]

The batna does not mean a course of action to use within the negotiation to achieve an agreement. The value of the no-deal alternative is a net value, including not only the gains to be achieved by following the alternative course, but also any costs that delay or deadlock impose on the party, such as costs a company will suffer by accepting a strike or losses a rebel army will suffer by spurning a deal with a government. The net value of the batna can be negative for a party, just as the net value of an agreement can be negative, relative to the status quo ante.

Two parties' batnas will not necessarily be equally attractive. If no deal means

---

[5] The acronym originated with Fisher and Ury 1981, 104. This central insight appeared at least as early as Zeuthen 1930, chapter 4. Also see Iklé 1964.

[6] Another form of this point in economics is the premise that an agent will consider the opportunity cost of a given choice, including the alternatives that would have to be foregone, as part of her decision calculus.

only discomfort for one but severe loss for the other, we expect the former to have an advantage over the latter in bargaining. Thus identifying the parties' batnas is basic for judging which side is likely to yield on issues in conflict. Thinking in terms of batnas rather than "bargaining power" helps avoid the circularity of so many discussions where the latter term is nothing more than another label for the outcome.[7]

We get closest to the reality of particular situations by thinking of batnas and resistance points as cognitive variables—alternatives as perceived and judgments located in negotiators' minds—rather than relying exclusively on measures defined by the observer. Objective data may be used as proxies, and sometimes we may not have any other information. But government negotiators also care about intangible interests and their rationality is limited. If one has to forecast next week's negotiation between Russia and China, ideally one would know what Wang and her team privately perceive as their alternatives and how attractive or unattractive they regard those alternatives. Do they have a crisp sense of their resistance point, or is it uncertain and subject to framing? If Chinese officials believe signing a commercial deal with Russia will cost more than a deal with other countries, say because of some bilateral political dispute, Wang's genuine resistance point will be higher than indicated by the Pakistani bid. If Pushkin looks only at world pump prices to estimate Wang's resistance point and dismisses Wang's firmness at the table as bluffing, he could lose the deal.

Now suppose a new conflict between China and Vietnam causes Wang to place 50 percent of her priority on improved relations with Russia and less weight on commercial gain. Now China's batna includes the quality of Chinese-Russian political relations in the absence of a trade deal, as well as the highest price China can get from the global pump market. Presumably Wang lowers her price demand.

Another unavoidable complexity in international bargaining arises from two-level games. When the negotiator's objectives include the chief executive's popularity at home, the perceived benefits and costs of each alternative include its effects on domestic politics. Suppose a major constituent in Pushkin's political party is the Russian pump industry, whose production costs are higher than the world average. If this constituent regards imported Chinese pumps as a commercial danger and threatens domestic political penalties, then Pushkin's combined batna is worse than it was before and his resistance point rises, other things equal. In international bargaining, batnas and resistance points can reflect domestic politics.

As we continue, let us set such complexities to one side to help us see the basics of negotiation more clearly. It is difficult to attach accurate numbers to actual negotiators' resistance points even for a single economic issue. Empirical researchers and practitioners must be satisfied with rough estimates.

---

[7] Noted long ago in Schelling 1960, 22.

Possibility frontier

A resistance point is only a minimum. On its own it does not tell how much can be gained from negotiation. To answer that question, a simple one-line diagram may be misleading. It may give the impression that the only way China can gain more is by taking more from Russia. Yet parties in some negotiations expand the pie as well as divide it; they create value that the parties would not enjoy without the bargaining. Commercial negotiations between firms do so every day. Tough bargaining can also destroy value for both if it leaves parties worse off than they would have been without the interaction.

A two-axis diagram (fig. 2) provides a more complete way to imagine diverse negotiating situations. Each point in the diagram represents an outcome, and the two axes give the value to each party. Points to the east represent gains for China, those to the north gains for Russia. The lines C and R mark the parties' resistance points. The outcome at their intersection represents the payoff to each if they reach no deal. At outcomes 1, 2, 3, and 4, each party gains relative to no deal. Suppose there are limits on the gains these parties can achieve by negotiation. Outcome 4 is not feasible, for technological or other reasons. Curve P depicts the theoretical *possibility frontier,* Pareto frontier or efficient frontier. This is an abstract concept of outer limits, not something that negotiators ever know exactly.

Another core analytical question, then, is where the possibility frontier is located. In plain English, "is additional gain feasible from here, and if so, how much? Have we reached the frontier yet, or can we find more gains?" One way to get approximate answers is to assume negotiators will define gains and losses objectively for different countries, but again, more accurate answers will come with better evidence about what possibilities and limits negotiators actually perceive.

The zone of agreement has become the area bounded by C, R, and P, and in figure 2 it is positive. Suppose this diagram depicts Minister Pushkin's perception of the situation, and suppose he and Minister Wang have sketched a provisional deal at point 1. This outcome creates a gain for each party and for the pair when it is

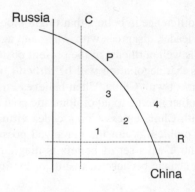

Fig. 2. The possibility frontier and the zone of agreement

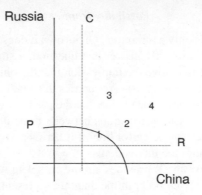

Fig. 3. Agreement near the frontier

compared with no deal. Moving to either point 2 or point 3 would create value for the pair compared with stopping at point 1. A move from 1 to 2 allocates most of the added value to China. Russia will clearly prefer 3 over 2 as well as 1. Any Russian effort to persuade China to abandon 2 in favor of 3 will involve not creating additional joint value but claiming a gain for Russia at China's expense. Outcomes 1, 2, and 3 all leave some potential gain on the table, namely that which would be realized at all points northeast of 2 and 3 but not outside P.

The possibility frontier reminds us graphically not only of possible joint gains but also that not all agreements are equally efficient. Outcomes 2 and 3 are both more efficient than 1. Where the parties' objectives are partly complementary, the negotiation process is partly an exploration for more efficient outcomes.

Suppose Wang, however, believes that previous negotiations have already discovered all possible exchanges and arrangements that benefit both parties, as they define their objectives. Wang believes the provisional deal is already on the frontier. That belief will look like figure 3. If Pushkin takes the initiative in this situation without considering the chance of a different outlook in Beijing, he will probably meet resistance.

This is not the only difference in beliefs that might block agreement. Suppose Chen, another Chinese leader, disagrees with Wang and agrees with Pushkin that the possibility frontier is well northeast of the present position at outcome 1. But Minister Chen believes that negotiation will be difficult because Pushkin is not serious about an agreement with China. Chen believes Pushkin is proposing negotiations to further another international or domestic goal and will not in fact accept any agreement with China unless China cedes virtually the entire gain to Russia. For Chen, the problem is not the perceived possibility frontier but the Russian resistance point. Chen's set of beliefs is diagrammed in figure 4. The zone of agreement can change because of a shift of the frontier or because of a shift in a resistance point.

This theory does not assume parties will always reach the efficient frontier. Attaining this theoretical ideal would be easy in a world of common knowledge,

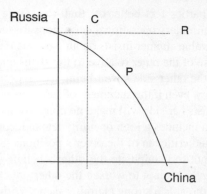

Fig. 4. High Russian resistance point

complete information, and unbounded rationality. In a hazy world of bounded rationality and incentives to misrepresent some of it, doing so is an arduous and uncertain task.

Strategies

Given a preliminary diagnosis of the situation—identifying the parties, issues, objectives, perceived batnas, resistance points and frontier—what should negotiator Wang do? And how is Wang most likely to behave? The negotiator's behavior is described as her *strategy,* a set of behaviors that are observable in principle and associated with a plan to achieve some objective through bargaining. Tactics are particular actions that make up a strategy. Any strategy, when applied, will necessarily be adapted to the special features of the situation; a strategy will not employ exactly the same tactics in every application.[8]

The term *strategy* is used in print to mean dozens of different behavior patterns and goals. Without some discipline, the notion loses its value. Suppose the options vary along the spectrum between two polar ideal types: distributive or value-claiming behavior, and integrative or value-creating behavior.[9] At one pole is the *pure value-claiming* or *distributive* strategy, a set of actions that promote the attainment of one party's goals when they are in conflict with those of the other party.[10] *Offensive* claiming tactics attempt to take value from the other, whereas *defensive* claiming tactics aim to prevent the other from taking value from the first. Distributive behavior is a rational response to a situation in which no settle-

---

[8] Note that *strategy* here does not carry all connotations that are customary in game theory. A strategy does not necessarily specify every possible response to every conceivable contingency. Nor will the choice of strategy necessarily follow directly and simply from objective national interests as attributed to nations by outside analysts.

[9] This continuum is inspired by the investigations by Walton and McKersie (1965 and 1994) on labor-management negotiation, where the separate concepts have proven valuable empirically, and by Lax and Sebenius 1986, who coined these terms and made valuable additions to the theory. Also see Sebenius 1992c.

[10] Walton and McKersie 1965, chapter 2 and Lax and Sebenius 1986, chapter 2.

ment can make both parties feel better-off than they were prior to bargaining. (appendix B offers preliminary operational definitions for these strategies.)

Concretely, a strict value claimer insists on an agreement under which one side will gain at the expense of the other relative to the status quo ante, or at least not lose.[11] Failure to cite the other side's well-being as a reason for negotiating is a sure sign of this strategy, even if the statement of such concern is not taken at face value. The claimer insists her side will make no concessions and resists doing so. The tactical menu also includes a high opening demand, concealing information about true priorities, and criticism of the other's positions. She may concede at a slow rate, delay, attempt to manipulate the other's beliefs about its alternatives and her own, and actually attempt to worsen the other's alternatives and improve her own. The explicit threat is a strong claiming tactic. With a threat, the claimer attempts to establish a commitment to a particular demand, in order to lower the other's resistance point, shift the zone of agreement, and rule out certain points inside it. Various ancillary tactics are used to increase threat credibility.[12]

The greatest risk of tough bargaining is stimulating manipulation and counter-threats from other parties, possibly convincing them that the negotiator is not serious about agreement—hence ending the negotiation, increasing resistance, or at least failing to uncover possibilities for gain that could have been revealed with a different strategy.

The United States has employed relatively pure distributive strategies many times to reduce another country's exports of particular goods. In these cases Washington demanded a concession from an exporting state but refused to make any compensating concessions of its own, such as increasing its imports of other products from the exporting country. In October 1969, for example, the U.S. government began a famous episode of claiming from Japan over textiles trade. Washington's aide-mémoire described its objectives concerning "the textile problem" not as seeking mutual benefit but exclusively by reference to American concerns. It notes:

> apprehension on the part of American management and labor over the rapid rise in imports of textiles and the adverse effect this can have on investment decisions and on employment; the importance which the Government of the United States attaches to the creation and preservation of employment opportunities for minority groups in the United States . . .

The message called on Japan's government to accept a comprehensive five-year bilateral agreement establishing a quantitative limit on exports of every wool and synthetic fiber textile and apparel product to the United States. This document pointed to "strong sentiment in the United States Congress for a legislated solu-

---

[11] The no-deal outcome may be equal to the status quo ante, but the perceived value of no deal may also change during negotiation, as is discussed below.

[12] Many sources develop lists of tactics, including the modern classics such as Schelling 1960, Schelling 1966, and Walton and McKersie 1965.

tion should the attempt to achieve a negotiated solution fail."[13] Later, after two years of fruitless bargaining with Japan, President Nixon escalated this thinly veiled threat to a public threat to impose such limits unilaterally, under the Trading with the Enemy Act. At that point Japan settled for such an agreement, as did Hong Kong, Taiwan, and South Korea.

Claiming is not restricted to the most powerful states. A poor country requesting a gift and declining to reciprocate is attempting to shift value from one party to another. Harsh offensive claiming by the weak against the strong is probably rare, but defensive claiming is common among all states. Delay and refusal to make unrequited concessions are forms of defensive claiming. To classify behavior as "claiming" is not to assume that it will succeed, that it will avoid all concessions or acquire the largest possible share of any gain. Often mutual claiming ends with an unequal split. The claiming strategy can include the tactical retreat—agreeing to accept less than demanded earlier or give up more than conceded earlier.[14]

At the opposite pole is the *pure integrative* or *value-creating* strategy. It involves actions that promote the attainment of goals that are not in fundamental conflict—actions designed to expand rather than split the pie. Many negotiations bring together parties that have some objectives that are not in conflict. Even parties fighting each other in a war sometimes have some overlapping objectives and mixed interests.

In a crystal-clear world of perfect information, each government would know its own and others' goals and priorities, and thus would know whenever a Pareto-improving deal was possible. Such governments would adopt the appropriate strategies and reach the best agreement permitted by their utility functions. Minister Wang, however, may know at the outset only that Minister Pushkin has offered a very low price, lower than she can accept. Pushkin too is often uncertain, prior to bargaining, about whether or how much potential exists to create value. Only by taking action to find out can most actual negotiators discover the limits of that potential. In this hazy world, even a purely self-interested negotiator may consider integrative tactics in order to clear away haze, to discover the parties' preferences (or on a new issue perhaps to crystallize them for the first time), and to search for ways to gain without claiming from the other.

Behaving as a pure *value creator*, Wang would propose that the two parties negotiate toward an agreement designed to make both, not just her side, better off. In Walton's and McKersie's formulation[15] based on U.S. labor-management negotiations, the ideal-type integrative process moves sequentially through three phases. At first the parties explore, discover, and reveal the nature of the problem,

---

[13] United States aide-mémoire of October 2, 1969, rpt. in Destler, Fukui, and Sato 1979, 339–41.

[14] Some theorists, e.g., Pruitt and Rubin 1986, postulate yielding or making concessions as a strategy separate from others. But this behavior is so common that it seems more fruitful theoretically to consider it a tactical adjustment, reserving strategies for more encompassing meanings.

[15] Walton and McKersie 1965, chapters 4 and 5. U.S. labor-management experience of the 1980s led these authors to modify their earlier theory and make it more complex in some respects (Walton et al. 1994). The simpler 1965 formulation seems better suited to present purposes.

their objectives, and their priorities. Throughout the process, openness about information is favored (except information about the parties' true reservation values). Wang will state positions to facilitate identification of rather than conceal underlying concerns and priorities. The negotiator operates less like an institutional role-player with a fixed brief to read and more like an individual assigned to take the initiative in solving a practical problem that affects both sides. In a hostile dispute, the pure value creator listens carefully and probes for underlying reasoning rather than immediately responding to attack with equivalent attacks.

The second phase is a joint search for potential solutions, which may include baking a different pie rather than splitting the existing one, and joint effort to estimate the likely consequences of various options. Desired solutions stated in specific terms replace sermons about abstract principles. Here too inventiveness is favored. In the final phase of a purely integrative negotiation, problem solvers combine their utility functions in some way and test the invented alternative solutions against them. At this stage, if not earlier, the parties explore for concessions that might be valued differently and thus exchanged. One legislator seeking the vote of a second in favor of a given bill might ask the second what other bills the second supports, to find one for which the first could offer to vote in exchange. The integrative bargainer treats all partial agreements as provisional until all issues are settled, to avoid excluding a possible repackaging of the parts that would move the outcome closer to the frontier.

Integrative strategy does not include making a threat and then proposing not to execute it if concessions are made, or actually seizing a hostage and then proposing to give it back in return for concessions. Such actions do not make the other better off than before the threat was issued or the hostage taken. In such cases the first bargaining move is issuing the threat or taking the hostage, and a subsequent proposal to exchange "concessions" is a step in a strategy designed to make the other worse-off, not better off, than before. The offensive claimer is not making any true concessions, giving up something she valued and possessed prior to bargaining. Likewise, if B makes unrequited concessions to claimer A, such concessions are not indicators that B is employing a value-creating strategy. Defensive distributive tactics include making concessions under pressure. Defensive claimer B might decide rationally that she prefers an agreement in which she made some unrequited concessions (a win-lose agreement) over an impasse under which something even worse would befall her.

Integrative behaviors do not necessarily indicate that the negotiator is motivated by altruism, though altruism is not excluded by definition. Nor does value-creating behavior mean failing to work diligently to gain value for one's own side. On the contrary, the concept denotes behaviors that are effective, at least in some situations, in the sense that they benefit the negotiator's own side when certain gains cannot be achieved (or losses avoided) without another party's participation.

In our example, the principal risk of pure value creating is that Pushkin will try to exploit Wang's openness to his own advantage, for example by taking one of her priority goals hostage, that is, by claiming rather than matching her strategy of creating. It is not assumed that B will necessarily reciprocate A's strategy; this is a matter for investigation.[16] Integrative tactics are discussed in more depth in chapter 7.

Nothing requires a negotiator to choose one of these pure polar strategies. Indeed, the ideal of pure integrative behavior has not been documented often in international economic negotiations—only occasionally, as a phase in a longer process[17]—and it is not investigated in this book. Some negotiators mix distributive and integrative tactics so that observed strategies vary by degrees between the poles. The actual strategy spectrum ranges from pure claiming, to claiming diluted by minor integrative moves, to a balanced mix, to mostly value-creative tactics diluted by mild claiming moves.

Concretely, to signal a decision to negotiate by *mixing*, Wang will commit her government to search for an agreement that benefits all parties and not rule out possible concessions by her side. She will invite Pushkin to express true Russian concerns and priorities as opposed to their public positions, and will avoid the harshest claiming tactics. Yet she will also delay her own concessions and attempt to bias the distribution of joint gains in her direction. She will defend her own proposal and resist claiming by others. She may propose a principle of fairness or a formula that would realize gains for both while also shifting their distribution her way.[18] Theoretical tit-for-tat can be seen as one variant of mixed strategy, wherein the negotiator rewards the other for favorable moves and punishes the other for harmful ones. Most, however, have conceived tit-for-tat more narrowly and mechanically, excluding the joint discovery and creative activity captured by the notion of integrative behavior.[19]

Two mixed strategies from the integrative side of the spectrum can be seen in 1942–44 during the process that resulted in the Bretton Woods monetary agreement. Both the U.K. and the U.S. governments took the initiative, each putting forward a proposal designed to benefit many parties, not only itself. At this time, ordinary means of private international payments were blocked and most national currencies were fluctuating as their values were not linked to gold. The U.S. plan

[16] For this reason I refer to distributive and integrative "strategies" or "behavior" rather than distributive or integrative "bargaining." Walton and McKersie originally defined each of the latter as a process involving at least two parties rather than a strategy undertaken by a single party. Their usage is common today. But it tempts us toward the fallacy of assuming that two parties described as engaged in integrative bargaining are each following the same strategy when they are not. Some experimental studies of integrative bargaining do not even report results for individual players; they analyze only the joint profit achieved by the pair of subjects. Kemp and Smith 1994 and Mannix, Tinsley, and Bazerman 1995 are examples.

[17] For example, see Winham 1986, 169–74, on the unusual process whereby E.C. and U.S. negotiators broke a deadlock over rules on trade subsidies and countervailing measures during the Tokyo round.

[18] See Winham 1977 for illustrations and Zartman and Berman 1982 for the useful concept of the negotiation formula.

[19] Most empirical studies of tit-for-tat in international relations have concentrated on military-political issues; see Hopmann 1974, Leng 1993, and Weber 1991. An exception is Rhodes 1993. Chapter 6 takes up threats of retaliation in trade bargaining.

essentially proposed that governments create a new, permanent, intergovernmental organization that, after the war, would deal with exchange-rate instability and payments blockage, and would offer short-term loans to members who agreed to follow common rules toward that end. The institution's capital was to come originally from governments, each paying its subscription in its national currency plus some gold. It was clear to all that the national currency in heaviest demand would be the U.S. dollar. Thus, the proposed fund was a way to loan dollars to needy governments under a set of international rules. The organization was also to be permanent, to operate in conditions that could not be foreseen completely. This relatively integrative U.S. position was a dramatic change compared with the earlier U.S. record. The strategy was diluted with mild distributive tactics to protect special U.S. objectives. The American negotiator initially proposed, for instance, that the United States must have a veto over the organization's decisions, and he firmly rejected John Maynard Keynes's basic scheme to create a new international money and expose the United States to far greater financial liability.

Treasury Secretary Henry Morgenthau launched the conference at Bretton Woods with words that hardly could have exemplified an integrative tactic more exactly:

> We can accomplish this task only if we approach it not as bargainers but as partners—not as rivals but as men who recognize that their common welfare depends, in peace as in war, upon mutual trust and joint endeavor. . . . We are to concern ourselves here with essential steps in the creation of a dynamic world economy. . . . On battlefronts the world over, the young men of our united countries have been dying together—dying for a common purpose. It is not beyond our powers to enable the young men of all our countries to *live* together—to put their energies, their skills, their aspirations into mutual enrichment and peaceful progress.[20]

Later during the conference, Morgenthau, Keynes, and others reiterated this idea of acting more like partners working toward common objectives than like "bargainers" in the selfish sense.

Washington used another strategy from the middle of the spectrum in a monetary negotiation one year after the famous 1971 Nixon shock (an instance of pure claiming discussed in chap. 4). At the annual IMF meeting in 1972, the United States offered a new plan for creating a more flexible monetary system, one still within the Bretton Woods framework of officially pegged exchange rates, which most member states favored. Unlike 1971, the U.S. position now explicitly addressed the shared interests of all members in smoother international adjustment and implied that Washington would not rule out changes to its own policy as part of a deal. One key feature would also have helped the U.S. claim value commercially—a requirement that would have caused surplus countries such as Japan to allow their currencies to appreciate more readily. Treasury Secretary George

[20] Van Dormael 1978, 172–73.

Shultz showed this proposal confidentially to finance ministers of other dominant countries in advance and asked for their comments,[21] another clear change from 1971.

The GATT Tokyo round later in the 1970s also illustrated mixed strategies. This round has been described as "a rulemaking exercise of major proportions."[22] The parties drafted six new international codes, one of which, for example, extended established GATT principles to government procurement. While bargaining to create this larger pie, the typical party also attempted to claim the largest possible share of the gain for itself. In still other cases, parties use mixed strategies from the other side of the spectrum—mainly distributive but diluted with some integrative tactics. Chapter 7 provides two examples.

Issue linkage is found in strategies of every type. When President Nixon imposed a special surcharge on imports in August 1971 and committed not to remove it until other governments revalued their currencies against the dollar, he was linking two issues—exchange-rate policies and the import surcharge—to worsen the others' batnas in an attempt to claim value from them. But in other situations adding a different new issue to a deal will create joint value.[23] When Malaysia asks Japan to reduce its tariff on small machines to 10 percent, and Tokyo agrees on the condition that Kuala Lumpur would cut its duty on large trucks to 15 percent, the negotiators have linked their tariff cuts, presumably because each regards the package deal as a net gain for her side. Some linkages combine issues from within a given area such as tariffs, while others link issues from different areas, such as tariffs plus commercial counterfeiting or human rights.

Likewise, delinking or subtracting an issue from a negotiation can be a tactic for either distributing or creating value. If linking a deal to a new issue will shift value from A to B as in the Nixon example, then subtracting that issue (the import surcharge) will have the opposite distributional consequence. If talking about an issue on which A and B have no zone of agreement will cause deadlock, whereas each negotiator would prefer to accept a mutually beneficial exchange of other concessions (think of China and the United States on human rights and trade), then subtracting the divisive issue, perhaps by moving it to another forum, can free both sides to create joint value on the other matters.

Defining issue linkage as a strategy in itself[24] can confuse analysis by implying that some strategies avoid it. Issue linkage is found in every strategy and negotiation except those that cover only a single issue, and very few negotiated international agreements pertain to a single issue. Whenever a demand or agreement covers more than one provision or issue, and gaining a benefit conferred by one

---

[21] Interview with George Shultz, Palo Alto, California, June 1995.

[22] Winham 1986, 12.

[23] Tollison and Willett 1979 and Sebenius 1983.

[24] E.g., Keohane and Nye 1977, 30, and many later works by others. In other respects my thinking owes much to this landmark study and its authors. Oye 1992, chapter 3, differentiates three forms of linkage.

element is contingent on observing the rest of the deal, issues have been linked. A particular linkage of, for example, trade with a human rights issue that may seem unrelated functionally, is a special case of a ubiquitous phenomenon. What varies from one negotiation to another is which particular sets of issues or issue areas are linked and excluded.

A few other caveats may avert misunderstandings. Value claiming is not the same as a fixed-sum game, and value creating is not the same as a positive-sum game. Value claiming refers to one party's behavior, whereas a game describes a strategic interaction. Nor is it assumed that the negotiator will necessarily perceive a strategic situation the way an observer does—say, as positive sum. Strategy is not simply a function of "interests" defined by observers. Nor is it assumed that if negotiator A perceives a situation as offering opportunities for both to gain, she will necessarily reject a strict claiming strategy. This is one plausible hypothesis, but other influences including domestic politics can be imagined. Chapters 3, 4, and 7 in particular expand on possible influences on strategy choice.

Outcome

Eventually the negotiation terminates in one of two broad states—impasse or agreement. The latter can include the tacit or informal settlement, a pattern of government behavior that is equivalent to compliance with an explicit agreement.

The outcome of an international trade or monetary negotiation refers to the terms of the governments' settlement rather than the behavior of markets after that settlement. In 1986, for example, the governments of Japan and the United States reached a bilateral deal concerning trade in semiconductors. The outcome refers to the terms of that official agreement, in which the government of Japan pledged among other things to take steps to help U.S. firms increase their sales in Japan. The actual magnitude of sales after signature of the agreement is not defined as part of the negotiation outcome, though it may well be an effect of that agreement. Market results such as quantities sold, prices paid, and market shares are of course central goals of both particular constituents and government negotiators. But government negotiators sometimes aim to influence political relationships, international institutions, and other things as well. Subsequent market behavior is typically affected by many economic and political conditions beyond the agreement, so that sound inferences about the effects of an agreement, disentangled from these other causes, can be reached only through careful analysis designed for that purpose. Other scholars conduct much research of that type, and much less has been done on the government behavior that produces these official settlements, which is important enough for some of us to concentrate on it.

Everyone is concerned not only with whether agreement is reached but also with the value of the outcome for the parties—their gains or losses—even though normally we do not measure them exactly. Gain, loss, and value may include intangible as well as tangible items such as exports and exchange rates. Thinking of outcomes as varying by degrees is better than attempting to reduce all negotiations to successes and failures, since the dichotomy discards valuable information. Later chapters will illustrate this point.

Any notion of gain or loss implies some reference point, and negotiation analysts use two different reference points at different times. One is the value of the status quo prior to bargaining. Observers often wish to assess how well a negotiator performed for her organization, and to do so they ask whether it is better off or worse off than before. By this definition an outcome can be described as win-win, if both parties come out better; win-lose, if one comes out better and one worse than before; lose-lose, if both parties come out worse; or zero-sum. This reference point is attractive in being easier to identify by consensus.

A negative evaluation in this sense can be unfair to the negotiator, however, as some of the following cases demonstrate. When a party's batna worsens (as perceived by everyone) after the negotiation process has begun, a rational negotiator may well decide to accept a win-lose agreement, if to refuse would make her side still worse off.

A second common reference point is her batna, her no-deal alternative at a given time, which can be the same as the status quo ante, better, or worse. A gain by this definition means a situation that will be better for her objectives than the situation that would have prevailed had she chosen her batna instead. This second definition brings us closer to understanding the choice the decision maker will probably make at any given time. If she believes she has a better alternative, why would she settle for the deal on the table? And why would she reject that deal if she can find no better alternative today, even when the deal will be worse for her side than the status quo last year?

A disadvantage of the batna reference point is that gains and losses are partly speculative and more difficult to identify by consensus. The negotiator must speculate about what will happen to her side under each scenario. The analyst, looking back at history, must try to discover what negotiators believed would happen under these alternatives, or must approximate by speculating what would have happened to the party had the actual outcome not been reached.

Another disadvantage is that no actual agreed outcome can be classified as a loss. Thus if a major power and a small state use purely distributive behavior on each other and reach agreement, by this definition the small government cannot be described as having lost even when it gives up substantial value it preferred to keep—such as cutting its exports. In this book I try to make clear which of these outcome meanings is in play.

Every outcome has distributional consequences, as figure 5 illustrates. Suppose the reference point for each party is the value of the status quo ante for that party. Points 1 and 3 are win-win and lose-lose outcomes, respectively. At points 2 and 4, one party gains at the expense of the other. Outcomes 1, 5, 6, 7, and 8 make both parties better-off than before. But agreement on 6 rather than 5 distributes more of the joint gain to B than to A. Naturally the negotiator can be expected to care not only about whether she and her counterparts achieve cooperation, but also about how much gain she will take home for her side. Thus it seems likely

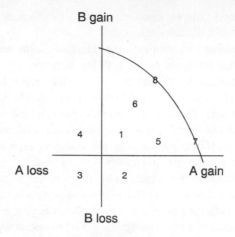

Fig. 5. The outcome distributes the gain

that some value-claiming behavior will appear in any negotiation process at some stage.

The Pareto frontier is therefore not the only region where gains will be divided between the parties—contrary to the implication sometimes taken from Stephen Krasner's much-cited work.[25] Note too that recognizing this simple point does not necessarily imply that we must adopt all the realist school of political thought or reject all other perspectives.

That absolute gains and losses must be split does not necessarily imply that the negotiator will seek relative gains in the sense that preoccupied political science in the 1990s. To conjecture that she will aim to increase the difference between her gains and others' gains, as well as to increase the former, is consistent with this framework. I do not emphasize this line of inquiry here, however, in order to concentrate on others. Each of the two reference points refers to the party itself, either its prior situation or its no-deal alternative at the time, rather than to the other party or the relation between them.

Structures limit outcomes but do not uniquely determine them. The same clearly defined background facts can lead to a wide range of negotiated outcomes. Experiments document such scattering. For example, experienced senior business negotiators and U.S. public officials attending an executive program at the Harvard Business School were randomly assigned roles in a two-party simulation, and each individual playing a given role received exactly the same instructions and fictional interests. Even so, outcomes of different pairs scattered widely across the outer three-fourths of the agreement zone, as shown in figure 6.

[25] Krasner 1991. Krasner 1993, 140, contends that "the basic issue is where states will end up on the Pareto frontier, not how to reach the frontier in the first place." Krasner suggests that political scientists' over-reliance on the simple prisoners dilemma game model, which presents only one outcome where joint gain is possible, may have contributed to overlooking distributional consequences.

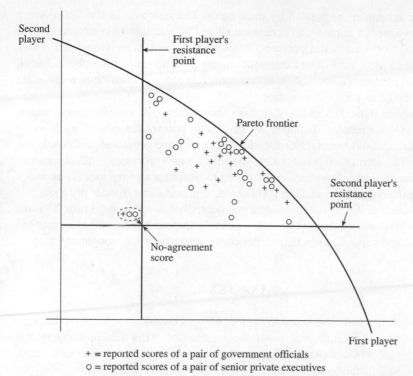

+ = reported scores of a pair of government officials
o = reported scores of a pair of senior private executives

Fig. 6. Outcomes scatter widely and many are inefficient. Adapted from Sebenius 1992a, 340.

Note two other interesting aspects: the variable distribution of gains and the inefficiencies. In some cases where both gained, player 1 claimed the lion's share of the joint value, while in others, player 2 exploited player 1. In a third, larger set the pair divided the gains more equally. The distribution varied even though each player 1 had the same interests, just as each player 2 had the same instructions. Many pairs also settled for inefficient agreements well short of the frontier, failing to realize all gains that were possible given the parties' payoff schedules. Three pairs deadlocked and "went home" completely empty-handed.[26] And these players were veterans of real, complex negotiations, not naive students.

Such results underline the need for research concentrating on the negotiation process. To understand outcomes well, we must investigate bargainers' strategies and how they interact, not just background conditions.

International agreements, once negotiated, often must be ratified before they enter into force. *Ratification* is a formal or informal decision by principals to ac-

[26] Sebenius 1992a, 339–41. Raiffa 1982 (fig. 23, 138) reports an earlier experiment having the same results in all senses—a wide scatter, imbalanced claiming in opposite directions, and many inefficient agreements. Brett et al. 1998 confirms that many negotiated agreements, even between members of the same culture, leave value on the table.

cept an agreement negotiated by their agent. The outcome in the fullest sense refers to either an impasse, an agreement signed by agents but not ratified by their principals, or a ratified agreement. Most of this book selects episodes where agreements were ratified and does not inquire into the ratification phase. Part 4, however, contrasts a ratification failure with a success, indicating how the main ideas may be extended to this stage.

A basic analytical checklist, then, asks about parties, issues, objectives, batnas, the zone of agreement bounded by resistance points, the possibility frontier, strategies, and outcomes. Over the years analysts have generated additional concepts of the negotiation process. One simplifies it as a process of mutual learning, concessions, and convergence on a midpoint.[27] Another sees the process as one of communication and persuasion.[28] Others have postulated a distinct prior stage of pre-negotiation.[29] Each of these ideas undoubtedly has value, yet I hope to show that the set presented here is productive of new hypotheses as well as a means of integrating diverse findings that earlier conceptions have not brought together.

CONTEXT

No book has sufficient space to explore all conceivable influences on the complex process of international economic negotiation. This one deliberately sets aside elements of context mostly for other investigations: variations in security, international institutions, domestic political institutions, and cultures. With one exception, this book does not attempt to observe variations of these types or support or refute claims about their effects.

Context refers to aspects of the situation that are normally beyond the influence of the monetary or trade negotiator, at least in the short term, and are taken as given. Military-political variations also may affect states' economic negotiations, at least under special conditions such as wartime. Yet we have reasons for questioning the cliché that economics and security are inextricably intertwined. The speaker is often either a defender or opponent of a particular proposed policy move and rarely provides comparative evidence to support the claim. There is also a theoretical reason to expect economics to be insulated from security in general. To use military threats or concessions to induce economic concessions, for example, is to assume that such military moves would have no important consequences for the security sphere—a dubious assumption. Surely security moves will be constrained by security conditions and goals and by the bureaucracies that embody them. Similarly on the commercial side, the proposal to bend trade or financial concessions or threats to security goals is likely to meet at least some opposition from the sellers, buyers, and investors who would pay the price—except

---

[27] Bartos 1978, Cross 1978, Hopmann and Smith 1978.
[28] Axelrod 1978, Jönsson 1990.
[29] Stein 1989 and works cited there.

when the commercial moves or opportunities are economically insignificant or perhaps when constituents believe war is imminent. Such opposition may be weaker in authoritarian polities than in democracies.

Some scholars who argue for military-security influence on peacetime economic bargaining provide little evidence. Robert Gilpin, for example, in his influential *U.S. Power and the Multinational Corporation*, asserts:

> In essence, after 1958, a bargain was struck between the three dominant poles of the international economy—the United States, Western Europe, and, to a lesser extent, Japan. Partially for economic reasons, but more importantly for political and strategic ones, Western Europe (primarily West Germany) and Japan agreed to finance the American balance of payments deficit. . . . Thus, after the late 1950s the United States in effect ran its foreign policy largely on credit. The willingness of Europe and, to a lesser extent, of Japan to hold dollars helped make it possible for the United States to maintain its troop commitments in Western Europe and elsewhere around the Soviet and Chinese periphery, to finance foreign aid, and of course to fight the Vietnam War. For its part, the United States, as we have already pointed out, tolerated discrimination against its exports and promoted the creation of the European Economic Community even though the success of the EEC would make it a direct and significant threat to American commercial interests.[30]

No concrete information confirms that the most important beliefs or objectives in states holding dollars were political and strategic ones. In fact many of those dollars were held by private European, Japanese, and other banks and corporations that needed increasing quantities of dollars to conduct international business. As for their governments, the chief reason they did not revalue their currencies after they developed payments surpluses (revaluation would have reduced the surpluses and the U.S. deficit needing financing) was commercial, not military. They did not want to see home goods lose competitiveness at home and abroad.

Vinod Aggarwal 1985, as another example, contends that negotiations in the 1950s and 1960s to regulate international trade in textiles and clothing were nested within a "higher level" international security system, meaning that states made the former conform with the latter if they found inconsistencies. "The best evidence of the paramount importance of the bipolar struggle" in the formation of textile trade policy, the author says (78), is a quotation from a strongly protectionist U.S. senator whose state was home to a concentration of textile workers. The senator bemoaned that exporting countries complain about U.S. measures taken to protect his constituents, and that the State Department, concerned about their protests, was doing too little to protect his constituents. But a legislator's complaint is hardly convincing evidence that the Soviet threat (or anything else) really did restrain American negotiators. Actually, the textile story is one of

[30] Gilpin 1975, 154–55.

steadily widening application of protection, against more and more countries and products, in the face of exporters' repeated protests and despite the Cold War—until the conclusion of the Uruguay round in 1994, after the breakup of the Soviet Union.

The most thorough case study of any bilateral trade negotiation yet published (Destler, Fukui, and Sato 1979) documents that in 1971 President Nixon was even willing to threaten American allies Japan and South Korea with economic sanctions under the 1917 Trading with the Enemy Act in order to extract a concession on textiles trade. Nixon took this remarkable step, moreover, in the midst of strategic nuclear negotiations with the USSR and a hot war in Vietnam—surely a moment when, if the security system really was higher in priority, one would expect special restraint for the sake of allied unity. The case study emphasizes that "high policy" arguments failed to keep allied governments from engaging in a long and damaging commercial dispute.

Many other case studies of peacetime economic negotiations indicate that the parties did not act in response to security conditions or introduce military linkages at all. A lengthy account of the GATT's 1960s Kennedy Round notes that the parties did not include China and the USSR, but otherwise makes no references to security conditions or linkages affecting the negotiation of this major agreement.[31] The same silence, except for peripheral references, prevails in case studies of U.S. trade strategy between 1887 and 1939,[32] the 1965 Canada-U.S. automotive trade pact,[33] Japan's bargaining over exchange rates in 1969–71,[34] the 1970s New International Economic Order bargaining between developing and developed countries,[35] Group of Five monetary negotiations at the Plaza Hotel and the Louvre 1985 through 1987,[36] and the GATT's Uruguay round.[37] Most of these studies were written by political scientists, who should notice possible military-political influences sooner than most observers, and all resulted from deep exposure to empirical evidence. Many of these negotiations took place during the Cold War and some during hot wars. If political scientists fail to find such influence under these conditions, will it be found when the risk of war is lower?

This brief review raises reasons for questioning security claims but it is not sufficient to dismiss them. Instead, the relationship needs more well-focused empirical investigation, and more than this book can provide.

We have theoretical reasons for suspecting that international institutions too may shape bargaining by member-states, and more empirical research on such

---

[31] Preeg 1970. Friman 1993 (404) argues that President Kennedy "played the security card" in U.S. politics, citing the communist threat as a tactic for generating support for passage of the enabling U.S. legislation in 1962. Preeg makes a passing reference to this domestic tactic (46–47).

[32] Lake 1988.

[33] Keeley 1983.

[34] Angel 1991.

[35] Rothstein 1979.

[36] Funabashi 1988.

[37] Hampson and Hart 1994.

connections is needed. At present, we have little comparative empirical research designed to check propositions about effects of institutional variables on the negotiation process, such as choice of strategy and how much each side gains or loses.[38] Long-lasting variations in national political institutions from one state to another might also make a systematic difference.[39] Cultural variations have attracted considerable interest in negotiation studies.[40]

Part 2, however, does not seek regularities of these types. Instead the evidence is selected so as to hold constant four types of context—security, international institutions, domestic institutions, and cultures—in order to uncover more clearly the operation of other possible causal relationships. Part 3 relaxes this restriction in part; there we will observe the effects of changing domestic institutions on the odds a negotiated agreement will be ratified. Part 4 identifies specific research opportunities concerning each type of context.

In sum, the strategy spectrum, the outcome and six other concepts describe basic features of any negotiation. Since the most distinctive aspect of international negotiation on economic issues is that the bargainer's behavior is typically sensitive to commercial markets, it seems sensible to develop implications of this insight next (chap. 3). Some of these market propositions will primarily address strategies, others the rest of the process and outcomes.

Thereafter part 2 will develop several additional hypotheses, each in greater empirical depth and mostly moving beyond market conditions. These may be relevant for negotiation on noneconomic issues as well. Chapter 4 helps explain strategy variation, and the other chapters are about outcomes. This part simplifies greatly, by looking only at two-party interactions where variations in context and in the ratification phase can be discounted as explanations for different results.

In part 2 the book concentrates on policy ideas and domestic politics as well as objective market conditions as major influences on strategies and outcomes. Figure 7 shows how these process variables fit together. It simplifies by representing the negotiation experience for only one party and by omitting the context. The horizontal line represents the sequence of interactions involving all parties, which transmits the influences that feed into it. Chapters 3 and 5 relate market variations to government negotiation strategies and, ultimately, outcomes. Chapters 4 and 5 show that negotiators' beliefs and biases influence strategies and condition strategies' effects on outcomes. Chapter 6 shows how domestic political variation can diminish or amplify gains from the offensive claiming strategy. Chapter 7 focuses on mixed strategies and the effect of strategy choice on the outcome, both of which are discussed further in chapter 9. This diagram depicts only major points

---

[38] Bates 1997, chapter 6, is an exception regarding member states' proposals in negotiations within the International Coffee Organization.

[39] Studies that concentrate on national institutions hypotheses, regarding foreign economic policy in general and not negotiation as such, include Katzenstein 1978, Johnson 1982, Hall 1986, Goodman 1992, Goldstein 1993, Henning 1994, Verdier 1994, O'Halloran 1994, and Destler 1995.

[40] E.g., Cohen 1991, Graham 1993, Faure and Rubin 1993, and works cited.

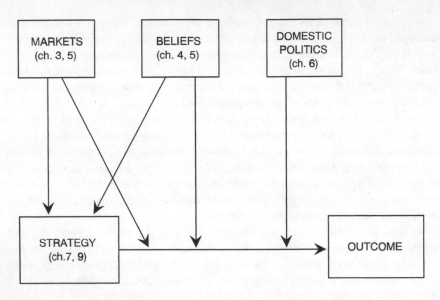

Fig. 7. Negotiation process variables

of this book. Other research could generate additional boxes and arrows, including feedback loops.

Chapter 8 (not shown in this diagram) relaxes two earlier simplifications. It extends these ideas to a pair of multiparty regime cases, and it relaxes the assumption that domestic institutions are invariant, showing how such a change can affect ratification prospects.

CHAPTER 3

Market Conditions

The most fundamental and obvious difference between negotiations over economic issues and other negotiations is that only the former are sensitive to changes in market conditions. Negotiations over airline hijackings, nuclear arsenals, and peace settlements are not sensitive to shifts in financial or commercial markets. Economic policy makers, except in centrally-planned systems, are in the business of promoting and regulating markets. A useful theory of economic negotiation could not ignore them.

Yet surprisingly little effort has been made to sketch out the relationship between market conditions and the rest of the bargaining process in general, beyond a particular episode. Some negotiation and cooperation studies limit themselves to political and psychological ideas developed for political-military issues and overlook some of the most consequential and useful points. Many case studies on monetary, trade, or investment negotiations, though well-informed in the particulars, overlook patterns that can be seen clearly only when economic negotiations are viewed as a set. Another way to miss these points is to work with extremely broad concepts like "interests" and "interdependence" and not theorize specific aspects of markets.

If any economic negotiation will have something to do with some market, which aspects of markets will cause official negotiators to respond in which directions? Which other elements of the process will market changes affect? Do different markets for goods, services, and money all have the same effects on the negotiation process, or should we expect systematic differences across markets? And in light of answers to these questions, how will future negotiators probably take markets into account in their strategies?

Answers will come, in this chapter, from certain insights inspired by economics. Tracing over the checklist of elements of the general negotiation process in chapter 2 generates ten hypotheses or ideas for international economic bargaining in particular. They are illustrated here briefly; this chapter is more exploratory and wide-ranging than those to follow, each of which concentrates on two deeper case studies.

These market propositions differ from other familiar ones, so several caveats may be helpful. First, unlike almost all economics, these ideas refer to a decision maker using bounded rationality. This means these points referring to objective markets give us a first approximation, not necessarily an unqualified prediction, of what he will do. The negotiator will attempt to respond to market conditions and to advance his economy's economic well-being as indicated by these propositions. But given the mind's inherent limitations, he will also rely on cognitive shortcuts and will satisfice. Thus average behavior, responding to interior as well as exterior reality, may not fully confirm hypotheses limited to the "objective situation." In the rest of this chapter each idea will be expressed in streamlined form without this qualification, to keep the presentation manageable. But each point should be interpreted as referring to a diplomat with only bounded rationality and incomplete information.

Second, the text says "market," not "free market." The markets discussed here are actual ones, not imaginary ones depicted in economics textbooks as free of all government influence. We are in a world political economy, where every actual market reflects the government institutions and policies under which it operates, ultimately. Of course we can still observe price increases and declines. These are examples of changes in actual market conditions. Describing them does not imply any particular claim about what produced them.

Third and related, the primary purpose is not to explain market performance— to trace market behavior to its own roots, further back up the causal chain. Many economics and other studies are designed to address those questions. This chapter concentrates instead on explaining what government negotiators do, and isolates features of their market environment as one possible set of clues.

Referring to a market does not, in itself, imply perfect competition, private enterprises only, or movement toward improved efficiency or welfare. Nor is it to contend that governments *ought to* respond to markets by changing their policies as these markets seem to be signaling. The primary inquiry here concerns what official negotiators *will* most probably do in the presence of market pressures, whether we like it or not. Ultimately we may hope that sounder knowledge of the process will also make possible better practical decisions.

Finally, this chapter, like all those in parts 2 and 3, is partial. Each claim should be understood as ceteris paribus. Even if a market proposition is valid on average while other influences are held constant, those other causes may vary as well, and they may override the market's incentives in a given case. Negotiator beliefs and domestic politics are examples of other causes that may be partly independent of market conditions. Official negotiators will not behave in every case as market propositions lead us to expect.

Let us begin by assuming that the market is exogenous for the negotiator, then relax this assumption later. The former is the simpler place to begin, even though in practice the distinction is a matter of degree.

PARTIES AND STRATEGIES

1. *Market conditions help determine the parties themselves in economic negotiations* as opposed to security and other negotiations, of course. The states that depend most on exports and imports of a good will be most likely to participate in a negotiation to liberalize trade in that good. The global distribution of supply and

demand of a service will determine the parties in bargaining over that service. An international debt crisis will tend to be dominated by key debtors and creditors. A major power, judged in terms of overall military and economic assets, may not participate actively in a negotiation concerning debt repayments if it does not hold significant distressed debt or credit. Likewise, market changes over time sometimes will add or subtract parties. Textiles, the first manufacturing industry, spread successively to more and more countries. After 1960 as investors set up export platforms in each new country, government negotiations to regulate textile trade predictably added each country as a party. In the mid 1980s, the computer industry was not typical of those seeking trade protection, and many were surprised in 1985 when Washington began complaining to Japan about semiconductors. Those monitoring this particular product market, however, had seen clear changes—growing supply, recession, and financial losses hitting U.S. producers at home, expanding Japanese exports to the United States, and the remarkably small share U.S. firms had carved out in Japan, despite the global technological lead of the United States. These market conditions influenced Washington's decisions, though not without controversy.[1] Bank regulators continually monitor commercial banks' inventions of new financial instruments and practices, and such market developments have caused the governments that host dominant banks to negotiate with each other over the consequences. Chapter 9 illustrates this change with the 1984–88 case of bank capital adequacy regulations.

Markets also vary as to the degree of concentration among firms. For negotiations over highly concentrated markets, it is more useful for the analyst to think of the dominant firm or oligopoly as a potential party too, at least informally, one whose actions are able to influence the behavior of other parties much as governments do. Influencing its moves might be an equally important element of strategy in such market conditions, and ignoring it might be highly misleading. Several examples are provided later in this chapter. In a negotiation between a host government and a multinational firm or firms over a direct investment, of course the firms are parties by definition.[2]

The negotiator's objectives and priorities will also presumably vary with his country's position in the world market, though possibly for other reasons as well, such as security or domestic political conditions. The average agent for a wheat-exporting country will emphasize higher prices and lower barriers to its exports more than other negotiators, while the importing country will probably aim for lower prices to the extent possible, at least as long as objectives mean those of the country as a whole. In monetary bargaining, the average negotiator for a country with a persisting payments deficit will give larger weight to liberal provision of international credit, while agents for countries with persisting surpluses can be expected to attach much lower priority to that objective.

2. When two countries are on the same side of a market, their governments are

---

[1] For other accounts see Prestowitz 1988, Tyson 1992, chapter 4, and Krauss 1993.
[2] Chapter 1 cited some literature on such cases. For analysis of policy implications of international and domestic corporate alliances, see Cowhey and Aronson 1993.

more likely to use integrative tactics in their strategies toward each other than when they are on opposite sides, where we should observe more distributive tactics toward each other. The analyst should certainly not overlook differences in objective market conditions as natural influences on future strategies either, even though beliefs and domestic politics could push strategies in other directions. For starters, two states A and B whose commercial goals will gain or suffer from the same price change are especially likely to succeed in reaching a mutually beneficial agreement between the two of them, including tactical agreement to form an alliance in a larger negotiation. A's negotiator is likely to want to avoid tactics vis-à-vis that would interfere with realization of this apparent common interest, and will probably emphasize tactics that are designed to uncover possibilities for joint gain. In the opposite situation, say state C is likely to lose in the market when B gains and gain when B loses, then C's agent is more likely to attempt to claim value from B for the same reason.

If so, then research on coffee trade during the 1950s, for example, should find that negotiators for Brazil and Colombia, coffee exporters that both stood to gain from a price increase, used mixed-integrative strategies with each other and tended to avoid harsh claiming tactics concerning international coffee prices. At the same time, a scheme to fix export quotas in particular would have established a fixed pie that would have to be divided, creating incentives for Brazil to attempt to claim from Colombia and vice versa. Coffee importing states stood to lose unambiguously from any price-supporting scheme, considering only their commercial objectives as coffee importers. They faced a win-lose situation in the prospect of an international coffee agreement that would raise prices, and so this hypothesis would expect them to display claiming behavior toward the exporters or decline to negotiate at all.

Bart S. Fisher's study of the 1962 London negotiations to create the International Coffee Agreement[3] provides some comparative evidence for these elementary ideas. The supply side of the world coffee market varied significantly both as to the size distribution of the exporting countries and as to coffee quality. Table 1 shows the market shares of exporting and importing countries in 1962. As to quality, the "milds" or highest quality beans came from Colombia and Central America. Brazil exported arabicas, ranking in the middle, and during the preceding decade several African countries had begun to export robustas, which buyers placed at the low end of the quality and price spectrum.

The main variance in negotiation behavior tracked what would be expected from the respective positions in the coffee market. Although the evidence on negotiation behavior is thin, in 1962 evidently all the exporting states (with the possible exception of the Africans) advocated and supported an international agreement to stabilize and raise coffee prices. With respect to the allocation of shares, the largest shippers, Brazil and Colombia, also attempted to claim from other exporters. The expanding African market share had come basically at Brazil's ex-

---

[3] Fisher 1972, chapters 4 and 8. Fisher, who had different purposes, only summarizes the evidence.

Table 1. World Exports and Imports of Coffee by Country, 1962

Exporters	Percentage	Importers	Percentage
Brazil	35.4	USA	52.1
Colombia	14.2	Canada	2.6
Guatemala	3.4	Other Americas	1.2
El Salvador	3.2	West Germany	8.3
Mexico	3.2	France	7.4
Costa Rica	1.9	Italy	4.0
Ecuador	1.2	Netherlands	2.3
Dominican Republic	1.1	Belgium-Lux.	2.0
Other Central America, Caribbean	2.4	(Total EEC	24.0)
Other Western hemisphere	2.9	Sweden	3.0
(Total Western hemisphere	68.9)	U.K.	2.4
Kenya, Uganda & Tanganyika	7.0	Other Western Europe	8.0
Ivory Coast	5.8	USSR, Eastern Europe	2.5
Angola	5.7	Africa	2.3
Ethiopia	2.2	Asia, Oceania	1.9
Malagasy Republic	2.0		
Cameroun	1.4		
Congo-Kinshasa	1.3		
Other Africa	2.5		
(Total Africa	27.9)		
Indonesia	2.1		
Other Asia, Oceania	1.0		
Total world	100.0	Total world	100.0

Source: Fisher 1962, tables 4 and 5, based on data from the Pan American Coffee Bureau.

pense. Meanwhile, Colombia was competing most directly with Central American states. Thus Brazil and Colombia attempted to preserve the status quo by proposing an export-quota arrangement with the largest quotas for themselves and smaller quotas to limit rising competitors. These small but expanding players pushed for one-state-one-vote governance and for quotas as large as possible, and opposed an effective enforcement mechanism that would prevent them from exceeding their quotas. There is some evidence that African exporters agreed to a limiting arrangement because they feared that otherwise, Brazil would use its substantial production capacity to flood the market and break them, and because the bargaining succeeded in keeping the enforcement mechanism porous. (The source does not report on bargaining strategies of particular exporters vis-à-vis other suppliers beyond these exceptions.)

The largest anomaly for this simple commercial analysis is that in 1962 the dominant coffee importing party, the United States, did agree to negotiate and ratify an international regime designed to place a floor under prices and lacking any mechanism to enforce a price ceiling. This decision reflected the substantial weight Washington gave at that time to broader political objectives, fostering political stability in developing countries and thwarting Soviet ambitions in Latin America after the 1959 Cuban revolution, according to Stephen Krasner.[4] Some

[4] Krasner 1971, 243–44.

elements of the U.S. coffee producing industry also favored an official agreement that would stabilize prices and supplies. Thus evidently Washington used a mixed strategy rather than pure claiming over coffee prices.

The most consequential price of all is the rate of exchange between currencies, which ultimately affects all current and capital transactions crossing borders. A well-known example of opposite economic effects is that when a country's currency depreciates, homemade products become more competitive and producers elsewhere lose relatively, at least in the short run. Competitors' governments can thus be expected to claim vigorously in exchange-rate bargaining if short-run commercial objectives dominate their decisions.

Similar and opposite market positions are not the only market basis for strategy choice. When two countries are in different yet complementary positions—when each would gain from an exchange of particular concessions between the two—the negotiator is more likely to use some value creation toward the other government. Market conditions produce not only common interests but also differences across countries that can be complementary, and hence concessions that might be traded. The most familiar economic examples come from international trade itself, where agents in different countries (typically via private rather than official negotiations) exchange surplus goods for goods they lack. Successive rounds of tariff cutting in GATT negotiations were analogous. Official negotiators exchanged contingent promises to cut barriers to each other's trade—also reflecting complementary markets. This hypothesis from complementary situations to negotiating strategy would be disconfirmed if, for example, research found that a government negotiator in a GATT round tended to use pure value-claiming behavior rather than a mix toward countries with which an exchange of concessions would have been beneficial.

History does present clear anomalies for this expectation, if we rely on tenets of economics alone. According to mainstream trade theory, for instance, many less-developed markets would have gained if their governments had exchanged their import restrictions for those of other countries. Yet many of their GATT negotiators during the 1960s and 1970s approximated the strict distributive strategy instead, defending high protection at home and demanding nonreciprocal concessions from the richer countries. Many of them believed that mainstream trade theory was defective. They were confident that their import protection would aid the expansion of infant industries and employment, and that liberalizing first would mean a severe loss, not a gain. We get closer to understanding and anticipating the negotiator's behavior by taking into account not only analysts' beliefs about markets' effects but also the beliefs of negotiators themselves.

BATNAS, RESISTANCE POINTS, AND STRATEGIES

3. The better the market alternative to a prospective government agreement, as viewed by the negotiator, the lower the odds he will decide to enter a negotiation toward that agreement, and if he does, the higher his resistance point, the harder

his claiming behavior, and vice versa. The economic diplomat's batna will vary
with market conditions, at least in part. In international trade and financial bargaining, one alternative to an official agreement, in principle, is to leave the matter to the market (operating under existing policies). The more the negotiator's
market alternative worsens during the talks, relative to his objectives, the softer
his claiming behavior will become, according to this hypothesis. Softer distributive behavior means scaling down one's demands, accepting demands from the
other that had been resisted, or both (see appendix B).[5]

Two historical comparisons suggest the validity of this familiar alternatives
principle for international economic bargaining. After the mid-1950s the international price of coffee fell sharply, worsening the exporters' market alternative to
official management of the coffee trade. Coffee is the primary commodity exported by the largest number of countries. Many countries are small players and
enjoy little individual influence over the prices of the goods and services they
trade. In the period from 1945 through 1954, the coffee market was characterized
by an excess of consumption over exportable production and sharply rising
prices. "The result of the heavy demand relative to current supply was relatively
little interest by producers in international collaboration to boost coffee prices."[6]
Over the next decade, however, the international price of green coffee (measured
as the Santos 4 variety) fell fairly steadily from the range of 70 to 90 U.S. cents
per pound to 30 to 35 cents by 1961 and 1962. At that time thirty countries exported green coffee. As their market alternative deteriorated, the exporters first
tried a producer-only deal to halt the slide, which failed. They decided to negotiate a deal with importing countries. The resulting 1962 International Coffee
Agreement included a system of export quotas and engaged the chief importers,
United States and the EEC, as partners to help enforce the quota obligations to establish a price floor and limit fluctuations.

After 1969 the coffee market changed back in the opposite direction for several
reasons, boosting the price into the range of 45 to 55 cents in 1970 through 1972.
As this hypothesis would expect, the improvement in market alternative encouraged the producer countries to harden their distributive tactics. In 1972 when they
demanded an increase in the floor price to compensate for the dollar's devaluation, the United States resisted. Rather than compromising on the price, the exporters (and importers) decided to allow the regulatory mechanism of their Agreement to lapse.[7]

This hypothesis also makes sense of monetary bargaining. During the late
1970s a market alternative improved enough in one sense to cause governments to

---

[5] This proposition, like many in the book, is stated in terms of an individual negotiator. This simplification should not be taken to imply that agents are completely autonomous from their principals
or that personal idiosyncrasies will necessarily determine policies. The negotiator's assessment of his
country's batna may in fact result from a collective deliberation in his capital. His views may represent
beliefs shared by fellow officials and citizens. Complexities arising from domestic constraints will be
added via later hypotheses.

[6] Fisher 1972, 16.

[7] *Wall Street Journal,* 21 November 1975.

terminate an on-going monetary negotiation entirely.[8] In 1978 the Federal Republic of Germany and Japan had balance of payments surpluses and held much of their official reserves in U.S. dollars. The dollar was declining in value. When the German Bundesbank intervened in exchange markets to slow the deutschemark's rise, markets sometimes swamped Germany with more dollars, complicating its fight against inflation. Bonn and Tokyo also worried that further dollar declines would lead more third parties to shift their own international balances from dollars to the mark and the yen, which they feared would disrupt their national economic management. The market's current alternative for Germany or Japan—a payments surplus and a falling dollar—had negative implications for important policy objectives. Simply refusing to buy dollars or even selling some reserves on commercial markets would have driven the dollar down further and destabilized business. The United States was no longer converting dollars into gold, and efforts to persuade Washington to change its macroeconomic policies were not proving sufficient to remove these problems.

In late 1978, Germany, Japan, the United Kingdom, the United States, and other states launched bargaining at the International Monetary Fund over the possible creation of an official dollar substitution account at the Fund. Holders of excess dollars could exchange them for these claims on the IMF. The Fund's leaders and the surplus countries sought some commitment from Washington to make good any losses the Fund might sustain by holding these dollar assets, either due to interest rate differences or future declines in the dollar. The United States initially resisted assuming any cost short of the account's liquidation, and European and Japanese negotiators resisted any deal without such a constraint on the Americans.

Meanwhile, however, market conditions, specifically in the world oil market, shifted with a vengeance. The price of Saudi light crude zoomed from $13.34 per barrel at the beginning of 1979 to $26.00 one year later, and on 1 January 1981 the price stood at $32.00, due to the 1979 revolution in Iran and international reactions. Because West Germany and Japan each imported a large share of its energy needs, those payments surpluses suddenly vanished. The second oil shock eliminated their excess dollar problem in a flash, and the dollar also stopped falling. With improvement of their monetary alternative, the negotiators dropped the subject of an IMF substitution account during the spring of 1980. IMF Managing Director Jacques de Larosière neatly summarized the reason for the collapse of these talks:

[W]ith the rise in the value of the dollar, which was already underway in early 1980, and with the second major increase in oil prices, we shifted from a situation where there . . . [were] too many dollars in the system very rapidly to a situation where there was a lack of dollars. It appeared clearly that the demand for substitution, at least

---

[8] This account relies heavily on Gowa 1984, a study designed to address different analytical questions.

from a number of countries who might have been interested in the project, was just fading away.[9]

Changes in market alternatives and negotiators' resistance points are part of the economic negotiation process. More complex market hypotheses about batnas, beliefs, and behavior could also be generated and compared with these empirically. Consider the possibility of a market change that affects two parties unequally. During bargaining already underway, an asymmetrical market shift that worsens A's alternative but not B's could shift the negotiation process toward greater claiming by B at A's expense. In advance of a prospective economic negotiation, if A anticipated such an unfavorable market shift, it might believe that B might think that now A will be willing to pay more to get agreement. Anticipating harder B claiming, A might decide not even to enter talks in the first place,[10] though only if A expects the diminished value of the deal to fall below his reservation value.

Some early readers objected that because actual markets are full of government intervention, "leaving it to the market" may be misleading as a description of the real policy alternative. But the presence of government intervention is beside the point being made here. The comparative claim is only that, if the actual market alternative improves, whatever the reasons, then the resistance point for an official agreement to achieve these objectives will be higher than before, all else being equal. Or suppose a deal on the table proposed mutual reductions in trade barriers and other regulations. This proposition claims that the negotiator will compare that deal too with allowing (regulated) markets to operate without the deal, and that when those market conditions improve—say GDP growth accelerates—the government negotiator will require a more advantageous deal than before.

THE POSSIBILITY FRONTIER AND THE OUTCOME

4. When international markets change, they sometimes move government negotiators' possibility frontiers outward or inward, expanding or limiting the possible gains from value-creating tactics. For example, over the nineteenth and twentieth centuries as transportation industries lowered long-distance costs per unit, they gradually expanded possibilities for distant countries such as Belgium and Japan to gain by exchanging tariff concessions. With air transportation and unit cost reduction on products such as fashion garments and computer parts, a given tariff cut presumably boosted trade by a greater magnitude than in the days of sailing ships. Thus if government objectives and gains are reckoned partly in commercial terms, the market change—the cost decline—created new outcome points to the northeast that were not possible before. A strategy aimed at creating joint value

---

[9] Interview by Joanne Gowa, 7 April 1983, attributed by permission, Gowa 1984, 679. Gowa's interviews with other participating officials confirmed this diagnosis.
[10] I am grateful to Peter Rosendorff for suggesting this idea.

then had more to work with. This market change and the outward shift of the frontier are not sufficient to guarantee that actual diplomats for Brussels and Tokyo will reach agreements to realize those gains. Nor are market conditions the only determinants of the frontier.

. The vast increase in the size of the world's foreign exchange markets after 1960 moved a frontier inward, by eliminating some possibilities for official gain through coordinated government interventions to manage those markets. When France's balance of payments moved into deficit, these markets began to put downward pressure on the franc, as traders covered themselves against the chance of a devaluation or actively speculated on the franc. Before 1960 when foreign exchange markets were small relative to central bank coffers, the central banks could absorb this selling pressure by buying up excess francs jointly, and thus help convince other firms not to jump on the bandwagon. For their governments, devoted to the objective of maintaining a stable system of pegged exchange rates, avoiding instability of this type was a gain—value they could create jointly. Today though, when the weekly volume of currency market transactions vastly exceeds central bank liquid assets, even an agreement among the largest countries to take excess French francs off the market can be overwhelmed by a tide of sell orders in hours.[11] This change reflects new market institutions—more rapid means of global communication and the creation of Eurobanks—among other things. Official gains from negotiation are less possible today, and a value-creating strategy following this conception of gain and these techniques alone is less likely to succeed.[12]

In practice, negotiators lack neat diagrams to show them where the possibility frontier lies; the limits of the possible are hazy. For this reason market behavior probably influences official bargaining by a more subtle route as well. My decision as to whether to attempt value creating in the first place, for instance, may well turn on whether I think my counterpart believes we are far inside the frontier or already on it. If I believe he sees no possibilities for further joint gain, I am less likely to try. Lacking full information about what he perceives, I may wish to estimate his beliefs using proxies. Market behavior provides one type of information for such estimates. I might rely on evidence from recent currency market crises to judge how much coordinated intervention other financial officials will probably accept. They may make assumptions about me based on the same common information. Of course, judgments based on incomplete information and assumptions can be inaccurate. This sort of judgment is notoriously sensitive to strong ideological preferences, for example. Nonetheless, market behavior, especially when everyone moves strongly in one direction, is likely to signal and co-

[11] Dabringhausen 1997 adds to this insight an inquiry into the variable profit strategies of particular industries as influences on likely government policies.

. [12] Actually the situation is more complex, as usual, in this case because governments can borrow additional resources for this purpose. Mexico did in so 1995 and some Southeast Asian states did so in 1997. The gains or losses realized by interstate bargaining on these issues depend critically on which other actions are coupled with foreign exchange intervention, including domestic measures by the borrowing country.

ordinate officials' expectations about what government agreements are feasible, creating subjective focal points, especially among officials who share the same predispositions.[13]

DOMESTIC DIVISIONS OVER OBJECTIVES AND STRATEGY

5. *When international market shifts affect different citizens of the same country differently, interest groups mobilize and domestic politics shapes the government's negotiating objectives and strategies.* To this point, we have assumed the parties have no internal differences over these issues. This simplification has helped us identify certain conjectures about the economic negotiation process that might prove valid across states with different cultures, historical experiences, and national political institutions. Yet often governments seem to depart from market incentives, at least incentives of their countries viewed as wholes.

For example, when the ruble falls, the change helps Russians who export and hurts Russians who buy foreign goods and services, at least in the first instance. Changes in these constituents' economic circumstances can be expected to shift their demands on their government's negotiator and affect his priorities. Over longer periods, some market shifts change the very distribution of the national population across economic activities, expanding new sectors at the expense of older ones. If so, disaggregating both markets and domestic politics will often be critical for a sophisticated grasp of a government negotiator's likely behavior. A valid theory of economic negotiation needs more than economics.

Economists and political scientists have established some connections between world markets, domestic politics, and government policies, especially on trade. What remains is to link these connections into the international negotiation process. During the 1970s political scientists began to track domestic political consequences of economic interdependence. Gourevitch showed how international depressions tended to fracture established domestic political coalitions, whose parts regrouped into different lasting alliances in many countries.[14] During the 1980s Destler and Odell called attention to how the expansion of international trade into American society had expanded sectors that stood to gain from trade and lose from new import barriers imposed by their own government. A substantial increase in domestic sectoral pressures against new product-specific protection occurred during the 1980s, along with rising pressures for it.[15] Milner converted the systemic notion of interdependence into an industry-level counterpart, and showed that industries suffering from import competition at home were less likely to press their government for protection if they were also exporters or foreign investors.[16] Likewise, as Goodman, Spar, and Yoffie found, the more U.S. industries

---

[13] Schelling 1960, chapter 3, introduced the notions of focal points and tacit bargaining.
[14] Gourevitch 1986.
[15] Destler and Odell 1987.
[16] Milner 1988.

became penetrated by inward international investment, the more the industry's expressed preference for U.S. trade policy shifted to reflect the market's new structure.[17] Meanwhile, Rogowski used the Stolper-Samuelson theorem of trade as a foundation for a worldwide theory of domestic political coalition formation.[18] Frieden emphasized that increased mobility of international capital, too, helped some citizens and hurt others and ought to affect their respective preferences regarding monetary policies.[19] Keohane, Milner and their collaborators offered a new general statement of this market logic and studied its fit with evidence from centrally-planned and developing countries as well as the developed world.[20]

Meanwhile, economists of the public choice school were developing parallel models of trade policy making. Many even postulated that politics itself is a market—with import-competing producers on the demand side and elected politicians on the supply side, auctioning off whatever policies are demanded on balance. This extensive literature has been surveyed elsewhere.[21] Much of it concentrates on the narrower question of which industries have higher or lower tariffs. An example is the finding that in the United States, greater and rising penetration of imports into a sector leads to higher tariffs and smaller tariff cuts offered in GATT negotiations, but not to a greater chance the International Trade Commission or the president will approve additional ad hoc protection for the same industries.[22] Over the longer term, U.S. tariff rates fell during the twentieth century as the aggregate ratio of labor to capital in the American economy fell.[23] A major weakness of most of these trade policy studies has been to overlook the influence of the international negotiation process, even though it is no secret that tariffs have been set partly through interstate bargaining since 1933. Trade policy research could be improved if seen from the negotiation standpoint.

Disaggregating international market conditions and their domestic political effects will also make for more accurate knowledge of governments' negotiating behavior, compared with what this chapter has said to this point. As an illustration, consider the most discussed shift in economic negotiating strategy in the world during the 1980s—Washington's turn to frequent offensive claiming over trade. The United States began issuing threats to impose new economic penalties on other countries unless they lowered barriers and subsidies that troubled American producers. This aggressive bargaining on behalf of market opening sparked much consternation around the world and affected the negotiation of the GATT's Uruguay round. Yet this sustained shift by Washington had not been predicted by experts. Most international economists and political scientists had little specific to say about why a government would choose one among alternative strategies for

[17] Goodman, Spar, and Yoffie 1996.
[18] Rogowski 1989.
[19] Frieden 1991. Related are Frieden 1987 and Frieden 1988.
[20] Keohane and Milner 1996.
[21] See Baldwin 1986, Cohen 1990, Odell 1990.
[22] Baldwin 1985, chapter 4 and pages 103–14 and 129–33.
[23] Magee and Young 1987.

negotiating market opening. So why did it occur? Under what conditions will such a shift happen again?[24]

Two possible answers proceed from international market conditions through disaggregated U.S. domestic politics. First, some worldwide industries experienced increases in production scale economies. One hypothesis says that in such a business, and when another government supports competitors abroad, the home firm exporting these goods is likely to change its expressed preference from tariff-cutting to strategic trade policy or offensive claiming, and its government will respond in that direction.[25] Greater economies of scale imply a few huge firms engaging in imperfect global competition. In such a business, it was argued that government support, for example Japanese restrictions against imports, might give Japanese firms a cumulative and eventually decisive advantage worldwide. Their competitors elsewhere fall behind if closed off from significant world markets, while the favored firms extract rents and invest the earnings into faster product development and other competitive moves. When faced with such challenges, U.S. multinationals in some sectors had commercial alternatives. They invested directly in factories behind the protective wall, or exported into it from lower-cost third-world economies. But in a business with large gains from scale and learning, spreading the factories around is less efficient. American chip firms needed to export from their large existing factories to Japan, or some U.S. industry leaders so argued. These industries called on Washington to adopt what is here called an offensive claiming strategy—threatening to raise import barriers unless the other government agrees to reduce its support, without any compensating U.S. concessions.

Comparative evidence from four manufacturing industries supports this interpretation. Because of technological changes, U.S. makers of semiconductors, commercial aircraft, and telecommunications equipment all experienced sharp increases in scale economies and steep learning curves from the mid-1970s to the mid-1980s. Governments in Europe and Japan helped national firms, U.S. companies pressed Washington to adopt strategic trade bargaining for their sectors, and it did so in those sectors. The change in market conditions was much less significant in the machine tool industry, which did not respond to foreign competition by demanding this type of policy.[26]

Yet Washington also used offensive claiming for a variety of other businesses

---

[24] Chapter 6 more specifically discusses this trend and two notable instances.

[25] Based on Milner and Yoffie 1989. This article concentrates on explaining companies' expressed policy preferences for trade policy, more than on what Washington does in response to these expressions.

[26] This summary omits some important refinements found in Milner and Yoffie 1989. Omitted there also, however, is a clear theoretical reason why U.S. firms would oppose continuation of the traditional U.S. mixed negotiating strategy—which included offers to *reduce* remaining U.S. barriers conditional on Japanese concessions, as the means of changing Japanese practices. The article says these industries had favored noncontingent "free trade" before the 1980s and then shifted to favoring conditional policy. But few American constituents had ever advocated unilateral liberalization, and Washington's negotiating strategy had been conditional, not noncontingent, since the nineteenth century.

including even corn farming, which is far indeed from what strategic trade theorists had in mind. Something more must have been happening. A second market interpretation begins with macroeconomics. Dornbusch and Frankel[27] and others point especially to the sharp rise in the international value of the dollar during the early eighties. This appreciation helped generate a huge increase in the U.S. trade deficit, which meant gains for American producers of nontradables and consumers but bad news for a wide range of export-dependent and import-competing producers. Those hurting shouted louder and louder for Washington to act against imports and members of Congress joined the chorus. The voices from the other side also rose but were held down by free riding. In this domestic political environment, for a U.S. leader to negotiate by a more integrative strategy including offers of new liberalizations may have looked like a ticket to quick political exile. Beginning in 1985 Washington instead shifted to the offensive claiming strategy in order not only to increase exports abroad but also to bleed off pressure in home politics for increases in noncontingent U.S. protection.[28] Rather than a response to other governments' changing behavior, this major U.S. strategy shift, in this view, reflected the way the dollar appreciation and the huge trade deficit reverberated through American domestic politics.[29]

Introducing domestic divisions does unfortunately make our analysis less simple, and it implies negotiating behavior that will diverge from the expectations of earlier propositions. But overlooking markets' differential effects would leave us with a misleading theory of economic negotiation. This implication is developed further in later chapters.

THE ENDOGENOUS MARKET

Now it is time to relax the simplifying assumption that markets are exogenous, and to incorporate more complex and interesting generalizations that become visible when we recognize strategic interactions between government negotiators and markets. Of course every actual market is endogenous to some political economy, ultimately. Observed market behavior is partially a reflection of official in-

---

There is a difference between the firms' preference over policies and their preference over bargaining strategies. Some additional premise seems to be needed.

[27] Dornbusch and Frankel 1987.

[28] This market perspective omits another important condition that makes repetition of this strategy less likely today. Prevailing international trade institutions changed in 1994, and the World Trade Organization offers Washington additional rules under which to file complaints and greater assurance of prompt and decisive remedies, compared with the GATT of the 1980s. On the other hand, no institutional change in the international monetary system has been adopted to restrain the tendency of major exchange rates to become severely out of line.

[29] A deeper analysis could work further back up the causal chain, asking in turn what caused the dollar to rise. There, government macroeconomic policy would be a prominent influence. But important as it is, the U.S. government is not the only player or influence in the foreign exchange markets.

stitutions and players' expectations about them, as occasional changes in those institutions reveal. The post-1960 expansion of the foreign exchange markets was itself the result of historic decisions by governments to open their economies to international capital flows again.[30] If market players forget this elementary background truth and assume that the political rules cannot change, they become vulnerable to painful surprises, as international investors in Mexico and Southeast Asia discovered when governments suddenly abandoned supposedly fixed exchange rates in 1994 and 1997, respectively. But for understanding the negotiation process, what difference does it make, in general, to introduce the reverse causal arrow, from negotiator to market?

Roberto Chang proposes a model of economic negotiations in which contemporary market behavior does affect and is affected by government negotiations while the two play out simultaneously. Chang uses the model in an article on monetary unions[31] to show that *(6) if markets expect a particular outcome and if they punish a government whenever its negotiating position deviates from the equilibrium path, then among the equilibria will be an inefficient one in which a rational government will delay a valuable agreement to form a monetary union, for an arbitrary number of periods.* Chang cites facts from European monetary experience that seem consistent with this model.

7. Suppose the negotiator favors a moderate proposal to shift policy to point M, but regards a larger shift in the same direction to E as worse than the status quo. *If he believes that proposing M will trigger large changes in market conditions and if under those conditions his government might well choose the more extreme E, he will probably rule out proposing the preferred M, even if other states might agree except for the intervening market shift.*

This idea comes to mind when reading evidence of beliefs and reasoning of Washington monetary negotiators in the late 1960s, when they faced the tension between a swelling payments deficit and the prevailing monetary regime. The United States had pledged to convert dollars to gold at $35 per ounce upon demand by other states. After the late 1950s the United States ran a persisting deficit in its overall payments, and other governments accumulated more dollars than the gold stock could redeem at that price. Moreover, the other governments were obliged to absorb more private dollars if markets wanted to sell them, so that a private run on the dollar could enormously expand governments' dollar claims on that gold. Maintaining this entire system unchanged depended on markets deciding, on balance, not to do that.

Meanwhile, after 1958 the world's major foreign exchange markets became increasingly open and likely to respond quickly to news of possible policy departures. Thus all governments took special precautions to insure the confidentiality of any proposals about possible policy changes. For any monetary negotiator it

---

[30] Helleiner 1994 develops this point.
[31] Chang 1995.

was second nature to consider how financial markets would react to any move under consideration.[32]

When countries ran substantial payments deficits or surpluses during the 1960s, market participants began to speculate on changes in official exchange rates. The more it began to look as though Britain was going to devalue or West Germany was going to upvalue, the stronger the net pressure downward on sterling or upward on the mark. With payments imbalanced substantially, a particular ministerial statement or government action could spark a surge of such trading, threatening to force the government unwillingly to change the parity to escape the costs of defending the old one.

Given a continuing payments deficit, the open gold window, and the insufficient gold supply, the worst policy nightmare for those sympathetic to the prevailing regime was that somewhere something would provoke dollar-holders everywhere to rush to the nearest central bank to unload their dollars, fearing the dollars were about to be devalued. Any central bank charged with the responsibility to protect the national currency's soundness would then be obliged to present its excess dollars for gold in New York while they could still get the promised ounce for every $35. As soon as the United States began to lose even more gold, which would provoke even greater loss of market confidence, the entire system would crash. Monetary officials in many countries, not only America, had the same nightmare.

During the first Nixon administration the senior U.S. technician in this area was Paul Volcker, Under Secretary of the Treasury for Monetary Affairs. Volcker's memoir tells the story of secret deliberations in the interagency committee assigned to discuss international monetary policy options. One alternative was to devalue the dollar unilaterally by announcing a marginal increase in the dollar price of gold. A committee member had asked a European Community official what Europe would do in that case, and reportedly the reply was, "All European currencies would be devalued by the same percentage on the same day."[33] The other governments would frustrate such a unilateral attempt to depreciate the dollar against their currencies.

> We concluded that a "small change" of perhaps 10 percent would be destabilizing without any clear prospect of achieving anything constructive because of the risk that other countries would simply devalue with us and additional changes would be expected. That would undercut the willingness of foreign central banks to hold dollars. A stronger case might have been made for increasing the dollar price of gold by a large amount, perhaps even doubling it.

---

[32] Other markets are less sensitive in this sense, and there government negotiators might devote less thinking to short-term market reactions. The contribution of this hypothesis could vary with market sensitivity. Lags are discussed below.

[33] Volcker and Gyohten 1992, 67.

He adds, however, that no one on the committee pressed this idea because the ultimate consequences for both exchange rates and aggregate international reserves were highly uncertain.[34]

A third proposal was a moderate shift to point M—to propose negotiations to modify the rules to give exchange rates greater but still limited flexibility. One proposed rule dubbed "the crawling peg" would have moved a pegged currency under pressure upward or downward as the case might be, by a weekly or monthly percentage not to exceed an agreed maximum. States under this rule would still have an obligation to intervene to hold the currency at the official rate prevailing for each agreed interval. But a deficit state could devalue its currency automatically and gradually rather than only through painful ad hoc political decisions and larger jumps. The committee adopted this proposal as part of its plan.

Volcker quotes a European ambassador who spoke after Washington had first publicly aired its qualified interest in these academic ideas: "If all this talk about flexible exchange rates brings down the system, the blood will be on your American head." Volcker continues:

> That remark was extreme, but in fact it would be difficult to talk publicly about increasing the flexibility of exchange rates without promoting speculation. The markets would move against the dollar because there was no doubt that exchange rate flexibility meant depreciation of the dollar. . . . Once the principle of easy exchange rate changes, however small, was agreed, it seemed to me that speculative pressures in the market would make it extremely difficult to resist larger changes and would probably cause them quickly.[35]

Though Washington did not rule this option out entirely, Volcker himself made public remarks undermining it, and negotiators from Japan and Europe resisted it during low-key IMF talks during 1969 and 1970. No agreement was reached before the Nixon shock of August 1971.

This is one example consistent with the hypothesis that the negotiator who favors a moderate negotiated change will rule out proposing it if he anticipates that offering it will trigger strong market pressure to overshoot. Actually Volcker in particular might not have preferred this moderate change in 1971, but some American specialists did.[36] The more limited change toward greater flexibility would have helped solve the underlying problem of payments imbalances and exchange rate stickiness without destroying the established par value regime, if it could have been implemented as designed. Implementation would have created common value for the negotiating states, as many of them defined their objectives at the time. A key reason why, some leaders believed, it could not be implemented was not only that key governments were cool to the idea, but also that official ne-

[34] Ibid.
[35] Ibid., 68.
[36] Interviews with participating U.S. officials, 1975.

gotiation itself, given low confidence already, would stimulate markets to destroy the new scheme and even the larger pillars on which it was to stand. This danger of negative over-reaction from endogenous markets may also have cooled the interest of other governments in discussing it.

8. More welcome to the negotiator, though not to his counterparts, is that *an endogenous market makes available an additional claiming tactic—namely, worsening another party's market alternative in an attempt to pry loose additional concessions.* During the subsequent era of floating exchange rates after 1973, for example, U.S. monetary negotiators intentionally "talked the dollar down" on occasion. In September 1985, after the dollar had risen so much, Treasury Secretary James Baker engineered a Group of Five agreement at New York's Plaza Hotel to nudge it back down (chap. 4). In addition, Baker wanted major surplus countries, especially West Germany and Japan, to stimulate domestic demand so their countries would buy more U.S. exports. Through 1986, as their currencies rose, Bonn and Tokyo stoutly resisted making these fiscal concessions. They continued to advise Washington to cut its own fiscal deficit, something it had promised but not delivered. But they also feared still greater appreciations of their currencies against the dollar, which would hurt business constituents competing in world markets. During the summer of 1986 American officials increased the pressure with public warnings that "if we don't see more growth in our trading partners, it will imply more exchange market adjustment," in the words of Beryl Sprinkel, chairman of the President's Council of Economic Advisers.[37] To a foreign exchange trader who did not see the domestic growth, this talk signaled that betting more against the dollar and on the yen would not be a bad move. To the extent that markets acted on these signals, they would bring about the dreaded yen appreciation whether Tokyo liked it or not. Washington was putting the squeeze on its friends, through the market.

In September Baker repeated at an IMF meeting that the U.S. trade imbalances "have got to be reduced, either through greater competitiveness of the dollar, or increased growth outside the United States, or a combination of these factors."[38] A year after the Plaza agreement, the dollar was already down by 40 percent against the German mark and 55 percent against the yen. The European Community responded promptly by pledging a joint effort to oppose any further dollar declines, "to stand up and speak with one voice toward the United States," as Luxembourg's finance minister said.[39] Japanese business was becoming feverish over the continued rise in the yen. Late in October, Japan's Finance Minister Kiichi Miyazawa flew to the United States to offer new concessions. The Bank of Japan reduced its discount rate and Miyazawa promised to submit a supplement to the government budget for the coming year and to seek future tax cuts. In exchange Baker reiterated earlier promises to reduce the U.S. budget deficit and fight pro-

[37] *New York Times*, 9 August 1986, 19.
[38] Ibid., 29 September 1986, 21.
[39] Ibid., 22 October 1986, 25.

tectionism, and he agreed that exchange rates were now "broadly consistent with the present underlying fundamentals."[40]

Nevertheless, in late December 1986 and early January 1987, currency markets resumed heavy selling of dollars for deutschemarks and yen, helping to force an embarrassing realignment of exchange rates within the European Community only weeks before German national elections. Tokyo bought an additional $1.5 billion dollars, attempting to halt the yen's rise, but still it rose even further.[41] The *Financial Times* observed that central banks were finding themselves "overwhelmed by the strength of speculative pressure in the foreign exchange markets."[42] U.S. officials now put out the word that they were not actively trying to talk the dollar down, but neither did they do anything new that would discourage further selling. Most observers saw "a big game of chicken"[43] in which nothing more needed to be said. Baker demonstrated his tactics again by meeting a nearly-desperate Miyazawa in Washington another time on 22 January and sending him away with little new to show for his trip.[44]

Soon, however, Baker ended the episode, perhaps because further currency instability would now be too expensive for the United States itself. Partly in reaction to the dollar's turbulence, U.S. interest rates had begun to rise, and this raised the Treasury's cost of financing budget deficits. A few days before a scheduled Paris G7 meeting, after nearly canceling the meeting, Baker reportedly extracted promises from West Germany and Japan to take additional expansionary measures in the future,[45] limited ones for Germany and substantial ones for Japan. Then at the Louvre on 22 February 1987 he and the other G7 ministers agreed on measures to stabilize exchange rates "around current levels."[46]

This episode illustrates a mixed strategy incorporating this tactic of stimulating markets to worsen the other parties' alternatives to making desired concessions, as well as some U.S. concessions. This process helped the U.S. claim more from Japan. But talking the currency down, even by the powerful United States, was sufficient to force only limited concessions. Washington had still failed, thus far, to deliver much macroeconomic restraint of its own, a concession that was not delivered but might have generated a larger deal.[47]

9. *With an endogenous market, strategic interaction between firms and negotiators can also create or eliminate possibilities for official agreement, moving the frontier outward or inward.* An interesting final illustration of reciprocal influ-

[40] Ibid., 1 November 1986, 1.

[41] *Journal of Commerce*, 14 January 1987, 3A.

[42] 15 January 1987, 14.

[43] *Wall Street Journal*, 15 January 1987, 3., quoting David Hale of Kemper Financial Services in Chicago. Also see *New York Times*, 15 January 1987, 1.

[44] *New York Times*, 23 January 1987, 1.

[45] Funabashi 1988, 180.

[46] Communiqué, 22 February 1987, rpt. in Funabashi 1988, 277.

[47] The U.S. government did reduce its fiscal deficit in 1987 to 3.4 percent of GDP from 5.2 percent in fiscal 1986. The deficit fell further in the late 1980s, rose in the early 1990s, and declined again during the mid-1990s (U.S. President 1995, table B78).

ence comes from the 1985 to 1987 multilateral bargaining over chlorofluorocarbons (CFCs). Some scientists and regulators feared lasting and possibly catastrophic damage to the earth's stratospheric ozone layer from continued industrial use of these chemicals. Until 1986 the industries in Europe and America that produced and used these chemicals had contended that scientific evidence did not demonstrate any risk to the ozone layer. They had significant political power with which to oppose restrictions.

From each producer's viewpoint, however, the prospect of a global CFC ban, if credible, also created a commercial incentive to be the first to market an attractive substitute. The prospect was especially credible for firms in the United States, where Washington had, in 1978, unilaterally banned CFCs in nonessential aerosol propellants. Proposals for additional unilateral restrictions were introduced in Congress during the ozone negotiations. For U.S. producers, deeper CFC restrictions affecting them alone, leaving their European competitors free to supply their customers, could be the worst possible world. Dupont, the world's largest producer, surprised the rest of the industry in September 1986 by announcing support for a negotiated multilateral limit on CFCs. Dupont's defection then helped advocates gain support from upper levels of the Reagan administration and Congress. One reason Dupont broke ranks was prospective competitive advantage in its own market. This firm was thought to be ahead of its global rivals toward the development of a substitute.[48] In turn, this giant's decision to pursue a substitute more aggressively drove its market competitors to do so as well. The government negotiations and the prospect of unilateral regulation thus shaped company behavior in the short and medium term, in their laboratories, marketing plans, and political stands.

In turn, company behavior and official beliefs about it may also have affected ongoing government bargaining. For diplomats, an agreement to eliminate CFCs entirely in the absence of a suitable substitute would have entailed economic and political costs. Invention of a substitute would reduce the cost of a CFC ban, moving that outcome above or to the right of their resistance points and probably moving the official possibility frontier northeastward. As it happened in 1987, ozone negotiators, despite lacking full information about the degree of ozone loss and about what might be causing it, did settle on new rules requiring gradual future reductions of CFC use, while also providing for future amendments in light of new science and new alternatives.[49]

In brief, the prospect of a market-generated substitute may have encouraged diplomats to agree to begin reducing CFC use, though not to ban them immediately, while simultaneously the prospect of such regulations stimulated firms to create that substitute. The general point, however, is not that the endogenous mar-

---

[48] Haas 1992, 205 and Sebenius 1992a, 358. Six months after the 1987 Montreal meeting finished the protocol limiting CFC emissions, Dupont announced it had decided to phase out its own CFC production completely, which boosted efforts, successful in 1990, toward interstate agreement to phase them out completely in dozens of countries.

[49] Benedick 1991 is the most complete account of this negotiation.

ket response will always expand the official agreement zone. Conceivably in another situation, government negotiations could boomerang in the opposite direction—encouraging firms to develop new techniques or products that in turn reduce an official zone of agreement.

These last three examples also remind us that markets vary as to the degree of concentration among firms. The foreign exchange market for the yen versus the dollar is highly competitive, with many players in the world having access and a huge potential supply of money. The acts of no single player, even George Soros, change the commercial behavior of other buyers and sellers for long. In contrast, the CFC market—with Dupont, a single firm, producing one-quarter of the world's output—departed much further from perfect competition on the seller side. The more concentrated the market, the more useful it will be to define the cartel or the dominant firm as a negotiating party. Doing so will yield the smallest payoff in a case like foreign exchange markets. In the CFC case, toward the other end of the spectrum, treating Dupont as a bargaining party seems well worth the greater complexity. This one firm was clearly in a much stronger position than others to profit from the incentive to create a substitute. In turn, the possibility of a Dupont substitute was highly significant for other firms and for government negotiators.

VARIABLE LAGS

These examples might also seem to imply that financial negotiation is fundamentally different from trade bargaining. Trade diplomats are not often heard attempting to "talk down" the international price of, say, steel beams. Nor do they typically fear market counterreactions to their negotiating moves the same day, which must be built into their strategies. Today's foreign-exchange markets may also be the most extreme example of a sensitive international market, where lags are short. Given low government barriers and electronic communications technology, a million dollars can be sent from Frankfurt to Tokyo in exchange for yen at very low cost per dollar a few hours or minutes after the decision is made. Producers of steel beams or coffee require much longer to make, sell, and deliver the goods to the destination, and actual transactions are sometimes determined by contracts running for multiple years.

Yet lag differences too are matters of degree, and variations are found within finance, agriculture, and industry. Establishing a network of bank branches in China will take longer and cost far more than sending liquid dollars to Shanghai, and economic negotiations today deal with investment and trade in financial services as well as goods. By contrast, Hong Kong's manufacturers of toys and garments are famous for switching from one product to another in very short order and delivering them around the world by jet. Inducing chemical firms to develop a substitute for CFCs took much longer than talking the dollar down, but not infinitely longer. A government announcement of an intention to raise a trade barrier or lower a managed price might still deter a decision to make a new investment or the signing of a new sales contract, though the effects would take longer to appear in observed trade data. It will be more useful to ask not whether the issue is finance or trade, but how long is the lag in the market under negotiation.

10. *Market lag variations may well have significant implications for the official negotiation process. Most obviously, when the lag is longer, the market will seem, in the short run, more like an exogenous force, which may alter the tactical mix.* A long lag will subtract the tactical option of worsening or improving another party's market alternative, or such moves will have weaker effects, and a long lag may add to the process the tactic of attempting to forecast market effects. The negotiator using a mixed strategy aimed at achieving reciprocal tariff cuts will typically attempt, during the process, to forecast market reactions to cuts under discussion, in order to place a value on each potential concession. The formulas for making such predictions can become a negotiating issue in themselves.

More important, a *longer lag may imply greater odds for success with the mixed-integrative strategy in particular.* Value-creating tactics require time if they are to soften long-standing biases and commitments to incompatible demands, encourage parties to reframe issues, explore unprecedented arrangements, and build political support at home. Making a market less sensitive, were that possible, would give the bargaining process more time in which to unfold. Quick market "vetoes" of certain solutions probably tend to constrain bargaining to a smaller issue space. If negotiators believe this is so, they may make fewer integrative attempts in the first place regarding more sensitive markets, unless they find a way to insulate the talks from market reactions or lengthen the lag, such as by imposing controls on liquid capital flows.

The longer the lag, the more probable are agreement terms designed to deal with uncertainty. The boundedly-rational creators of the 1987 ozone protocol did not yet have a practical substitute for CFCs at hand, and science had not fully confirmed that CFCs were causing an ozone problem. Thus they committed only to gradual and partial reductions in CFC use, and included rules for later modification to the emissions limits and chemicals to be covered in light of new information. In trade too, when subsequent exports fall short of expectations with a lag, the new information may trigger a request for additional negotiations from the disappointed party. For this reason trade negotiators may write monitoring and renegotiation provisions into their deals in the first place. U.S., Japanese, and Chinese trade negotiators have illustrated this phenomenon many times in recent decades.

In seeking to understand governments' international economic negotiations, we need to appreciate the most fundamental difference between bargaining over economic issues and all other international negotiations: the former are sensitive to the nature and changes in relevant market conditions. This chapter outlines a menu of hypothetical linkages between particular market dimensions and particular elements of government negotiation, with causality running in both directions.

These propositions offer substitutes for the slippery notions of interests and preferences. They give us some essential starting points from which to understand why conflicts and official talks will break out and break off when they do; which parties will step forward into a given economic negotiation, and what their top-priority commercial objectives and strategies will be.

The market batna is a key clue to the finance or trade negotiator's resistance point and propensity for claiming tactics. Some exogenous market changes will move the official possibility frontier inward or outward, helping to determine the outcome of a value-creating strategy. Changes in a world market often affect different groups in the same country differently, however, so that a more complex disaggregated analysis of both markets and domestic politics will often be critical for a sophisticated grasp of international economic negotiations.

Ultimately real markets are endogenous to a political environment, and even in the short run, negotiators sometimes move markets as well as the reverse. In markets with short lags, the negotiator's moves may cause reactions that in turn delay valuable official deals, or fears of such reactions may cause negotiators to withhold a preferred policy recommendation. On the other hand, a new claiming tactic becomes available. And negotiations themselves may spur companies to generate new market possibilities over the medium term that in turn enlarge or shrink the government negotiators' possible agreement space.

Using this market perspective, we can recognize patterns in negotiations over different economic issues that are not apparent when we look at sectors and episodes one at a time. A bargaining approach also shows a way to improve the literature on national trade policies. A global market perspective also will deepen studies that begin with interest groups and domestic politics that are not viewed as embedded in that changing market environment.

While a valid theory for economic bargaining will surely need components from economics, such ideas will not be sufficient. The next two chapters turn from the objective to the subjective. Chapter 4 proposes that even when objective market conditions, international power structures, and domestic institutions are essentially constant, variable negotiator beliefs about strategy feasibility will exercise a key influence on the choice of strategy at the opening of the negotiation process.

PART TWO

TWO PARTIES WITH
FIXED INSTITUTIONS

Beliefs about Feasibility and Strategy Choice

If economic diplomats vary their strategies across different negotiations, then it would be useful to know what will determine those strategy choices.[1] Launching a negotiation in one direction rather than another is likely to shape the other side's response, and hence the remainder of the interaction and who gains or losses. It stands to reason, for example, that Russia or the United States will get a different response from the European Union depending on whether the initiator begins the process by demanding unrequited concessions and threatening penalties, or by inviting the European Union to negotiate an agreement designed for its benefit as well. In turn, a planner in Brussels naturally will have an advantage if she knows what strategy Moscow or Washington will use, or has at least some sound basis for estimating what is most likely. Suppose the strategy options are arrayed, as in chapter 2, along a theoretical continuum between pure value claiming at one extreme and pure value creating at the other.

The previous chapter offered one objective clue, the hypothesis that countries on opposite sides of a market will attempt to claim value from each other, while those on the same side will tend toward mixed-integrative strategies vis-à-vis each other. While this might turn out to be true on average, in a world of bounded rationality things often become more complicated.

Another clue is suggested by a major recent comparative study of labor-management negotiations. It found substantial variations in managers' strategies, sometimes within the same industry where international competition and other pressures for change were similar. One of the most powerful explanatory variables was a subjective one—whether managers expected the union to be receptive or hostile to the management's business rationale for proposed contract changes. When managers believed labor would be skeptical, they used a more distributive strategy, and when they anticipated a more favorable response, managers were more likely to attempt value-creating tactics.[2]

The same implicit hypothesis about players' beliefs might help account for variations in international economic relations. That is, given incomplete information, the more diplomat A believes B will resist or exploit a value-creating strat-

---

[1] Particular negotiators may stumble into an interaction without undertaking any careful choice among strategies. This theory will be useful to the extent that actual negotiators do make deliberate choices over strategies or act as though they did so.

[2] Walton et al. 1994, 250. The strategy terms used in this book are "forcing" and "fostering" change, respectively. Strategy choices also varied according to the nature of managers' goals and their perception of power relations between the parties.

egy, the less likely A will be to choose such tactics, other things equal. B's response to integrative attempts will vary according to her subjective priorities and beliefs about bargaining with A, as well as her beliefs about objective interests. If B's secret goals are entirely antithetical to A's, B will be tempted to exploit the openness of A's integrative tactics, but if goals are not entirely antithetical, then B will be constrained from pure exploitation and more tempted to explore whether or not she can gain through joint value creation. A will not know B's priorities and attitudes completely and will have to make a judgment. A will ask herself how B is likely to respond, all things considered, and A's belief will then bound a choice regarding value creating.[3] This proposition introduces the reciprocal nature of the negotiation process into the theory by assuming that parties will anticipate it when making strategy decisions.

Consider two monetary cases in which Washington chose quite different strategies. On Sunday night, 15 August 1971, during a currency crisis President Richard Nixon shocked the world. For years Washington had pledged unequivocally to defend the dollar. That night Nixon announced the United States had unilaterally suspended its convertibility into gold, and he also slapped a temporary ten percent surcharge on all dutiable imports, to be collected until countries with payments surpluses allowed their currencies to rise against the dollar. The country with the largest surplus by far was Japan. Nixon's speech blamed foreigners for the dollar's problem and demanded that they solve it. "The international money speculators" and "unfair exchange rates" were responsible for the crisis. "When the unfair treatment is ended, the import tax will end as well."[4] In Tokyo this speech was a shocking bolt from the blue. It was the first word from Nixon indicating he wanted Japan to revalue the yen. There had been no earlier secret communicating toward this end. Nixon and the chief U.S. negotiator, Secretary of the Treasury John Connally, refused to make any concessions and offered no proposals characterized as benefiting others, unlike previous and later U.S. monetary negotiators. Washington chose pure offensive claiming, even skipping over threatening a sanction to impose one preemptively at the outset.

Fourteen years later, the United States again had a large payments deficit, Japan again had the largest surplus, and Washington again decided it wanted the yen to rise. In sharp contrast, however, Washington in 1985 did not attempt the pure distributive strategy to achieve the same goal. Instead President Ronald Reagan, Treasury Secretary James Baker, and their team chose a mixed strategy with prominent integrative elements. Baker began by talking privately to Japanese leaders about possible joint action on a common problem. He kept the initial

---

[3] This is not to say that the negotiator is expected always to prefer value creating over value claiming whenever the other side will play the mutual-gain game. The present proposition only identifies a variable condition under which a negotiator is expected to avoid value creating. Other conditions, objective or subjective, might bias a negotiator toward or away from claiming. If any do, a more useful theory will include propositions identifying those causes as well.

[4] U.S. Department of State, *Bulletin* 65 (1975): 253–57.

phase of communication secret, opened it in an exploratory manner,[5] listened to the Japanese carefully, and avoided criticizing Japan publicly for causing the exchange-rate problem. He avoided threats, efforts to worsen Japan's batna, and public commitments to any point in the agreement zone. He did not rule out American concessions. This strategy was mixed, though, not purely integrative. He did seek Japanese concessions that would benefit the United States, and there was much complaining by Washington about Japan's trade practices. The outcomes of these two attempts will also be described in a moment.

This pronounced variation in negotiating strategies cannot be explained by any of a host of general ideas that have been suggested at one time or another. It cannot have been due to fundamentally different financial market conditions; in both cases the United States had a large and growing external deficit and an overvalued dollar, and Japan enjoyed the largest surplus. The United States had the same economic interest in both cases, and international monetary economics does not predict the observed strategy variation. The 1971 instance fits the objective market hypothesis described in chapter 3 but 1985 diverges from it.

Nor do we see different strategies because we are looking at a different deciding country, or because the United States faced a different target country. It can not be because the cultures, the military-security conditions, or the domestic political institutions had changed, since they too were essentially the same. Even the same political parties ruled during both episodes—the Republicans in the White House, the Democrats in the congressional majority, and the Liberal Democratic Party in Tokyo. The United States had a divided government during both episodes. Both treasury secretaries were politicians who had reason to be concerned about constituency demands and elections, yet they did not choose the same external strategy. The U.S. negotiator had to consider other states' payments positions and likely responses in addition to Japan's, but equally so in the two cases.

A key reason for the difference was a difference in policy ideas. The American negotiator in 1971 believed that Japan's government would relentlessly oppose a mixed-integrative strategy that would revalue the yen. In 1985 U.S. negotiators believed there was a good chance Tokyo would respond favorably.

CLAIMING VALUE IN 1971

In 1971 the president and the chief negotiator chose pure offensive claiming. Watching the widening deficits early in 1971, the Under Secretary of the Treasury for Monetary Affairs, Paul Volcker, privately warned Secretary John Connally, his new superior, that the coming year could conceivably force serious consideration

---

[5] Funabashi 1988, 10. Funabashi conducted over 100 interviews with government and central bank officials in Japan, Europe, and the United States for this account of monetary negotiations from 1985 through 1987. For those events this is the most important single source published in English.

of devaluing the dollar.[6] During the spring and summer, the staffs of the U.S. Treasury, the International Monetary Fund, and the Organization for Economic Cooperation and Development all estimated independently and secretly that a depreciation of 10 to 15 percent would be necessary and sufficient to return U.S. payments to equilibrium.[7]

These same three agencies estimated that a large appreciation of the yen would also be needed to restore international balance. By 1970 even Japan's own Ministry of Finance had secretly concluded that Japan's payments balance had moved into a fundamental surplus for the first time since World War II.[8] The Ministry denied this publicly, just as firmly as the U.S. Treasury promised never to devalue the dollar. The bilateral deficit with Japan constituted the largest share of the U.S. global deficit. Other currencies were also out of line with each other, especially the Europe/Japan rates. In short, market trends were making it ever more likely that a major currency realignment would occur somehow, by virtue of some strategy or lack thereof.

In July 1971 the treasury secretary, the under secretary, and the president agreed secretly that currency exchange rates had to shift; the yen and certain other currencies had to rise relative to the dollar. Accomplishing this shift was their primary international bargaining objective. Nixon and Connally undoubtedly also thought about protecting Nixon from domestic criticisms and winning the 1972 elections.

Nixon considered more than one negotiation strategy, and the choice was not fully determined by objective market and power conditions. The treasury secretary advocated bold, hard claiming. The game was nearly over, he told Nixon. We should seize the initiative before world markets attacked the dollar massively. One of Connally's most salient beliefs was that other countries were hurting U.S. business. At one private 1971 cabinet-level meeting with the president, he delivered "an unbelievable diatribe" against Japan and the European Community, implying they were America's real enemies.[9] Connally said Washington should impose domestic wage and price controls and announce it was suspending dollar convertibility into gold, without specifying a time or conditions for resuming convertibility. Washington would call on surplus countries to revalue their currency against the dollar, and Connally added, we should simultaneously slap their exports with the import surcharge. Volcker had strongly objected in private to adding an import surcharge, which he saw as antagonistic, protectionist, and contrary to the goal of depreciating the dollar.[10] Other economists voiced these objections before the decisions were made. Volcker also urged Nixon and Connally (again unsuccessfully) to include a plan for a reformed world monetary system at

[6] Volcker and Gyohten 1992, 72.

[7] Odell 1982; Angel 1991, 61–62.

[8] Angel 1991, 61–62.

[9] Interview with a participant in the meeting. For fuller evidence and discussion of this episode, see Odell 1982b, chapter 4 and Odell 1982a.

[10] Interview with a participating U.S. official, Princeton, New Jersey, 1975. Interviewees spoke on condition of confidentiality unless specified otherwise.

the same time.[11] This would have added a prominent element of value-creation, producing a mixed strategy instead. Connally dismissed this idea, firing back, "It'll be a year before they know what the problem is."[12]

Some information available to Washington prior to the American decision supported the belief that Tokyo would resist value creation and claim vigorously in any exchange-rate negotiation, even if Japan did not cash in its dollar reserves. In 1969 and 1970, mid-level American officials had canvassed for support in the IMF on behalf of rule changes that would have permitted wider but still limited flexibility of exchange rates within the established par-value system. Governments of Japan and other states firmly opposed even these limited schemes,[13] and no reforms were adopted during that period.

Reinforcing this belief in early 1971 was the behavior of the Japanese finance ministry in response to renewed market pressures: it adamantly rejected yen revaluation at every opportunity. Each succeeding month brought another sharp further accumulation of dollar reserves, as market participants probably began to prepare themselves for a yen appreciation. Each report touched off public discussion about how to satisfy foreign complaints about the payments surplus, with front-page discussion of the possibility of yen revaluation.[14] By March, the most prominent Japanese business leaders began to indicate even publicly that they no longer had confidence that the "stand fast" policy of the Ministry would solve the problem. In mid-April, the chairman of Keizai Doyukai, a prominent business association, said yen revaluation should be given more serious consideration as one policy alternative.[15] The controversy could have been taken as contrary evidence that Japan would in fact agree to a negotiated deal. In May, West Germany responded to similar market pressures by allowing the deutschemark to float upward. In Tokyo, the Ministry of Finance responded to still more inflows by repeating its denials that the yen could be revalued, and by quickly organizing an "Eight-Point Program to Avoid Yen Revaluation."

Some U.S. monetary officials, viewing the same evidence from objective markets and power structures, disagreed with Connally and advocated mixed strategies with value-creating elements. Firm defense of the parity was standard operating procedure for all finance ministries, right up to the moment of change. The superpower was staunchly affirming its own determination to defend established exchange rates, and it was offering Japan nothing in return for a revaluation. Observed behavior does not establish how Tokyo would have responded to a secret combination of demands, threats, and carrots.

Earlier in January, William B. Dale, the long-time U.S. delegate to the IMF

[11] Interview with a participant, Princeton, New Jersey, 1975; Volcker and Gyohten 1992, 78.
[12] Interview with a participating U.S. official, Washington, D.C., 1975.
[13] Interviews with participating U.S. monetary officials, Washington, D.C., 1975.
[14] Angel 1991, 74.
[15] Ibid., 78. This was also the period of the long bilateral conflict over textile trade mentioned in chapter 2. Japan's resistance on textiles was highly frustrating to Nixon, and this experience could have colored his expectations about how responsive Japan would be on exchange rates, though no specific evidence documents such a connection.

board, had sent Connally a long memorandum declaring that "interruption of convertibility and a major change in exchange rates would be necessary in the not-too-distant future."[16] In Dale's proposed scenario, the next September, one week before the annual IMF meeting, the president would suspend gold sales and currency trading and seek Congressional approval to change the dollar's par value. At the meeting, the United States would ask surplus governments to stand still for a substantial dollar depreciation, but the United States would take political responsibility for leading and make a contribution of its own. Dale would have further proposed a way of "deliberately working our way out of the reserve currency business," a regime change that would have been a welcome concession to some Europeans. Dale thought the bargaining could be completed and markets reopened within two weeks.[17]

At the August meeting at Camp David where Nixon made his decision, Arthur Burns, veteran Washington economic adviser and now chairman of the Federal Reserve Board of Governors, spoke tenaciously for a mixed-integrative strategy that would keep the gold window open. Burns favored taking unilateral domestic measures to restrain inflation—something Europeans had been calling for—and simultaneously negotiating an exchange rate realignment without suspending convertibility. He told Nixon that the surplus governments would respond favorably if the United States took these difficult measures at home and conceded an increase in the dollar price of gold (a dollar devaluation in terms of gold) in exchange for their revaluing their own currencies against the dollar.[18] He warned Nixon they would not like Connally's harsh strategy and could retaliate.

Volcker told Nixon he doubted Burns's expectations of foreign government restraint with the window open. He feared other central banks would not be able to resist an immediate rush to convert dollars to gold before the dollar was devalued. A central banker has a legal duty to protect the value of his nation's reserves. Volcker maintained that this approach would result in an embarrassing collapse of the commitment under pressure.[19]

Nixon, having opened himself to competing arguments but enjoying neither complete information nor unlimited time to deliberate, agreed with Connally that value creating would not achieve their objectives, rejected all integrative tactics, and chose pure claiming. Approving Connally's entire recommendation, he decided the import surcharge was "not too damned aggressive, just aggressive enough."[20]

To carry this story forward to the outcome, Japan's government responded to Washington's shocking, pugnacious strategy by attempting to defend tenaciously,

---

[16] Interview with William B. Dale, Washington, D.C., 1975.

[17] William B. Dale, "Scenario III: Exchange Rate Realignment and Related Matters" and "Time Sequence of Events for Scenario III," 28 January 1971, U.S. Treasury Department files, Washington, D.C.

[18] Safire 1975, 514.

[19] Volcker and Gyohten 1992, 78. He adds that Connally "certainly" did not share Burns's optimism.

[20] Safire 1975, 512, 515.

first buying enormous quantities of dollars for two weeks to hold the yen at its peg, and then, after allowing it to float upward, intervening further to brake the yen's rise as much as possible. Four months of tough multiparty negotiations ensued before the parties settled at the Smithsonian Institution in December.[21] There, Washington did claim some value from reluctant partners. They agreed to a dollar depreciation averaging 8 percent relative to OECD currencies. The 8 percent was probably more than other governments had been prepared to accept prior to negotiations, yet substantially less than what the Treasury and international organization staffs had estimated would be needed to stabilize financial markets. The yen's appreciation at the Smithsonian averaged 11 to 13 percent against the other currencies as a group.[22] In the end Nixon did concede a politically-visible U.S. devaluation of the dollar from $35 to $38 per ounce of gold and removed the import surcharge. The major IMF member states reaffirmed their pegged exchange rate rule, but Washington did not pledge to defend these new pegged rates. In 1973 they abandoned that rule in practice.

CREATING VALUE IN 1985

In 1985, in contrast, the U.S. negotiator chose value creating diluted with mild claiming tactics. During the early and mid-1980s the external current deficit expanded again together with Japan's surplus. The dollar, rather than falling to correct the imbalance, rose dramatically. Extraordinarily high interest rates, reflecting Federal Reserve policy, were drawing capital inward from other markets and thus pulling up local interest rates elsewhere, higher than those countries preferred. By 1983 financial officials in Europe were criticizing this policy and demanding changes. The first Reagan administration (1981–84) bragged about the strong dollar, held staunchly to a laissez faire policy, and took little direct action to bring it down or otherwise accommodate these complaints. Meanwhile, extraordinary increase of the dollar encouraged imports and intensified competitive pressure on manufacturers and growers of traded goods, stimulating political pressures on Washington for higher import barriers.

After the 1984 elections, James Baker III, Reagan's new Secretary of the Treasury, decided to try to accomplish another dollar depreciation.[23] Baker chose a sharply different negotiating strategy to achieve the same objective with the same country. Far from springing a fait accompli and opening with a sanction, Baker began with a Paris speech on 12 April 1985 offering to host an international conference to make incremental improvements in the world monetary system.[24] Next, at a preparatory session in Tokyo on 19 June 1985, prior to a meeting of the Group of Ten finance ministers, David C. Mulford, Baker's Assistant Secretary of

---

[21] This subsequent process and settlement are described in Odell 1982b, 271–91.
[22] Odell 1982b, 287–88.
[23] Destler and Henning 1989, chapters 3 and 4.
[24] *Washington Post*, 13 April 1985, 1; *New York Times*, 13 April 1985, 34.

the Treasury for International Affairs, gave secret advance notice to Tomomitsu Oba, Japan's Vice Minister of Finance for International Affairs, that Baker was thinking specifically about a cooperative dollar-yen realignment, adding the key assurance that the Europeans also would be asked to contribute.

Two days later, when Baker made the suggestion to his counterpart privately, Finance Minister Noboru Takeshita gave a favorable reaction. He even suggested that they have their central banks actively sell dollars during periods when market forces were already moving in that direction—a tactic known as "leaning with the wind."[25] According to Takeshita, Baker responded with caution to the latter suggestion. Baker maintained that the key to currency realignment was domestic macroeconomic management, and he specifically wanted Japan to boost domestic demand. The Japanese minister declined, as did many others after him.[26] The two, while exploring objectives that evidently overlapped, also were attempting to protect other goals that were partly inconsistent. Overall, a Japanese participant reported a sharp change in U.S. negotiating tactics compared with Baker's immediate predecessor as well as Connally. He recalled especially that Baker personally took notes while listening patiently to Takeshita. "What a difference from the table-pounding [Treasury Secretary Donald] Regan!"[27]

This bilateral negotiating process continued to play out secretly during the subsequent three months. At the next bilateral meeting on 23 July in Paris during an OECD conference, Mulford told Oba of the Reagan administration's plans for countering the remarkable surge of U.S. domestic pressure for trade protection that filled front pages at the time (chaps. 3 and 6). This objective—quelling U.S. domestic protectionism—was shared by the Japanese. Moves would be timed for mid-September, after Congress had returned from its August vacation. Mulford said that joint monetary actions could be coupled with planned trade policy initiatives and presented as a coherent package. Once again the Americans insisted on Japanese demand stimulus, either via tax reductions or spending increases. Again the Japanese responded with familiar defensive claiming, citing reasons why the government could not make any commitments at that time, though they did not firmly rule out fiscal adjustments.[28] Mulford and Oba met again on 21 August in Hawaii, where the Japanese committed to some capital market deregulation but continued to decline to lower tax rates. During a subsequent trip to Europe, Mulford heard only lukewarm responses to Baker's call for participation. The Germans sounded especially skeptical, insisting that the main causes of the large, disruptive international imbalances were the U.S. federal budget deficit and conflicts between Japan and America.

This second case also ended in an agreement. During the summer the dollar rose even higher, after having drifted slightly downward early in the year. A wide-

[25] Funabashi 1988, 11; interview with Oba, "The Political Economy of Money Diplomacy," *Toyo Keizai*, 22 May 1987.
[26] Funabashi 1988, 11.
[27] Ibid.
[28] Ibid., 12.

spread fear was that without some change in government management, the dollar could at any moment drop suddenly and generate panic selling, a cumulative free fall, bankruptcies, and needless unemployment. In these conditions, the Europeans did join to some degree in the emerging Japan-U.S. deal, which finance ministers and central bank governors from France, Germany, Japan, the United Kingdom, and the United States completed at New York's Plaza Hotel on Sunday, 22 September 1985. In a joint press conference, the first public disclosure of what had been going on, the Group of Five ministers declared that large external imbalances could destabilize the world economy to the detriment of all. They said the yen and the deutschemark should move up so as to better reflect fundamental economic conditions, and they repeatedly announced their willingness to "cooperate more closely to encourage this when to do so would be helpful."[29] For four years Washington had insisted that a strong dollar was good for America and the world and had shunned international negotiations to regulate currency values. This leadership of concerted action to depreciate the dollar marked a sharp change.

At the Plaza the G5 agreed secretly to coordinate intervention for six weeks. They would mainly sell the dollar whenever the market pushed it up and intervene progressively less at lower dollar levels. Sharing the objective of avoiding a costly free fall, they also declared their willingness to support the dollar if necessary. Baker proposed a target of 10 to 12 percent depreciation by the end of October, and this target was broadly accepted. The parties engaged in some claiming over whom would have to buy how many yen and deutschemarks. They did not reach agreement on how much further the dollar should fall after October, if at all, nor did they agree to coordinate interest-rate cuts. Germany and Japan still declined to commit to the additional fiscal stimulus Baker had sought—he settled without these concessions—just as the United States did not commit to new fiscal deficit reduction. Each minister reiterated intentions to carry out previously decided measures and to do better in general.[30]

The mixed-integrative strategy had worked in the sense of bringing about a limited agreement that each government counted a gain. Washington and Tokyo each would have counted a dollar "hard landing" or new protectionist trade measures as a serious loss, and both were avoided. By year-end, according to the Federal Reserve's measure, the dollar was down by 12 percent against all major currencies since the Plaza and by 25 percent since the February 1985 peak. It was down from 240 yen at the Plaza to 200 yen.[31]

---

[29] Communiqué, 22 September 1985, rpt. in *New York Times,* 23 September 1985; *Los Angeles Times*, 23 September 1985, 1.

[30] Funabashi 1988, 11–25.

[31] Some skeptics of the Plaza accord have contended that the dollar would have fallen without it. One, who would have preferred domestic American budget reform over international diplomacy, is Nau 1990, chapter 9. During 1986 Japanese leaders would become more and more alarmed as the yen continued to rise much further than they had intended. Subsequent monetary negotiations are discussed in chapter 3.

ANALYSIS

The main reason for the clear difference in strategy choice seems to be that in 1971, the U.S. negotiator believed Tokyo would not respond favorably to value creating, and in 1985 his successor believed the reverse, even though objective financial market conditions were generally similar. Close observers had three reasons to expect Tokyo to respond favorably to mixed-integrative tactics in 1985. Beliefs in Tokyo about the yen had changed markedly during the 1970s and early 1980s. The 1970s experience with *endaka* (yen appreciation) had turned out to be not nearly as bad for Japan's trade and profits as had been feared. For one thing, a higher yen gave Japanese firms that rely heavily on imported components a break in the prices they paid, which offset the competitive disadvantage on export prices, quite substantially in some cases. Japan after yen revaluation had registered trade surpluses again in 1977 and 1978 that vastly exceeded those of 1969 through 1972. Then during the early 1980s, following sharp declines due to the 1979 world oil price jump, the trade surplus promptly bounced back once again.

Second, after the late 1970s Japan's Finance Ministry adopted an almost unshakable opposition to deficit spending and a commitment to tight fiscal policy. This was a result of unhappy experience after the Carter administration had pushed Japan to stimulate its economy like a "locomotive," to pull the world out of the international imbalances of that period. This firm fiscal commitment gave Ministry leaders a preference for yen appreciation over tax cuts and spending increases as ways to reduce Japan's external surplus.[32] If U.S. negotiators were aware in 1985 of this ranking of possible concessions—direct evidence is thin on this point—the knowledge would have given them an additional reason for expecting a favorable response to a proposal to create joint gain by currency realignment.

On the Japanese side a third, special circumstance also intervened. Yasuhiro Nakasone had become Prime Minister in 1982. This leader, unlike many LDP colleagues, had supported the objective of a strong yen as a mark of national prestige and pride since the beginning of his political career. Years earlier he had advocated a foreign policy based on "yen in the right hand and Zen in the left." In a December 1982 press conference soon after becoming Prime Minister, Nakasone had "made it clear that he would manage the Japanese economy in a way compatible with yen appreciation."[33] *Fortune* magazine published an interview in February 1983, on the eve of his state visit to Washington. Asked about the recent strengthening of the yen, Nakasone replied:

I believe it is important to further strengthen the yen in order to stabilize prices and to revitalize economic activity. Japan imports huge volumes of raw materials. If the yen weakens, raw material prices will go up and apply pressure on corporate profits, which will deprive the private sector of its vitality.[34]

[32] Funabashi 1988, 93–95.
[33] Ibid., 89.
[34] *Fortune*, 7 February 1983, 8.

After leaving office in 1987, Nakasone said that in 1985 he had deliberately planned a strategy for strengthening the yen. He was supported in this planning by an informal group of business and former government leaders. Beginning in 1982, he said, the yen's opening and closing values were reported to him every day. As Japan's external surplus grew larger, leaders of Japan's international business sector transmitted ever greater concern about the political hostility it was generating in the United States, their most important market by far. By mid-1985, Nakasone said, he had decided that trade liberalization measures would be insufficient to moderate this surplus:

> I made up my mind to launch a comprehensive scheme to tackle the issue with U.S. support. It, of course, included yen-dollar currency realignment. I told my idea to Takeshita and Oba. They both agreed.[35]

Nakasone not only aimed to achieve greater international influence and prestige for Japan, but also saw *endaka* as a means for building a new, strong domestic political constituency for himself and his party. Part of the broader thinking was to restructure Japanese society away from dependence on exports and more toward reliance on internal growth. A higher yen would benefit the better educated, more affluent urban consumer voters who paid the price for Japan's protectionism, special-interest regulation, and cheap currency, and who seemed to welcome a more modern, outward-looking Japanese leadership.[36]

OTHER INTERPRETATIONS

Could other interpretations better explain this variation in strategy choices? Case selection essentially ruled out several possible answers: that it was due to fundamentally different market conditions or a different deciding country, negotiating objective, or target country. The 1985 case seems to confound one sensible market hypothesis that one should expect claiming with respect to a market change that would affect two countries in opposite directions. It confounds IR realists who expect countries always to beggar their neighbors by depreciating their currencies.

It would be difficult, as well, to attribute this difference to a change in any of the four contexts of economic bargaining. The national culture and political institutions were basically the same in 1971 and 1985 in the United States (and in Japan too for that matter). Both episodes occurred during the Cold War, when each state regarded the Soviet Union as its most important possible enemy. In 1985 no major increase in external military threat or decline in U.S. military power vis-à-vis the USSR can be cited as a reason for Washington's turn toward integrative bargaining with Japan. In fact, in 1971 the United States was fighting a hot war in Vietnam, which should have constrained offensive claiming from al-

---

[35] Funabashi 1988, 88, based on a personal interview with Nakasone.
[36] Ibid., 88–93.

lies if any security condition would do so. Whether or not the subsequent decline of the Soviet threat has freed allies to engage in more economic conflict, the Cold War and the hot Vietnam war were not sufficient to prevent these allies from engaging in fairly vigorous economic conflict and value claiming occasionally. Economic bargaining has a dynamic of its own.

Could a change in the international monetary rules have accounted for this strategy difference? Actually the monetary regime gave an observer precious little help in anticipating which bargaining strategy diplomats would use in either episode. The 1971 démarche was a plain instance of breaking the rules. And after 1977, the international monetary regime prescribed almost nothing with respect to exchange rate practices, and nothing at all with respect to bargaining behavior. It required states to maintain neither pegged rates nor floating ones, and only forbade antisocial behavior in general terms.

True, in 1971 the gold window was open and exchange rates were pegged, and in 1985 the window was closed and major rates were floating. The open gold commitment did make a practical difference to U.S. policy making in 1971, but it did not dictate which negotiation strategy Washington would use with other governments. The prevailing international rules and market conditions did not require the president to suspend gold convertibility the way Nixon did—together with complaints blaming foreigners for the dollar's problems, demands for one-way concessions, no acknowledgment of others' objectives, and a surcharge on their exports. Rules and markets did not exclude a mixed negotiating strategy with integrative elements, as proposals by Burns, Dale, and Volcker showed. Each was a veteran monetary policy maker with access to the same objective facts. If the president and the chief negotiator had been convinced, like these advisers, that other governments would respond favorably to value-creating, and if they had placed greater weight on maintaining the international regime (relative to a larger dollar depreciation) as the advisors did, they might have suspended convertibility temporarily as part of an invitation to an immediate conference of the major IMF members on measures to adjust and stabilize the monetary system in the interest of all. With Japan, a mixed strategy could have begun in secret talks as in 1985, even without suspending convertibility.

There was another complex technical difference between the rules and market conditions in these two cases. The 1971 official commitment to maintain pegged exchange rates gave the market player a "one-way bet." When a country had a payments deficit, traders could bet against its currency without fear that it would rise and cost them money. With rates floating, capital flows could carry a currency upward somewhat in the short term even while its country was running a large deficit. As a result, short-term currency market pressure on the dollar may have been concentrated more heavily on the sell side in August 1971 than in August 1985, even though the aggregate payments balances were similar. If so, it may have been somewhat easier for governments collectively to bring the dollar down in the short term, or to bring it down farther, in 1971 than in 1985—with the help of somewhat more one-sided market pressures waiting in the wings. But what does this consideration predict about the strategy choice of a government that decides to negotiate toward an agreement with other governments, given that its information is incomplete? In 1971, if Washington could count on more imbalanced market pressure to help it claim more from Japan (when Japan opposed yen appreciation more strenuously), would this have predicted that Washington will use fewer integrative tactics than in 1985? Or does it imply that precisely because markets might do more of the heavy lifting to move current exchange rates in the short term, then the government would likely mix in more tactics of its own for discovering and creating joint value for the longer term? This consideration also seems insufficient to explain the mix of tactics used vis-à-vis Japan and other governments. Current rules and markets did not fully determine Washington's bargaining strategies.

A final skeptic might ask whether the American negotiator in 1985 had an inferior batna, because of this difference in the rules or other factors. Did Baker need an agreement on balance more than Connally, and did Baker avoid offensive claiming and use more integrative tactics for this reason? This too would be a difficult case to make. First, not being vulnerable to an open gold window would seem to give Baker a preferable, not a worse, bargaining position. And on closer inspection, the alternative of acting alone, without a negotiated agreement with other governments, was conceivable in both instances but also carried risks in both. If the United States tried to force other currency rates up by itself, markets could be expected to add pressures in both instances, since the United States had a large deficit and Japan and others had surpluses, which signaled the directions in which rates were likely to move in the medium term. After all, in both instances U.S. official defense of the status quo was a key reason currency rates had not moved already. While Baker in 1985 could not stimulate a market run out of dollars by slamming the gold window shut, more subtle moves were available (chap. 3). Yet, on the negative side, a purely unilateral course raised the risk of retaliation. In neither instance were other governments powerless to oppose movements by their currencies. Even if they did not retaliate, merely the perceived possibility of government conflict over these sensitive markets could set off global economic turmoil. Recall, too, that in 1971 the U.S. government's goal was not to smash the fixed rate system, but to engineer finite shifts in pegged rates within that system while containing the disruption to business. (The December 1971 agreement did establish a new set of pegged rates, not floating rates.) In 1971 as well as 1985, Tokyo had a substantial capability to oppose yen appreciation or prolong disorder. Restoring the par value regime for the yen required Tokyo's agreement. All in all, Connally's alternative to a negotiated deal was not clearly more attractive than Baker's in terms of their respective policy objectives.

SOURCES OF VARIATIONS IN BELIEFS

Some might question this chapter's beliefs argument on the grounds that it sounds ad hoc, it stops short of telling us what produces belief variations themselves, but this objection would betray a double standard. Every supposed cause is itself a result of other things, of course. The question "but what caused that?" is never answered completely. If this test were applied uniformly, all social science theories would be rejected.

This being said, an empirically valid theory that explained behavior by reference to beliefs and also went deeper to explain belief variations themselves, would be even more powerful and useful. In this spirit, chapter 3 proposed objective market indicators that might on average reduce the likely range of dominant beliefs and strategy choices. Other possible sources (not necessarily suggested by these two episodes) can be imagined. For example, the more favorable responses A has received from B to past integrative attempts, the more A will expect a favorable response the next time. Or the stronger the domestic support for negotiator B, the more likely is a favorable response and the more A is likely to expect one. When negotiator B is under attack at home, A might reason, B is more likely to welcome an international conflict that will help B depict herself to her constituents as a brave defender of the in-group. Following this line of thinking, it might be supposed that when a country's population is suffering economic distress—widespread unemployment, falling incomes, collapsing firms—its negotiator will expect counterparts from other governments, international organizations, or firms to try to take advantage of her country's great need. This expectation of tough claiming by others might lead B to avoid integrative moves, which would expose information that could be exploited. Ideas such as these could be investigated as well.

Naturally negotiator A's beliefs or judgments could be inaccurate in a given situation, or biased predictably across the board. Valid knowledge of a negotiator's culture or predictable judgment biases might be another valuable arrow in the analyst's quiver. Chapters 5 and 9 explore these insights.

An analytical focus on the negotiator's beliefs need not mean that random personal idiosyncrasies will determine these choices. Relevant policy beliefs may be shared by a group, reflecting evidence gathered and evaluated by the group. The relative importance of individual idiosyncrasies is an empirical question. Even if they have some effect in history, as they surely must, that does not mean that no generalization can be valid.

If bargaining strategies are significant and they vary across negotiations, a useful theory ought to help explain this variation, and if possible help us anticipate future strategy choices by others. One useful thing to know, as in labor-management relations, will be the negotiator's belief about how the other side will react to integrative tactics. This contrast between two international monetary episodes supports the hypothesis that in a world of bounded rationality, the more negotiator A believes B will resist or exploit a value-creating strategy, the less likely A will be to choose that strategy, other things equal. To that extent, A will lean toward value claiming. The evidence strongly suggests that these strategies were not fully determined by objective background conditions, and thus that strategy choice, a process variable, made a significant difference of its own. Many alternative interpretations have been ruled out. This controlled contrast suggests that this hypothesis from policy ideas merits more extensive testing. Chapter 9 will point to additional possibilities for research on strategy variation, and chapter 10 will highlight practical lessons from these and other experiences.

CHAPTER 5

Biases, Compensatory Tactics, and Outcomes

Beliefs about strategy feasibility are not the only subjective variables in the negotiating process. More generally, negotiators, like people in other settings, will normally think with the help of shortcuts and biases. Facts reach the negotiator surrounded by much noise, so that to interpret incoming data and make a decision requires some intellectual structure. Cognitive heuristics and biases constitute some of the most consequential boundaries on real human rationality. By studying these biases and what is done or not done about them, we can develop other valuable ideas for the analytical tool kit. This chapter and those to follow will move the focus from strategy choice to the rest of the process and the outcome. The main new hypothesis is that the gains from bargaining with any strategy will increase as the negotiator uses tactics designed to compensate for his own judgment biases.

During the late 1970s Mexico negotiated toward bilateral trade agreements with the United States on two occasions, in each case using a mixed strategy to increase Mexican exports. Mexico clearly gained more from the second than the first negotiation. Early in 1977 the Mexican government decided to sell a large quantity of natural gas to its northern neighbor. As Petróleos Mexicanos (PEMEX), the state-owned firm, was increasing oil output and laying ambitious plans to increase it far more, it was simply flaring surplus associated natural gas at the wellhead, wasting it into the atmosphere. PEMEX decided to lay a large pipeline, called the *gasoducto*, from the fields northward to the tip of Texas. Completing an export deal meant negotiating not only with private U.S. pipeline companies but also with Washington, since the U.S. energy market was regulated by law. The December 1977 outcome was an impasse. Mexico's negotiator gained nothing commercially, relative to either the status quo ante or Mexico's best no-deal alternative at the time. Hundreds of millions of dollars in potential annual revenues were lost, and the bilateral political relationship was marred subsequently by angry reproaches, especially from south of the border. In an epilogue two years later, Presidents Jimmy Carter and José López Portillo attempted to soothe bruised feelings by signing a gas agreement at their September 1979 summit meeting. The amounts to be shipped, however, were only a fraction of what had been planned. Commentators regarded this tiny, delayed deal as slightly favorable for the political relationship but of little economic significance.

In the second case, Mexican representatives persuaded Washington to settle a 1978–79 dispute threatening its exports of another primary commodity—vegetables, mostly tomatoes. Large farms in northwest Mexico grew vegetables in conditions favored by nature during the U.S. winter, again suggesting significant potential joint gains from trading. Northbound exports of fresh and frozen winter vegetables grew substantially to a new plateau in 1969 and expanded further beginning in 1977. By 1978 these exports were worth about $300 million annually. Increasing market penetration provoked appeals for government protection from the only other winter competitors in Florida, both in 1969 and later. In October 1978 Florida growers filed a complaint in Washington under the antidumping statute, alleging that Mexican firms were selling tomatoes at less than fair value and demanding imposition of an antidumping duty. If Mexico had not responded effectively, the U.S. Treasury would surely have imposed such a duty. When a defendant ignores one of these allegations, Washington typically accepts the American complainant's version of the facts. The duty would have been substantial enough to cause serious damage to Mexico's trade. In the end, however, the Treasury announced that Mexican producers had not sold their products at less than fair value, and Washington did not impose any new duty. Mexico's *tomateros* succeeded in keeping the U.S. market as open to their rapidly growing trade as it had been before the petition was filed.[1] Although the commercial size of this market was smaller, Mexico's agents gained all they could possibly have gained by negotiating, relative to no deal. They gained commercially not relative to the status quo ante but by evading a loss that surely would have befallen them had they not responded effectively to a new threat. Politically Mexico (and the United States) also gained by removing an irritant from the bilateral relationship. This settlement was implemented.

Why then did Mexico clearly gain less in the first episode than the second? Exploring this contrast reveals another family of answers that probably will be valid in many future cases as well. First, however, we may set aside at least seven possible answers that have been thought to explain bargaining outcomes in general. The answer cannot be that Mexico was dealing with a less powerful party the second time; the power structure was equally and highly asymmetrical in both episodes. Nor were the issues qualitatively different, as would have been the case with a security or an immigration question; each episode concerned an export trade issue. It cannot be because Mexico's two negotiators used different strategies; both used a mixed strategy. Nor was the exogenous context materially different. Neither the military security threats facing Mexico or the United States, nor their security relationship, changed significantly during this time. The relevant international trade institutions remained essentially constant. There had been no change in either country's culture. The same domestic political institutions, and even the same two presidential administrations, were in place. Additionally, both episodes became politicized in the sense that mass media in both countries

---

[1] The case did not end legally until a few months later. Under the 1979 trade act, jurisdiction for such complaints passed from the Treasury to the Commerce Department, and in response to Florida appeals, the Carter administration reopened this investigation in Commerce in early 1980. The resulting decision, however, was the same. The Florida growers association also filed an appeal with the U.S. judiciary, but also to no avail.

published many stories about them and legislators and editorialists spoke out. Nor did Mexico fail to stimulate U.S. citizens to exert their own influence on its behalf in the gas case; transnational allies inside the United States were active in both disputes.

Two key differences will explain this outcome variation. Mexico's team in the second episode used debiasing tactics to a greater extent and with greater effect than in the first, helping them to reach agreement. This answer is quite different from those given by other accounts of these events.[2] Second, the United States' objective market alternative to agreement worsened between the two events, which probably helped spur Washington toward the second deal.

JUDGMENT BIASES AND DEBIASING TACTICS

A long tradition argues that psychological variables and policy ideas shape foreign policy decisions, especially on security issues.[3] Although many such studies have not applied psychological claims to an analysis of bargaining, several on the security side have done so more or less explicitly.[4] We have little good evidence, however, about the roles of cognitive variables in international economic bargaining.[5]

For our purposes, one well-established heuristic is anchoring, a special case of framing. When assigning a value to an object such as an alternative to agreement, a concession, or a deal, we tend not to conduct a comprehensive search for all conceivably relevant information and then perform an elaborate calculation. Instead, the average person saves time by starting with some subjectively-available reference point, the anchor, and adjusting the value from there. Negotiation experiments have found, for example, that when a seller is not well informed about how much a buyer will gain from a given deal, the seller tends to let the buyer's initial bid anchor the final agreement. The seller is uncertain how much gain is reasonable to expect. Thus when the buyer's initial offer is lower, the seller is less optimistic and tends to settle for a lower price than when the initial offer is more favorable but all else is the same.[6]

Researchers took professional real estate agents in Tucson, Arizona, to view a house that was for sale at the time. They asked each realtor, after viewing it and its

[2] In addition to works cited below, Cottam 1985 offers a different psychological interpretation of the first episode, one that pays no attention to parties' alternatives to agreement and how they were perceived, among other things.

[3] E.g., De Rivera 1968, George 1969, Holsti 1972, Janis 1972, Jervis 1976, Larson 1985, and Levy 1997. Young and Schafer 1998 is a recent review.

[4] E.g., Snyder and Diesing 1977, chapter 4; Jervis and Stein 1985 on deterrence.

[5] Exceptions are Stein and Pauly 1992 and Berejekian 1997. Haas 1980, Odell 1982b, Goldstein 1993, Goldstein and Keohane 1993 include policy ideas as influences on foreign economic policy-making, but usually not from a psychological viewpoint and not applied to negotiation specifically.

[6] Liebert et al. 1968. Bazerman and Neale 1992, 28, add that initial offers have a stronger influence on final agreements than the other's subsequent concessionary behavior. Thompson 1990 and Rabin 1998 provide useful critical reviews of this psychological literature.

neighborhood, to estimate a reasonable price to pay for the house, as well as the lowest offer you would accept if you were the seller. Each agent was given the same ten-page package of information about the house, including the value of neighboring houses that had sold recently—with one exception. Different realtors were given different seller's listing prices, which varied randomly from $119,900 to $149,900. Realtors given a higher asking price assigned the house a significantly higher average value, after each had inspected the same building and had the same information otherwise. Likewise, the higher the listing price, the higher the agent's measured resistance point. Although most realtors said they had reached their estimated values by comparing the house's features to those of neighboring homes and adjusting for differences in square footage, and did not say they had anchored on the asking price, clearly they had tended to do so. Experienced experts whose livelihood depends on such decisions behaved no differently from amateur subjects.[7]

A second bias is the endowment premium, another case of framing. The hypothesis is that the seller of an object tends to frame the transaction as losing something he already owns. Thus sellers price an object they own above the value set by a independent party such as a market, to compensate for breaking this relationship to the object and losing the so-called endowment. As a result, market-clearing transactions expected by economic theory actually fail to occur. In an experiment, every second subject was given a new specialty coffee mug, was told he now owns the mug, and asked whether he preferred to sell it for cash or keep it at each of a schedule of prices. The experimenters asked the other half of the subjects to examine one of the mugs and decide whether they would prefer to buy it with their own money or keep their money at each price. Subjects had been told to bring their own cash, and were then invited to make any trades they wished to make. The median seller reservation price was $5.25 and the median buyer reservation price was $2.25. Very few trades took place. Buying and selling prices also tended not to converge over repeated trials with full feedback each time. The endowment effect persists in market settings with opportunities to learn.[8]

A third documented bias is a tendency to remain committed to an initial course of action or even increase the stakes after it has generated negative consequences, out of reluctance to admit error or concern for reputation with some audience. In another study, for example, business students were asked to make simulated investment decisions, allocating funds between two divisions of a firm. Control subjects did not make an investment decision in round 1. After the first and prior to a second decision, each subject was told that one division had performed badly. Subjects who had invested in that division in round 1 committed significantly

---

[7] Northcraft and Neale 1987. The study ran amateur (student) subjects through the same experiment separately, and the two sets of evidence led to the same conclusion. Two experiments using different houses with different values replicated the findings. The realtors in the second experiment had an average of nine years experience, participating in an average of sixteen transactions per year. A check for possible effects of demographic variations among the subjects found no significant differences.

[8] Kahneman, Knetsch, and Thaler 1990.

more new resources to it in the second round on average, than those who received exactly the same information but had not invested in it the first time. As usual, individual subjects were assigned randomly to the treatment groups.[9]

Lest this seem like an error that experienced negotiators outside the laboratory will surely avoid when the stakes are much greater, recall Robert Campeau, the prominent Canadian corporate leader who in 1987 bid to purchase Federated Department Stores, Bloomingdale's parent firm. When a competitor, Macy's, was on the verge of victory in a bidding war, Campeau raised Macy's already high offer by another $500 million, winning the contest. Meanwhile, however, Federated had been losing value as key executives departed, which should have indicated lowering the offer if anything, not raising it. Two years later, having borrowed and paid far too much, this experienced business negotiator declared bankruptcy.[10]

Fourth and perhaps most general is partisanship bias. Each negotiator is a partisan for his side. The partisan subject in experiments, compared with a neutral subject given the same information, tends to overestimate the value of his own alternative to agreement[11]—which can eliminate the zone of agreement, especially if both negotiators do so. The partisan recalls more information that supported his own position, even when negotiators on different sides are given the same information.[12]

The partisan, without debiasing mechanisms, also tends to use a self-serving concept of fairness, believing it to be impartial, and then interprets aggressive behavior of the other as an effort to gain unfair advantage. In one experimental study subjects were given the facts from a true tort case and asked to predict the value of the settlement (between $1 and $100,000) that a neutral judge would award. Subjects who had been framed to think of themselves as plaintiffs predicted significantly higher awards on average than control subjects given all the same information. Asking the subject to list weaknesses in his own case first proved to be an effective debiaser.[13]

A recent field study of strikes and contract negotiations between teacher unions and school districts in Pennsylvania asked each party to list other districts they regarded as comparable for purposes of salary negotiations. Union presidents listed districts whose average salary was $27,633, while school board presidents listed districts whose salaries averaged $26,922. The difference between partisans was significant, statistically and economically.[14] Research indicates that self-serving assessments of fairness are likely to appear in morally ambiguous situations with more than one focal point—which are widespread in international relations.

The partisan also tends to underestimate the degree to which the other negotiator's objectives are compatible with his own—to assume a fixed-sum situation

---

[9] Staw 1976. The study was designed to eliminate several conceivable rival interpretations.
[10] Bazerman and Neale 1992, 9–10.
[11] Lax and Sebenius 1986, 58.
[12] Thompson and Loewenstein 1992.
[13] Babcock and Loewenstein 1997, 111–13.
[14] Ibid., 116–17.

when the truth is otherwise. In another recent study, a nonpartisan observer of a negotiation between two other subjects was more likely to make accurate judgments about the compatibility of the negotiators' payoffs than were the negotiators, who perceived incompatible objectives when they did not exist. Additionally, high subjective involvement with the negotiation worsened judgment accuracy among partisan observers, while it improved accuracy among nonpartisan observers. Making an observer feel more accountable also worsened judgment accuracy among partisans but increased accuracy among the nonpartisan.[15]

Many economists have been skeptical of these psychological findings and have offered several rationales to buttress their skepticism. One is that while naive experimental subjects might be biased, trained professionals will resist bias. The research with realtors and the field study of Pennsylvania school personnel are two of many careful studies that cast doubt on this conjectural source of comfort.[16] Another complaint is that the stakes in experiments are too low. But this complaint also does not apply to studies like the latter, where the subjects were professionals engaging in their normal business.

A third complaint is that experimental studies overlook the possibility that people learn from experience, and this learning will tend to correct biases. But some experiments confirming these biases have used experienced subjects. Other studies have responded to this objection by providing for feedback and learning during experiments, and have still failed to eliminate the biases. In general, learning in the real world is not so simple. Each actual negotiation is different from each other in some salient respect. Even in a single episode, participants from different agencies and firms are exposed to a somewhat different mix of information coming from the experience. Even all of those who receive the same information receive a complex mixture that must be interpreted. Facts normally support more than one inference about why it unfolded as it did and who deserves credit and blame.[17] Learning from experience is itself a function of the judge's predispositions, the public commitments he has made, and his concerns for reputation. Learning can reinforce biases and errors as well as offset them.[18]

---

[15] Thompson 1995. The subject playing a negotiator role was given a payoff schedule for an employer-employee negotiation task entailing six issues, and told to earn as many points as possible. Neither negotiator saw the other's schedule. The payoffs were constructed to create a positive zone of agreement. Subjects playing the observer role were framed either to focus on one negotiator's problems (partisan observers), or to try to understand each side's viewpoint objectively (nonpartisan observers). After the negotiation, each observer was given one side's payoff schedule, and each subject was asked to estimate the payoffs of the other party. Accuracy was measured by comparing the subjects' answers with the other's actual payoff schedule.

[16] Eisenberg 1994 provides similar evidence from a survey of bankruptcy attorneys and judges reporting on each other's behavior.

[17] Babcock and Loewenstein 1997 also respond by complaining that economists' alternative experiments described as free of contaminating context are in fact not free of context, that the advice to observe "behavior" and not "perceptions" is not followed consistently even in economics, and it would rob us of valuable information if it were.

[18] Rabin 1998, 31–32. Rabin adds that "experts who have rich models of the system in question" are even more susceptible than lay people to overconfidence in judgments and confirmatory bias. "Economists, take note," says this economist.

These four biases—anchoring, the endowment premium, escalating commitment to a losing cause, and partisanship—have several implications for bargaining. They imply that unless steps are taken to offset them, a seller will attach a higher value to his concessions or possessions than a neutral party would assign. He will anchor a bargaining position on a cognitively available analogue rather than relying on an exhaustive search and calculation. He will adopt a definition of fairness that is biased in favor of his own side and against that of the other. On average he will tend to under-weight common interests that exist but are partially masked by distorted information. He will use more claiming tactics relative to value-creating tactics, and run higher risks of impasse despite negative feedback during the process, than would a debiased negotiator.

Tactics for offsetting these biases may include the following:

- assigning some team member the task of reporting privately on biases that could in principle affect our own side, and recommending steps that could counter these risks, rotating members through this post so as to sensitize each in turn;
- tasking some team member or agent to specialize in reporting on the other's subjective goals, priorities, causal beliefs, biases, and apparent resistance points, and rewarding him specifically on the eventual accuracy of the judgments about how the other will react to scenarios, however unwelcome such predictions might be;
- sending one team of negotiators to "technical working group" meetings with the other party prior to politically-sensitive high-level talks, with the assignment of searching the other side's views for possible common objectives, while assuring that this team will not have responsibility for claiming value later, perhaps selecting team members known to have special talents for these functions;
- exploring true preferences directly and openly with the counterpart, by asking, for example, which issues rank highest and lowest for him, or asking for reactions to hypothetical alternative package deals constructed to elicit preferences more accurately; and
- inviting a consultant, who enjoys relevant expertise and independence from the negotiator, to report privately his own judgments and to suggest courses of action.

In principle these tactics could be applied in varying degrees—from repeatedly and at several levels and with strong support from the chief negotiator, to intermittently or nominally but without such support, or not at all.

NATURAL GAS EXPORTS, 1977

On 21 December 1977, a meeting at the White House ended with acrimony. Santiago Roel, Mexico's Foreign Minister, and Jorge Díaz Serrano, the Director General of PEMEX, met with James Schlesinger, the U.S. Secretary of Energy, but failed to achieve their purpose—to win Schlesinger's approval of the natural gas deal. Reportedly Schlesinger expressed strong reservations to their terms but said he was willing to continue talking.[19] The next day Mexico's President José López Portillo directed PEMEX to abandon the negotiation. Early in January 1978 Schlesinger was quoted as telling American firms that "sooner or later" Mexico would have to sell its gas to the United States,[20] which provoked additional angry Mexican attacks.

The universal public interpretation at the time was that Schlesinger had personally ruined an obviously lucrative deal with unreasonable demands and insensitive tactics. On 25 November the *Washington Post*'s editorialist, having gotten wind of the standoff, opined:

> Mexico has large resources of gas and oil, and it makes altogether good sense for the U.S. government to develop them. . . . What's a fair price for the gas? Mexico's wealth per capita is one-twelfth that of the United States, and Mexico is entitled to full market value. That means a price no less than that of oil.[21]

Nine months later the *Wall Street Journal* denounced the outcome as a "fiasco." It sympathized with the chairman of one of the interested pipeline companies, who said:

> We thought it was a hell of a good program for Mexico and the United States. With Mexico's problems, we couldn't have expected them to sell to us at below world prices. Why should they? . . . Our entire relationship to Mexico is involved here. . . . I don't understand why we didn't take a more enlightened view of this thing instead of approaching it as just an energy question. We could have been of tremendous assistance to López Portillo in getting things underway, even if it was a bad price—which it wasn't.[22]

The *Washington Post* concluded that "the United States has badly mishandled the preliminary test case involving natural gas."[23] *Forbes* agreed that "Mexico offered favorable terms." But "the U.S. . . . tried to beat Mexico down below OPEC prices on its asking price for gas. . . . Instead, it fell on its face."[24]

These early reactions glossed over critical elements of this situation, including some facts that were not known publicly. They fail to pose some of the decisive questions asked by a sound negotiation analysis of the type outlined in part 1. Without necessarily exonerating Schlesinger on all counts, a fresh, comparative look at it through the lens of negotiation theory puts the outcome in an interesting new light.

In December 1976, López Portillo began his presidential term announcing

[19] Vietor 1982, 1.
[20] *Journal of Commerce*, 6 January 1978, 1; *New York Times*, 6 January 1978, D5.
[21] *Washington Post*, 25 November 1977, A20.
[22] *Wall Street Journal*, 28 September 1978, 22.
[23] *Washington Post*, 16 October 1978, A22.
[24] *Forbes*, 22 January 1979, 29–30.

large new discoveries of petroleum reserves and an ambitious plan to invest in increased production.[25] The United States had been abuzz since 1973 with worries about limits to growth, energy shortages, and vulnerability to Arab boycotts. During the winter of 1976–77, the United States suffered the worst natural gas shortage in its history. Industrial plants were closed and some 1.8 million people had been forced out of work by the weather and gas shortages, at least temporarily.[26] In February 1977, López Portillo, just before departing for his first state visit to Washington, authorized emergency petroleum shipments to the United States, and during the visit played up his view that "friends must help friends."[27] Mexico itself was facing high unemployment and a balance of payments crisis and also needed short term help.

In February, PEMEX began negotiations with six American gas pipeline companies on a plan to export 2 billion cubic feet per day (cfd) of natural gas to the American market. The PEMEX plan called for construction of an expensive new pipeline from Cactus in southeastern Mexico along the Gulf coast to Reynosa on the Rio Grande, where it would connect with the U.S. pipeline system as well as one in northern Mexico. In March, López Portillo announced more exciting new discoveries of oil and gas reserves. Mexico's head negotiator was Díaz Serrano, the PEMEX director, a close friend of López Portillo, and an activist who took advantage of this relationship to operate relatively independently of the economic cabinet and even the president.[28]

The United States had a new president, Jimmy Carter, and energy problems were front-page news. His chief energy negotiator was James Schlesinger, soon to become the first Secretary of Energy. In April, Carter and Schlesinger announced their National Energy Plan, a proposal for new legislation. U.S. law and regulations at that time capped the price of domestic gas moving across state lines at $1.42 per thousand cubic feet (Mcf). U.S. energy prices generally were lower than those in the rest of the industrial world, though no "free" international market for gas really existed. Schlesinger reasoned that low price ceilings were discouraging supply, and his main approach to increasing supply was to allow producers to charge higher prices. The Carter bill would have raised the wellhead price of new interstate gas from $1.42 to $1.75 and phased out regulation of new domestic gas prices by 1985.[29] This proposal was welcomed much more in the southern states that exported petroleum than in the colder northern states that had to import it. Substantial political opposition to the price hike began to mobilize.

Meanwhile, the United States was importing huge quantities of natural gas from Canada under an earlier bilateral agreement. The amount reached one trillion cubic feet that year. During the spring of 1977, Washington agreed to a Cana-

---

[25] Bailey and Vega Canovas 1989, 6.

[26] *Facts on File*, 1–14 February 1977, 91; Gilmer 1980, 140.

[27] *Christian Science Monitor*, 17 February 1977, 3.

[28] Interview with an economic adviser to López Portillo, Mexico City, 13 July 1982. In 1981, López Portillo asked Díaz Serrano for his resignation after he had reduced oil prices without seeking approval first.

[29] Vietor 1982, 8. Gilmer 1980 explains the eventual 1978 law and its economic significance.

dian price hike from $1.80 to $2.16 per Mcf. Canadian reserves were estimated at 71 trillion cubic feet, and in light of Canada's own modest demand, many observers were optimistic that the present volume of exports could be increased.[30]

The PEMEX chief made trips to Washington in April and June, each time meeting with Schlesinger. Privately Schlesinger and others manifested the general enthusiasm of the day for Mexico's petroleum development. He offered to help PEMEX get the necessary technology, and even to intercede with the IMF for permission to increase borrowing sharply to finance the gasoducto.[31] A member of the second Mexican delegation reported, "He was very interested in the gas pipeline project. He kept asking 'how long will it take to complete?' and so forth. When I told him we were under an IMF program that restricted our spending, he asked: 'How on earth did you ever sign that thing?' "[32] Schlesinger was not passive or hostile to Mexican gas exports; he welcomed them.

Yet on both occasions he also warned the Mexican team that Washington approval would be necessary, and that there would be a problem if the price were higher than $2.16. He also warned against an escalator clause pegging the gas price to that of No. 2 fuel oil in New York (the OPEC price). U.S. negotiators did not make these private warnings public during the negotiation. John O'Leary, administrator of the Federal Energy Administration met with officials of Tenneco and Texas Eastern Gas Transmission, two of the firms negotiating with Díaz Serrano. O'Leary indicated that Washington would prefer a price of $1.75, the upper limit for domestic gas in Carter's bill.

In August 1977, PEMEX signed a letter of intent with a consortium of six pipeline firms and announced the pact to the media. The six-year, renewable accord provided for initial delivery of 50 million cfd, rising to 2 billion cfd by 1979—roughly 3 percent of total U.S. gas consumption. Mexico reserved the right to interrupt deliveries whenever national requirements so indicated. Three other provisions proved decisive. First, the price would be pegged to the price of high-quality No. 2 fuel oil delivered to New York harbor, representing the world OPEC price, and the gas price could change every six months. Second, on this basis the initial price would be $2.60 per Mcf. Third, the firms also agreed to "take or pay" for the gas; they would have to pay regardless of supplies that might be available elsewhere. The letter of intent would expire on 31 December 1977.

Although the new pipeline would cost $1 billion, a half-dozen nations' official export banks quickly lined up to offer to finance the construction and export the related goods and services.[33] Part of the pact was nearly $600 million in loans from the U.S. government's Export-Import Bank. So lucrative was the deal that PEMEX expected to pay for the entire pipeline construction cost with the equivalent of only 200 days of full export operation at this gas price.[34]

---

[30] Vietor 1982, 11.
[31] Ibid., 13.
[32] Interview, Mexico City, 15 July 1982.
[33] Grayson 1980, 187–89.
[34] *Comercio Exterior*, Nov. 1977, 1291.

Media commentary in each country treated this as "an absolutely golden deal," in the words of one international banker.[35] The United States seemed to have a gas shortage and was worried about dependence on Arab suppliers. Mexico was a next-door neighbor and its economy was already entwined with that of the United States. Mexico was in desperate need of short term foreign exchange and long term economic development. In addition, the marginal cost of producing most of this gas would be close to zero. The gas was going to come right up with oil anyhow, and much was simply being wasted.

On 6 October, before securing Washington's approval, PEMEX also decided to begin construction of the pipeline to San Fernando and Monterrey.[36] Complaints about the terms had been brewing in the United States, however. On 19 October, Senator Adlai Stevenson of Illinois took the lead when he introduced a resolution disapproving the Export-Import Bank loan, objecting to the gas price. Stevenson, like the Carter administration, did not oppose an agreement to pay $1.75. He contended:

> At $1.75 per Mcf, PEMEX would have ample funds to cover operating costs of the pipeline and principal and interest payments on its proposed loan from the Ex-Im Bank and still make a handsome profit. The difference between $2.60 and $1.75 is pure windfall to PEMEX and would add $620 million per year to our gas import bill. And that amount is small by comparison with the costs of other fuels, including Canadian gas, that would rise with the cost of Mexican gas. . . . Natural gas prices in excess of $1.75 produce no more natural gas. They do produce more inflation, recession, political instability, and windfall profits.[37]

Carter and Schlesinger needed congressional support for their pending legislation. Signing a deal with Mexico that would raise gas prices even higher would not make Carter's level-two battle easier to win.

In late November, middle-level officials from the two governments worked out a tentative compromise agreement. Mexico would accept $2.16 for the first two years and the United States would accept an increase to $2.60 at that time. But reportedly López Portillo and Díaz Serrano rejected this deal.[38]

Meanwhile, the Mexico City newspaper *UnoMasUno* was asking:

> Since Mexican demand for natural gas does not exceed 1.4 billion cubic feet per day, and when it is sold, moreover, at a subsidized rate 8 times smaller than the export price, is it worthwhile to invest 11.5 billion pesos for the gasoducto, whose real local utility has not, after all, been clearly demonstrated by PEMEX? If the gas definitely will not be sold to the United States, and we will not receive the annual revenues of $37.973 billion pesos that had been projected for the first year, is it justified to con-

[35] Quoted by Fagen and Nau 1979, 400.
[36] *Análisis Político* (Mexico City), 31 October 1977, 331.
[37] *Washington Post*, 12 December 1977, A22.
[38] Fagen and Nau 1979, 406–7; Bailey and Vega Canovas, 21.

struct a pipeline whose only value apparently will be to cover a deficit of 400 million cubic feet daily, and at a subsidized rate at that?[39]

When Díaz Serrano committed publicly to a price of $2.60 in August, he must have judged that Schlesinger was bluffing, that the true U.S. resistance point was at least this high. Several judgments bolstered this bet that Washington could be pulled up to $2.60. The Mexican team reportedly was convinced that the United States faced a critical gas shortage, judging from the problems during the 1976–77 winter and earlier.[40] Second, the Mexican team was impressed that the American firms negotiating with them were willing to pay $2.60, and these firms had to make a profit. Third, Mexico's negotiators observed that the price for gas sold within U.S. producing states had reached $2.70 in 1977, even though the lower price cap on interstate shipments was presumably bottling up some supply. Fourth, they doubted the refusal to link Mexican gas to other fuel equivalents, because of inferences from recent U.S. decisions on other fuels. In September, Carter and Schlesinger worked out an agreement with Canada for construction of another gas pipeline that would deliver gas from Alaska's north slope to the lower forty-eight states, beginning in the mid-1980s. The price of Alaska gas at that time was likely to be higher than the Mexican price.[41] Finally, Mexico's negotiators evidently framed accepting Canada's $2.16 export price as surrendering Mexico's sovereign authority to the political process of a foreign government.[42]

In fact, the true American reservation value may well have been no higher than about $2.16, as far as U.S. commercial objectives were concerned. If Schlesinger had wanted more foreign gas in the short run, he probably could have gotten it from Canada for about that price. That would seem to have been his batna. What was his incentive to pay Mexico more? In particular, if he had paid Mexico more, Canada surely would have demanded an equal price increase, and Canada's price covered more trade. The magnitudes were 2 billion cubic feet per day from Mexico and 2.7 billion cubic feet from Canada. Paying Mexico more than $2.16 would have cost the United States much more than it would have benefited Mexico.

But what of the Mexican team's supporting technical beliefs? As for the recent shortages, U.S. officials believed the primary cause was maldistribution of U.S. gas due to prevailing regulations. During the last crisis, when they permitted interstate shipments at temporarily higher prices, local shortages disappeared quickly. Gas producers had been holding back reserves from the regulated market ever since regulators had cut their prices in 1969.[43] Higher prices ought to stimulate greater supply. For the longer term, they were also thinking about dampening

[39] *UnoMasUno*, 31 December 1977, 1 (my translation).
[40] Bailey and Vega Canovas 1989, 21.
[41] Ibid., 25. This source also reports that during this negotiation a U.S. federal agency made a series of decisions authorizing imports of liquid natural gas with oil-linked price escalator clauses, further encouraging a hard line. Later one of these decisions would be reversed.
[42] Ibid., 24–25.
[43] Gilmer 1980, 140.

demand—conservation and greater efficiency due to higher prices—as part of the solution to shortages.

U.S. regulations also meant the private pipeline companies lacked strong incentives to bargain firmly over the gas price. These regulations fixed the company's profits as a percentage of its investment in physical plant, and allowed it to average high prices of new gas into the lower regulated prices prevailing under long-term contracts. Its profits, under these rules, were constrained more by lack of supplies than by a high unit cost of those supplies. Alaskan gas was American domestic gas, insulating its price from OPEC influence or strategic threats, which was worthy of some premium in Schlesinger's view.[44] Washington's team, then, applied different beliefs and policy values to the available noisy information and reached a different U.S. resistance point, and apparently Díaz Serrano did not discover these Washington beliefs or take them seriously.

Meanwhile, what was PEMEX's batna and hence its own true reservation value? When President López Portillo responded to internal critics in his fall 1977 annual Report of the President, he explained: "Our gas comes forth associated with petroleum . . . we cannot separate them. We cannot stop extracting petroleum. . . . Therefore either we sell [the gas] or we burn it."[45] And where could it be sold? Díaz Serrano reported to Mexico's Congress on 26 October that that the alternative of liquefying the gas and transporting it by sea to Rotterdam in specially designed ships would be much less desirable for Mexico. The transportation cost to ship liquefied gas would be $2.34 per thousand cubic feet, compared with $0.40 via the gasoducto.[46] The annual net income for Mexico from exporting to the United States at $2.60, after discounting for infrastructure costs, would be 37 billion pesos, while the net income from exporting the same amount by ship to Europe would come to only 4.5 billion pesos.[47] By PEMEX's own public accounting, Mexico really did not have a better alternative, or even one close to his asking price, on economic grounds. It seems that any U.S. deal at a price above roughly $0.40 per thousand cubic feet would have produced a positive return. In October Díaz Serrano concluded: "Based on this, the economic decision with respect to this matter is clear: the methane gas should be exported by gaslines to the only feasible market, which is the United States of America."[48] (Selling surplus gas to domestic users in northern Mexico through the new pipeline may have been even worse financially than flaring it, since the domestic price capped at $0.26 was subsidized. By paying for this pipeline and then using it only to ship gas internally, PEMEX probably *lost* money.[49])

[44] Bailey and Vega Canovas 1989, 22–23.
[45] Quoted by *Análisis Político*, 31 October 1977, 330. Translation by the present author.
[46] Moler and Bruce 1979, 115; also in *Comercio Exterior*, Nov. 1977, 1293.
[47] Moler and Bruce 1979, 116.
[48] Ibid., 116.
[49] PEMEX statements, made after the pipeline was already under construction and the deal had collapsed, claimed that going forward still made sense, or at least that some of the loss could be offset. Some of the dry gas now being used could be saved in the ground, some national industry could shift from fuel oil to wet gas, and the oil they would have consumed could then be exported.

Thus given some reasonable assumptions, the two parties enjoyed a positive zone of agreement on the price issue roughly between $0.40 on the low end and $1.75 to $2.16 on the high end. If so, it was indeed a golden deal. There was much joint value on the table as well as a conflict over its distribution—as in many other negotiations. Each side naturally used a mixed strategy, combining elements of distributive and integrative behavior. In this instance though, the seller committed to a price above the agreement zone, it turned out the buyer was not bluffing, and the seller did not adjust.

The evidence is consistent with the conclusion that Díaz Serrano's decisions were affected materially by all four documented judgment biases, while those of the later Mexican agents benefited more fully from compensatory debiasing tactics. Díaz Serrano defined a fair price by anchoring on the readily available OPEC oil price—just like the realtors and the listing price. The *Washington Post* editorialist also stopped thinking at that point. In estimating the true U.S. maximum, the Mexican team did not fail to do technical homework. But they discounted inferences from the same evidence that conflicted with their presuppositions. The gas was part of Díaz Serrano's endowment, and like the experimental subject with the mug, he was reluctant to part with it unless offered a price higher than any customer was willing to pay.

Díaz Serrano responded to negative feedback—early private warnings from his U.S. counterpart and later in public from Senator Stevenson and others that his preferred price was too high—by escalating his public commitment to that price, like Campeau, rather than making a tactical retreat that would have closed a lucrative deal. He signed the letter of intent and publicized the OPEC-based price and even began construction without having Washington's approval. Doing so also may have inadvertently shaped Mexican politics, and hence might have indirectly constrained his own or his president's subsequent behavior. To retreat now and accept a lower price—after so visibly defining $2.60 as the minimum acceptable measure of Yankee fairness—would have generated embarrassing domestic political attacks on Mexico's president—especially in a negotiation over petroleum—even though walking away meant declining a substantial economic opportunity for Mexico.[50]

The two international negotiators, partisans both, chose definitions of fairness more favorable to each's own side. Mexico's agent claimed more exclusively and used value creation less than he would have done had he taken Schlesinger's batna and perspective more seriously. Consistent with excessive confidence, Díaz Serrano did not communicate his offer in a form that would appeal as precisely to the thinking that was actually most salient on the U.S. side, or explore relatively openly (like the management negotiator with the engineers' union to be discussed in chap. 7) toward a different arrangement that would come closer to satisfying U.S. requirements as well as those of Mexico. We will see that Mexico's agents in

---

[50] Coming home empty-handed is not a plus in domestic politics either, unless a scapegoat can be found. Ironically, Schlesinger's undiplomatic remarks inadvertently helped to clothe him in exactly the costume Díaz Serrano needed at that political moment.

1979 did explore more openly, used value creation more, communicated more directly to party B's thinking, and gained more from negotiation.

WINTER VEGETABLE EXPORTS, 1979

Mexico's negotiators in the second case also used a mixed strategy. However, this time the Mexican side used debiasing tactics more thoroughly and to greater effect.

A group of Florida growers, not the U.S. government, had filed the legal complaint concerning vegetable trade under the U.S. Antidumping Act of 1921. In response, the Treasury Department's attorneys informed the Carter administration's leaders privately that they saw no legal alternative to finding the Mexican growers guilty of dumping.[51] The administration then pressured the Florida growers to take the issue to the bargaining table. Several months of direct talks between the grower groups proved fruitless.[52]

Meanwhile, however, Mexican growers also retained special consultants and agents in Washington: Arnold and Porter, the prominent law firm, and specifically the well-connected Robert Herzstein, who soon thereafter became a high official himself in Carter's Commerce Department. Herzstein and his associates brought deep, specific expertise in U.S. trade law and policy-making, and probably fuller knowledge than even well-prepared Mexican officials enjoyed concerning U.S. gas markets and regulations. Washington trade attorneys such as Herzstein were relatively close to the American officials who had a decision to make, and hence were in a good position to report coolly and credibly on how U.S. officials privately framed their own situation, to steer their clients away from biased judgments of what was feasible, if necessary, and to fashion a settlement the Washington side would accept.

The crucial legal problem for the Mexican growers was that in past dumping cases, normally concerning products that were not perishable, the technical question had been whether any import transaction was deemed to have occurred at "less than fair value," for example, at less than the price charged in the home country or less than production cost. Producers of perishable vegetables naturally must sell each crate as soon as it is harvested or let it spoil, even if the price available that week is lower than their costs. American vegetable growers also unloaded their crops at a loss on particular days.[53] Yet an import transaction doing so triggered a finding of international dumping, according to established practice.

Mexico's negotiating and legal team understood how U.S. officials framed the matter: "our duty is to enforce the law." But they also knew that the Antidumping Act did not define "fair value"; it left the Secretary of the Treasury some discre-

---

[51] *New York Times*, 15 June 1979; *Wall Street Journal*, 19 July 1979, 40; Mares 1987, 212.

[52] *New York Times*, 9 September 1979, A1, and 27 October 1979, 29.

[53] A study by Professor Robert S. Firch on the California lettuce industry was submitted. Mares 1987, 214.

tion, subject to judicial review. The Arnold and Porter team first attempted to convince Washington officials that the statute was not meant to cover agricultural products. Research showed, however, that Congress had so intended it, and that it had been applied to perishable items three times in the previous decade.[54]

Eventually Mexico's agents proposed a new technique for defining and interpreting "sales at less than fair value" of these perishable products. Some reference point for "fair value" was needed, but these particular vegetables were not sold in Mexico. In such cases it was customary to refer to prices charged for the same export to a third country. Herzstein and the Mexican growers suggested that Treasury compare prices paid for Mexican vegetables in the northern half of the United States with prices paid in adjacent regions of Canada on the same day, to see whether U.S. prices were lower. They should also investigate transactions over an entire season; prices might fluctuate in both adjacent regions due to temporary market conditions. They argued that if an exporter charged less in the United States than in the reference market repeatedly, this would constitute reasonable proof of the price discrimination the law was designed to counter.

The Mexican side also retained Professor Richard L. Simmons, a consultant to the U.S. Department of Agriculture on fruits and vegetables, who conducted and produced a statistical study showing a high correlation between vegetable prices paid in Canada and in the United States on the same day during the past season. They offered these findings as evidence that "sales at less than fair value" had not taken place in this case, even if some individual sales took place below cost. In October, Alfred Kahn, chairman of the Council on Wage and Price Stability and chief inflation fighter, sent a memo urging Treasury to adopt this technique.[55] He contended that limiting Mexican tomato sales could cost the U.S. public an additional $800 million.[56]

In the end Treasury decided to accept the Mexicans' new technique, and as a result, they ruled on 5 November 1979 that Mexico had not sold winter vegetables in the United States at less than fair value[57]—the opposite of what everyone, including these Treasury officials themselves, had expected to find back in July. The technical innovation gave U.S. decision makers a way to raise their subjective resistance point to the status quo level of trade, while still defending their actions in court. Florida's attorney promptly challenged this determination, but the court declined to overrule Treasury and later the Department of Commerce as well.[58]

The Mexican negotiators in this second case avoided traps often set by judgment biases. They avoided a public commitment to a point outside the zone of agreement with Washington, nor of course did they respond to negative feedback by increasing the stakes on that commitment. They worked largely out of the public eye, though some American allies were speaking out. They did not perma-

[54] See U.S. *Federal Register* 44: 63588–92.
[55] This paragraph draws on Mares 1987, 212–14.
[56] *Business Week*, 23 July 1979, 79.
[57] U.S. *Federal Register* 44: 63588–92.
[58] Mares 1987, 216.

nently anchor their demand to an available analogue, as far as is known; mainly they proposed a creative *departure* from precedent. If the Mexicans' judgments of their alternatives to agreement or their preferred fairness norm were biased in a self-serving direction in this second case, ill effects on their negotiating performance are difficult to find.

We do know they used a compensatory technique: they hired expert consultants who specialized, among other things, in understanding how the other party in this case thought, at both the technical and the political levels. These experts gathered nuanced, accurate information about U.S. regulatory rules and history, as well as the perceived batnas of the officials who would decide the dumping case. With this understanding in hand, they attempted to invent a proposal that would satisfy not only their clients' objectives but simultaneously those of the officials and in this case the courts of the other country. The use of the law firm can be understood not only in the obvious way as acquiring technical and political assistance, but also as one means of guarding against and correcting biases that normally affect the negotiator's own decisions. While debiasing tactics are no guarantee of a favorable settlement, in this case they did seem to facilitate an outcome that created, or better, preserved joint value in the eyes of both governments that otherwise would have been lost.

OTHER INTERPRETATIONS

It might seem that this second case differed from the first because negotiations over an antidumping investigation are constrained by applicable legal rules, which denied each side some potential offers and demands that would have been options in a theoretically-unconstrained negotiation. Often at least one of the parties has incentives to depict antidumping proceedings not as bargaining but as adjudication—a neutral judge decides according to the law and "the merits."

In fact this difference between the two episodes is a matter of degree, and its direction makes the outcome variation more rather than less surprising. The energy negotiation was also highly regulated. The gasoducto proposal required administrative investigation and testing against established rules. On the other side, some dumping cases do end with a negotiated agreement under which exporters agree to change their commercial behavior in the future and their U.S. competitors agree to withdraw the complaint. Indeed this has been the intended outcome behind some prominent dumping petitions. Sometimes American officials encourage a negotiated settlement. Thus ex ante, the international exporter cannot rule out the possibility of bargaining. Even when this is not the outcome, dumping decisions of the U.S. Treasury Department, and later the Commerce Department, have always been subject to some influence, using legal, economic, and political arguments. The law allows some scope for interpretation.

What is more, most observers would have thought the difference implied less scope for bargaining over vegetables than over gas, ex ante. Both sides agreed that some shipments of Mexican tomatoes were in fact sold in the United States at prices less than their costs of production. A conventional reading of the law's language would have classified these as dumping. This reasoning would imply that Mexico should have gained less on vegetables, not more. If the actual outcome shows anything, it is how much room for interpretation this law actually allowed.

Another obvious difference is that energy is strategic. Might the United States have refused Mexican gas in order to avoid possible future blackmail by a supplier? The facts certainly do not support a U.S. security interpretation of this gas stalemate (nor of the settlement on tomatoes, even tasty vine-ripened ones). It is true that the Carter administration was preparing a major revision of gas policy to encourage demand reduction and conservation, probably in part for security reasons, and this plan would raise Washington's reservation price for Mexican gas. But of course the United States with its own hydrocarbon reserves (plus agreements with Canada) was hardly on the ropes. Moreover, for security purposes Mexico was a relatively attractive foreign supplier, compared with Saudi Arabia, Iraq, or Kuwait. The U.S. negotiator showed from the beginning that he was interested in the gasoducto project. What he rejected were the particular terms.

Nor was the net U.S. domestic political opposition facing Mexico significantly greater on gas than on tomatoes. The U.S. opposition to the gas deal was wider and probably stronger politically than that of the Florida tomato growers. But U.S. forces pressing *for* approval of the pipeline—six major companies and allies like Senator Lloyd Bentsen of Texas—also were more formidable than constituents defending Mexican vegetables—essentially some Arizona shippers and the Arizona congressional delegation. Even the leading domestic critic of the gas deal, Senator Adlai Stevenson III, did not oppose Mexican gas at all prices, only at prices above $1.75.

What about judgment biases in Washington? Could they have been lower in the second case than the first, opening a positive agreement zone only in the second, or leading to more accommodating U.S. tactics? Surely U.S. negotiators are as vulnerable to such biases as any. U.S. officials in 1977 were certainly partisan in rejecting the OPEC anchor for gas pricing, for instance. And it does take two to tango, no matter what tactics the other uses. But was the true U.S. maximum—as judged by a neutral observer—really higher than $2.16, if the gas could have been purchased from Canada at about that price, and if paying more would cost far more than it would help Mexico? Was Schlesinger's judgment biased in that sense? It seems that paying more could have been justified only by the opposite bias—altruism—or by a decision to use gas trade to supply a form of foreign aid in support of U.S. political goals. The latter argument turns on negotiating priorities and trade-offs rather than cognitive biases.

In 1979 were U.S. negotiators' judgments less biased in their own favor than in 1977? It is equally arguable that they found no dumping because they were persuaded that that decision was the best course for the United States itself. Applying precedent instead to these perishables would mean raising prices to American consumers for no good policy purpose—burdening them to prevent a practice (occasional below-cost sales) that would occur anyhow whenever the seller was domestic.[59]

One other major answer should be added, however, to account fully for this particular historical contrast. U.S. market conditions worsened between the two negotiations. In 1979 the rate of consumer inflation rose to 13.3 percent (December to December), compared with 6.7 percent in 1977.[60] The public debate surrounding the tomato question made clear that U.S. officials were increasingly concerned to avoid steps that would worsen inflation.[61] This condition probably made them more receptive to arguments against measures that would raise food costs than they would have been during a period of price stability.

In turn, a principal cause of faster inflation was the dramatic jump in the world oil price that began in early 1979 with the Iranian revolution, again focusing American opinion on the risk of energy shortages. Meanwhile, in 1978 Mexico had uncovered even greater new petroleum reserves offshore. An unspoken element of the antidumping context was said to be a greater reluctance in Washington to anger Mexican opinion.[62] Oil prices and general inflation led American leaders to perceive that market alternatives to agreement with Mexico had worsened somewhat, though not catastrophically. The United States after all remained a major petroleum producing country itself. But these shifting sentiments, as evidenced by Alfred Kahn's intervention, added a reason for U.S. officials to accept the creative proposal and not insist on strict application of precedent in the vegetable dumping case.

Mexico's agents dealing with the same U.S. administration used basically the same mixed strategy in two export negotiations, yet Mexico clearly gained less in the first case. Had Díaz Serrano used debiasing tactics in 1977 to a greater extent, he almost certainly would have gained more for Mexico, even if all else had been the same. The gasoducto case illustrates all four of the biases documented by experimental research: anchoring, the endowment effect, partisanship, and escalating commitments to a strategy that has generated negative feedback. In 1979 Mexican agents used one debiasing tactic: they hired experts independent of the Mexican government who specialized in understanding how the other party thought at both the technical and the political levels, and who had a strong position from which to evaluate their principals' ideas and suggest their own. These techniques helped Mexico avoid an impasse and create, or in this case preserve, joint value. The second difference helping with vegetable trade was that U.S. leaders saw their market alternative to agreement worsen after 1977.

---

[59] While it is possible that some officials felt altruistic toward Mexico, no evidence has been found that would separate this value from U.S. national objectives.

[60] U.S. President 1994, table B-62.

[61] In addition to other press coverage cited, see *New York Times*, 20 June 1979, A22 (editorial), 16 July 1979, D2; and 27 October 1979, 29; *Wall Street Journal*, 31 October 1979, 39.

[62] *Wall Street Journal*, 19 July 1979, 40.

Thus this controlled comparison provides empirical support for two hypotheses, the market batna proposition of chapter 3 and this chapter's main idea. Two observations are not sufficient, of course, to show which of two causal variables is more important. For purposes of generalizing, additional research is needed, as usual, but this contrast indicates that wider testing will be worthy of investment.

Judging from this evidence, advocates of familiar theoretical approaches also need to recognize their limits. International cooperation is more than multilateral regime-building. Models assuming complete information cannot account for evidence, like 1977, that veteran bargainers do sometimes fail to reach the frontier or even to reach agreement and leave gains on the table even when they enjoy a positive zone of agreement. For power thinkers, the obvious power advantage the United States had over Mexico is not sufficient to explain this variation. Nor does the difference seem to follow from a difference in transaction costs or in fears of future reneging. Nor do prevailing military-security conditions, international institutions, domestic government institutions, or cultural variations help account for this difference. Prospect theory is not the only relevant idea from psychology. This evidence shows that neglecting the economic negotiation process can blind us to significant influences on outcomes.

One obvious implication for bargaining practice follows from the experimental evidence that judgment biases are at least as common in the United States as in Mexico. If efforts to offset negotiator biases will pay dividends for Mexico, they will do so for any capital and any company.

Less obviously, recall that part of the problem for Díaz Serrano, in the end, was that his earlier public commitment tactics at level one also had altered his own domestic politics in a direction that amplified the probable effects of his judgment biases. Their technician's tactics had caused the Mexican lay public to believe that the lowest price consistent with fair treatment of Mexico was $2.60 per thousand cubic feet. If he had told his public and president instead that the rock-bottom fair price was $2.00 and if he had taken similar steps to make credible a threat not to back down from that price, it is highly unlikely that the lay public would have regarded a final settlement at $2.16 as unfair. Then if PEMEX had preferred in the end to reap large export revenue by settling for less than $2.60, making this tactical retreat would have cost the president little or nothing in domestic politics. Note that the decision to terminate the negotiation was announced not by the appointed expert but by the elected president. Of course Díaz Serrano was not wrong to try to claim value from Washington within the agreement zone; that was part of his duty. The problem for his constituents was that in the end he brought home no value at all.

Interestingly, though unfortunately for negotiators, Díaz Serrano was facing a dilemma not peculiar to him. In any two-level game the tactics most suitable for claiming at level one also tend to interfere with ratification at level two if they

the most thorough preparation. It would be a mistake to assume that subsequent credibility problems cannot arise.

The gains from offensive claiming also depend on the target's internal politics. The second claim, theoretically independent of the first, is that the higher domestic players in B raise the political costs of complying for their government (relative to the political costs of impasse), the smaller the concessions their negotiator makes, reducing A's gain. Even assuming a credible threat, when a plausible reading of B's national interests dictates complying, minister B is less likely to do so the more she believes making a concession will cost her politically at home on balance. Negotiators, even in authoritarian states, care about domestic popularity. Threats can generate internal hostility to international agreement as well as fear of the costs of refusal. In state B a firm refusal could be popular and accommodation risky, or the opposite could be the case, or either stand could yield a net zero in domestic politics. According to this proposition, as domestic pressures against concessions rise relative to domestic pressures for them, negotiator B's claiming tactics will stiffen, all else being equal. The opposite domestic shift should produce more accommodative behavior. The negotiator's resistance point will depend on domestic politics as well as the external batna in this more complex view.

The Reagan administration attempted the offensive claiming strategy in two episodes between 1985 and 1988. In September 1985 they threatened Brazil with economic penalties if it did not change its program designed to promote a national computer industry and displace foreign firms. In March 1986 Reagan threatened to punish exports from the European Community[2] if the EC did not compensate it for new barriers to U.S. feedgrains in Spain and Portugal. These restrictions had just been raised due to the treaty making the Iberian states new members of the Common Market. Both Brasília and Brussels angrily threatened counterretaliation.

Paradoxically, the same U.S. strategy gained more commercially from the European Community, the largest trading unit in the world, than from the weaker player. The European case ended after ten months with a written agreement breaching the enlargement treaty, which had been ratified by twelve parliaments, and making substantial commercial concessions to the U.S. relative to the status quo in January 1986. (The U.S. made no concessions in the other direction; this was a clear win-lose agreement.) The Brazil-U.S. dispute dragged on for thirty-six months, and Reagan finally gained only a tacit agreement worth little commercial value to the United States beyond the status quo ante. Yet the claimer was the same superpower, with the same institutions, operating under the same international rules, led by the same President and the same negotiator during the same period.

How can we understand this paradoxical contrast? Much international relations theory begins with power and assumes states are monolithic actors. But the European Community was indisputably a more powerful player than Brazil—with the

---

[2] This chapter will follow the language of the day rather than the later title "European Union."

wherewithal to do far greater harm to the American economy in a serious trade war. The United States seemed to have a much better alternative to agreement with Brazil. In 1986, the European Community purchased 24 percent of U.S. exports while only 2 percent of U.S. exports were sent to Brazil. A more refined measure of dependence would consider exports as a share of the economies' total production, since some economies rely on trade much more than others, and also would examine dependence in both directions. This measure points to the same conclusion. In 1986 EC exports to the United States were equivalent to 2.3 percent of combined EC gross domestic product, while the United States exported 1.3 percent of its GDP to the European Community. At the same time, Brazil's exports to the United States also came to 2.3 percent of Brazilian GDP, but U.S. exports to Brazil were only 0.09 percent of the vast U.S. economy. By this general trade measure, the European Community was almost twice as dependent on the United States as the United States was on the EC, but Brazil was 26 times as dependent on America as vice versa.[3] Furthermore, Brazil was a much less developed country, and during the mid-1980s it was struggling with a serious international payments and debt crisis.

Moreover, the European Community had established a reputation for a willingness to stand up to threats from Washington and even retaliate, since the infamous "chicken war" of the 1960s. In that early challenge to the EC Common Agricultural Policy (CAP), Washington had threatened and then implemented modest economic sanctions against the Community, which nevertheless had refused to compromise, despite a GATT panel ruling in favor of the U.S. interpretation. In 1982 and again in 1984 Brussels had explicitly threatened counterretaliation if the United States imposed unilateral restrictions on European steel. The year before the enlargement dispute, the EC had countered U.S. penalties on European pasta by targeting American citrus products. Brazil had very little reputation for retaliation that might have bolstered the credibility of its counterthreats. From the standpoint of power assets it would have been reasonable in 1984 and 1985 to expect the U.S. to extract greater value from Brazil.

LOWER U.S. CREDIBILITY IN BRAZIL THAN IN EUROPE

A central explanation for this paradox is that Washington's threat against Brazil was less credible than that directed at Europe, fundamentally because of much greater domestic U.S. opposition to implementing the threat in the Brazil case. The negotiators in Brazil and Europe estimated their American counterpart's credibility from America's level two and acted accordingly. The first threat failed to convince Brazilians unambiguously that their no-deal alternative really had worsened very much, but the second threat left no doubts in Europe.

---

[3] Trade data from International Monetary Fund, *Direction of Trade Statistics Yearbook* 1989, and GDP data from United Nations, *Statistical Yearbook* 1987.

Differences in Washington's tactics may have contributed to the credibility variation, though this tactical difference itself probably flowed from the same source. The threat toward Brazil was less precise, concrete, and automatic. The administration did not publicize an estimated value of harm that Brazil was alleged to have done to U.S. interests, and at the outset Washington did not identify the Brazilian industries that would suffer if the sanctions were carried out. There was no specific action by the Congress regarding Brazil urging the President to carry out this threat. These threat tactics were more typical for Washington than those used in the 1986 EC case.

On Saturday, 7 September 1985, President Reagan made an announcement during his weekly radio address. His administration was concerned about unfair trade practices and had ordered three investigations under the authority of section 301 of the U.S. Trade Act of 1974. Restrictions in Japan, in South Korea, and the informatics law Brazil had adopted in 1984 to codify its decade-old informatics *reserva de mercado* (market reserve) program were targeted. This was the first time a President had initiated such an investigation without a petition from an U.S. industry. Section 301 permitted the President to impose penalties on Brazil's exports if his investigation determined that Brazil had maintained "unjustifiable or unreasonable" import restrictions or other policies damaging U.S. commerce. Washington set a deadline for decision for one year later. Reagan's speech said "we will take trade countermeasures only as a last resort." His chief negotiator, Trade Representative Clayton Yeutter, told reporters that under the law, "for all practical purposes the President can do essentially what he wishes by way of retaliation," if foreign governments do not cooperate.[4]

Washington moved more concretely against the European Community from the outset, detailing target industries and setting extremely tight deadlines. On 31 March 1986 Reagan announced that the United States would impose huge trade sanctions almost immediately unless the EC rescinded new quotas on oilseeds and grains in Portugal and provided compensation Washington considered adequate for higher feedgrain tariffs in Spain. "We cannot allow the American farmer, once again, to pay the price for the European Community's enlargement," he declared.[5] The Office of the U.S. Trade Representative (USTR) promptly issued a "hit" list of EC products that would be the victims.[6] The magnitude of EC export loss was designed to total an unprecedented $1 billion, which would make this the most severe trade war the two had ever fought by far. Separate penalties were designed for the Portugal and Spain issues. In this case Reagan did not merely start an investigation; he lit the fuse immediately. The U.S. *Federal Register* announced that penalties would be applied automatically beginning on 1 May for Portugal's issues and 1 July for Spain's practices unless the European Com-

---

[4] For a fuller narrative of these events and their background, also see Odell and Dibble 1992, Evans 1986, Adler 1986, Felder and Hurrell 1988, Evans 1989, and Bastos 1994.

[5] *Agra Europe*, 11 April 1986.

[6] Ibid., 4 April 1986.

munity backed down.[7] The cannons would fire without further action unless steps were taken to disarm them. U.S. Agriculture Secretary Richard Lyng commented dryly that "our intention is to bring the EC to the negotiating table as soon as possible."[8]

Underlying the difference in American tactics was a basic difference in the relevant U.S. markets and domestic politics. American constituents' preferences regarding strategy toward Brazil—even those of computer firms themselves—were divided, with some firms opposed to Reagan's strategy. The EC measures unified U.S. feedgrain producers behind a harsh claiming strategy with a vengeance.

Stronger net U.S. internal opposition on computers

In 1984 U.S. computer companies had mixed feelings about the new Brazilian law. All regarded the country as a great potential market and some hoped for an eventual policy shift. Despite obstacles, some had learned how to operate profitably in segments lacking local competition, while others were suffering. The giant IBM had been producing office machines in Brazil for decades, and its subsidiary there was reported to be highly profitable at this time. Located on the inside, IBM do Brasil benefited somewhat from the market reserve, which kept U.S. competitors making minicomputers, such as Digital Equipment, from setting up local manufacturing subsidiaries, and made it more difficult for Japanese mainframe producers to export into Brazil. Most U.S. firms did not see the new law itself as a major change but more as a codification of existing practice, which for many meant a long story of irritations and profits. One spokesman summed it up thus: "If a company is in Brazil it will tend to stick it out, but if a company is not now operating there, it is a place to avoid."[9] The industry as a whole was not lobbying for a shift to a more aggressive strategy in 1985 prior to Reagan's speech.

At the end of the summer, however, the administration decided to make major changes in its approaches to exchange rates and international trade in general, as it saw a gargantuan trade deficit firing an intense head of steam for greater protectionism (chap. 3). Indignation about trade had spread well beyond the Democratic opposition to Republican members of Congress, corporate executives, and even farmers dependent on exports. The 1985 negotiation to get the yen up, discussed in chapter 4, was part of this plan.

As another part, an interagency committee headed by the U.S. Trade Representative prepared a list of possible 301 cases for initiation. After having identified Japan and Korea, according to one well-informed participant,

---

[7] U.S. *Federal Register* 51 (3 April 1986): 11532–33

[8] Letter to U.S. Feed Grains Council, 15 April 1986. For a full account of this episode, see Odell and Matzinger-Tchakerian 1991.

[9] This section is based on an interview with a U.S. industry representative, Washington, D.C., 1987.

we needed a non-Asian LDC, we needed a "new issue," and we needed one where you could avoid going to the GATT. . . . With these 301 cases we were putting these issues on the international trade agenda. And to that degree, I would say that this 301 case was a success. The intellectual property rights issue was agreed to at Punta del Este [where GATT opened the multilateral Uruguay round in 1986], and if we hadn't been attacking the Brazilians on this, I don't think we would have had as much support from the Europeans and the Japanese to do that.[10]

According to this official, Brazil was chosen early and by unanimous agreement. "The view was that Brazil was an outlaw country, never following the rules on anything." Not all were enthusiastic about picking the informatics sector in Brazil, however. At least one policy-maker preferred a different bilateral trade issue because it seemed more "winnable." But a key participant said of the informatics case,

I thought we had broad industry support. I was convinced it was the right issue. Now, whether we would win or lose was not so clear. And what we would do if they didn't make concessions, we didn't quite figure out at that time.

Reportedly negotiators held an emergency meeting with U.S. industry representatives the day before Reagan's speech, more to notify them than to learn from them. A well-informed industry representative recalled, "The companies were shocked. I'm not sure, but I would guess the companies told them not to do it. I doubt any lobbied them to do it." Another grumbled, "There was *never* any enthusiasm for the case from those who knew Brazil."[11]

Immediately Brazilians discovered that supposed major beneficiaries of the threat had not demanded it and might well oppose actually carrying it out. A few days after the speech, IBM and Burroughs officials, attending a private symposium with Brazilians in Washington, told Brazilians they thought Reagan's action was inopportune, according to a Brazilian present.[12] Later a Brazilian government negotiator who had been assured of confidentiality recalled:

The U.S. companies were divided. IBM was neutral. They passed the word that they had not asked for the 301; it was really government inspired. The companies knew better than the U.S. government how difficult it would be in Brazil.[13]

IBM made a point of staying away from meetings with U.S. negotiators for many months. If the President were to have carried out the threat, and Congress had then called these firms to testify in public hearings, the results could have been embarrassing, which implied that USTR could have a difficult time convinc-

---

[10] Interview, Washington, D.C., 1987.
[11] Interviews, Washington, D.C., 1987. Emphasis in the original.
[12] Interview, Brasília, 1987.
[13] Interview, Washington, D.C., 1987.

ing the White House to approve implementation of the threat. Brazilian clients retained former U.S. policy makers as advisers, who explained this to them. Constituents undermined Reagan's and Yeutter's credibility as soon as they had issued their threat.

Two major organizations represented the U.S. computer and electronics industries. A few large multinational firms dominated the Computer and Business Equipment Manufacturers Association (CBEMA). IBM and Burroughs (later Unisys) each had a major investment stake exposed in the country, and Hewlett-Packard had established a small foothold in the 1960s. IBM was highly dependent on world markets, especially earnings from its overseas subsidiaries. The large firms had the capital to weather storms and hold out for long-term gains. CBEMA testified on their behalf at Washington hearings on the Brazil case in October 1985, advising strongly against trying to change the Brazilian law itself. Instead CBEMA wanted negotiations to prevent the market reserve from being extended to products not yet restricted, to improve the way the law was implemented, and to assure that the program would be phased out eventually.[14] Otherwise CBEMA sought, if anything, to restrain the Reagan administration, not to whip it into fiercer attacks. CBEMA avoided contact with the press on this issue.

Some companies other than the largest were in different positions. Some were not inside but wanted to get in. Others such as Tektronix had been in Brazil and then had been shut out. Still others, such as many in the much larger American Electronics Association (AEA), had no stake there, did not expect to have one, and did not know Brazil. Some of these paid no attention, while others wanted to set a global example. The AEA, representing 2,800 companies in electronics more broadly, had been more aggressive than CBEMA. For instance, in August 1985 the AEA had urged the administration to strip ten countries, including Brazil, of their zero-duty treatment under the Generalized System of Preferences unless they indicated a willingness to halt violations of intellectual property rights at home. After Reagan launched his 301 initiative, however, the AEA, like CBEMA, called for mutually beneficial negotiations to improve Brazilian informatics policies, at the industry-to-industry level as well as between the governments.

Weaker net U.S. internal opposition on feedgrains

In contrast, EC enlargement in early 1986 drove American feedgrain producers into furious, unified protest. To them this was yet another blow in a long history of unfair European agricultural policies. U.S. farmers were already suffering through a painful period of declining exports and declining income. Corn exports from the United States to the EC twelve had already plummeted from 14.2 million tons in 1982 to 6.0 million tons in 1985, before Spanish and Portuguese ac-

[14] Letter, Vico E. Henriques, President, CBEMA, to Office of U.S. Trade Representative, 11 October 1985.

cession and the new barriers. Even so the Iberian countries remained their third largest export market in the world. Corn farmers, the primary affected group, were not a multinational industry with overseas investments that could become hostages, nor did they depend on exports to the same extent as some sectors. While about two-thirds of U.S. wheat and cotton was exported, between 60 and 70 percent of the corn crop was sold at home. Feedgrains probably would suffer in a major international political conflict, but not to the same potential extent as the more extended multinationals.

Three weeks after the enlargement treaty took effect, major elements of the general U.S. farm lobby joined forces with feedgrain producers to demand that Reagan take immediate action, "to respond promptly and forcefully . . . to gain full compensation; . . . lack of firmness now would encourage a greater surplus of EC grain production and might well lead to more sweeping trade restrictions of this type in the future."[15] On 17 April the Senate passed a concurrent resolution urging the President to retaliate in the absence of prompt and complete compensation, notwithstanding an EC threat of counterretaliation.

No constituents, least of all prospective beneficiaries of the threat, took any known actions to undercut Yeutter's credibility in this case, to put it mildly. The four associations representing all producers of corn, barley, and grain sorghum unified their lobbying positions throughout these talks by speaking through a Trade Policy Coordinating Committee. Far from restraining Yeutter, they pressed him repeatedly to raise his reservation value. These producers wanted Washington to demand that the European Community eliminate its subsidies on European exports, which the Community used to move its surpluses into third markets, where they could displace other U.S. exports.[16] This demand would have been more difficult for the Community to accept than what Washington did demand. The U.S. growers feared that any sales recovery they achieved through a compensatory EC import quota would be offset immediately by increased subsidized competition in third markets (which did occur later to some extent). A delegation of American farm leaders traveled to Europe during the summer to deliver their message personally to farm and government leaders there, further demonstrating American unity and firmness.

In early July Brussels and Washington reached a temporary truce extending the time for negotiation until 31 December.[17] In return, Yeutter achieved special EC agreement to import U.S. feedgrains for six months, though at levels well below the compensation he had been demanding. For his American constituents, this compromise was "a bitter pill to swallow."[18] In the fall the growers stepped up

[15] Letter to the President from National Grange, U.S. Feed Grains Council, American Soybean Association, National Association of Wheat Growers, and eleven other organizations, 21 March 1986.

[16] Letters from U.S. Feed Grains Council to U.S. Secretary of Agriculture, 5 May 1986 and to the U.S. Trade Representative, 14 May 1986; letter from Acting Secretary of Agriculture to U.S. Feed Grains Council, 29 May 1986.

[17] The two also agreed to set the small Portugal issues to one side and concentrate on the Spanish market.

[18] Letter, National Corn Growers Association to U.S. Trade Representative, 11 July 1986.

their demands, urging Washington to hold hostage the possibility of a GATT agreement covering all agriculture in the Uruguay round until the EC paid additional corn compensation.[19] In December, the Feed Grains Council lectured U.S. negotiators again in no uncertain terms:

> Our membership has clearly indicated that the feed grains sector is willing to face the possible consequence of EC counterretaliation. What they are not willing to face is anything less than full compensation for the Spanish market, or a lack of resolve by our government if such compensation cannot be achieved. . . . The time has come to draw the line and take a strong stand against the unfair trading practices of the European Community. Any further delay in the settlement of this dispute is totally unacceptable.[20]

When asked whether other U.S. groups, especially those facing possible counterretaliation, pressed for accommodation, one U.S. negotiator replied:

> Sure, we heard from them. We got a few letters saying they were concerned about it, but they were not beating our door down. It was not heavy-duty political pressure. The corn gluten feed people [targeted by Brussels] have their own zero [duty] binding in the EC They know that if they want U.S. to go to bat for them, they have to play along sometimes when we're working for somebody else. We did hear a lot from the import interests—representing the French products, Belgian endive, and so forth.[21]

These relatively quiet, routine efforts were no match for the corn growers, and not comparable to those of the computer multinationals in the Brazil case.

Subsequent interviews with Brazilian and European negotiators revealed a significant difference in U.S. threat credibility. One official in Brasília, for example, when asked whether actual retaliation had been expected, replied:

> We had mixed expectations in Brazil; some people said they did, others that they didn't. Those who were opposed to having negotiations in the first place said they did not expect retaliation, and so forth.[22]

No mix was found in Europe. No European official consulted in Brussels, Paris, London, or Washington reported thinking that the U.S. threat against the European Community had been a bluff. All said they had taken it quite seriously indeed. "I think everyone was pretty much convinced that they would do it," re-

---

[19] Letter from U.S. Feed Grains Council to U.S. Trade Representative, 8 October 1986.
[20] Letters to USTR, 2 December and 17 December 1986
[21] Interview, Washington, D.C., 1988.
[22] Interview in Brasília, 1987. A different official, evidently belonging to the first group, recalled that in the early months of the dispute, he had feared the U.S. government would retaliate even without strong industry support, but that events in 1986, discussed below, seemed to ease this risk. Interview in Washington, D.C., 1987.

called a participating Commission official.[23] Two pointed to Washington's sanctions the year before in the pasta-citrus dispute. A French official, when asked what had convinced him, replied that he had visited several different agencies in Washington that often express different views on the same issue. This time he had heard the same complaint about Spanish accession in the same terms, even from the Department of Commerce. "It was very clear that a very powerful lobby was working the agencies on this issue."[24] The U.S. threat was more credible in Brussels than in Brasília.

GREATER INTERNAL POLITICAL COSTS
OF COMPLIANCE IN BRAZIL THAN IN EUROPE

A second reason for the paradoxical outcomes is that Washington's threats stimulated different mixes of internal pressures on the threatened negotiators. Inside Brazil Reagan triggered an explosion of angry hostility against compliance and little pressure in favor. In Europe, powerful actors quickly began to press for accommodation.

In Europe, stronger demands for making concessions

It is true that all EC member governments including Britain, led by Margaret Thatcher, denounced Washington's "Ramboism." The entire Community defended the enlargement treaty as consistent with their obligations under GATT without any further compensation to the Americans. However, although Bonn and London felt Washington clearly was in the wrong, they proved far from prepared to suffer a trade war over this issue. Washington's credible threat raised their subjective resistance points and split them off from the coalition, leaving France isolated.

The European Community's first reaction to Reagan's harsh ultimatum was symmetrical pure defensive claiming. On 9 April the Commission approved a list of U.S. farm products for counterretaliation. Commissioner for External Affairs Willy de Clercq, the chief negotiator, told U.S. journalists in Brussels, "We do not like Rambo-style diplomacy. There is no reason to confront us with deadlines, with ultimatums." Professing a desire to settle the issue amicably under GATT rules, he cautioned: "But I must underline our firm determination to defend the legitimate interests of the EC." Counterretaliation would follow any U.S. measures "in complete symmetry."[25] In response to U.S. measures concerning Spain, the EC wheeled out three of the biggest cannons it had for agriculture: counterthreats to cut U.S. exports of corn gluten feed, wheat, and rice.

---

[23] Interview in Brussels, 1987.
[24] Interview in Paris, 1988.
[25] *International Trade Reporter*, 16 April 1986.

In the first two weeks, however, differences appeared among the most powerful EC member states. French Minister for Agriculture Francois Guillaume described the U.S. demands as "completely unacceptable,"[26] and demanded that Brussels not cave in. West German Economics Minister Martin Bangemann, in contrast, warned that "an escalation of trade restrictions" could "spill over into the industrial area with unforeseeable consequences for growth and employment. . . . The Community should not take part in verbal muscle flexing, but should rather make unmistakably clear its readiness to negotiate and its interest in a settlement."[27] When the EC Council met on 21 April to approve the Commission proposals, the French and Portuguese governments supported the Commission's approach without reservation, but they were the only states to be so enthusiastic. Denmark, the Netherlands, and West Germany were noticeably reticent about counterthreats.[28]

Understanding the European responses requires a brief comparison of their national markets. While trade within the Community was free, the sector with the most to lose from compliance with Reagan's demand was French maize growers. France was the largest maize producing country—growing nearly half the EC12 crop in 1984–85—and the only state producing a corn surplus relative to domestic consumption.

During the mid-1980s, European farmers, like their U.S. counterparts, were suffering a painful decline in real income, despite the EC Common Agricultural Policy. In 1985 agricultural real income dropped to its lowest point in fifteen years. French cereals growers suffered a 20 percent shrinkage in net revenue that year, as costs rose while output prices slid.[29] Urgent pleas were mounting on the desks of national parliamentarians and EC officials in Brussels, just as in Washington.

French farmers had an interest in the Spanish corn market in particular. Community enlargement would increase competition for them in other products such as fruits and vegetables. Gains for corn exports in the Spanish market had been a crucial offset earning their political support for enlargement itself.

On the other hand, West Germany and the United Kingdom both imported corn. Thus the other two of the three largest powers stood to lose virtually nothing commercially from compliance with Washington's demand. But the Reagan threat raised the commercial cost of no-deal for both of them as well as France. The USTR office carefully selected sanction items that would hit most member states, while concentrating roughly half the total burden on France. White wine, one of the EC's leading exports to the U.S. with sales valued at $204 million in 1985, came from France, Germany, and Italy. Brandy and cognac were major French exports, and their producers and distributors were known to be politically well organized. Cheese was for France and the Netherlands; gin and whiskey

[26] *Agra Europe*, 4 April 1986.
[27] *International Trade Reporter*, 16 April 1986.
[28] Yannopoulos 1988, 122.
[29] Association General des Producteurs de Mais, *Rapport D'Orientation 1986*, 5.

were for Britain and Ireland; olives would cover all the Mediterranean countries. Wags soon dubbed the dispute "the yuppie war."

London and Bonn did face relationship and reputation costs from complying. The enlargement treaty had been ratified and was in effect. The U.S. threat directly challenged the fundamental EC legal and negotiating position on enlargements in the GATT. The Community had long interpreted the General Agreement as requiring parties forming a customs union to compensate third parties only if those nations' interests are damaged on the whole, not on a product-by-product basis. They maintained that EC "debits" on cereals were offset by "credits earned" by third countries on other products. Spanish and Portuguese industrial protection was quite high, and Brussels showed that after accession was completed, the average level of protection—combining industrial and agricultural sectors—would clearly be lower, not higher, in both countries. London and Bonn agreed with Paris that the United States already was receiving enough compensation via other products. Furthermore, their joint reputation for bargaining firmness would suffer if they yielded in this instance, and might encourage challenges in others. These governments shared their general commitment to Community institutions and mutual support, for broad political reasons. Still, the heavy U.S. threat placed great strain on these common political objectives.

When asked why trade war had not broken out in July, one Commission negotiator replied in part by reflecting on the problem of managing internal divisions in Europe:

> From the U.S. side, the EC was beginning to give up on its principle that we did not owe any compensation. For the European side, once we realized that there was a risk of a major trade war and possible strains on cohesion in the Community—our tendencies were far from unanimous—we saw that probably we would not have successfully resisted a trade war. It was decided that it would be better to drop something on the table, something limited, that would not prejudge our position later, but would allow time for people to realize that such a thing was a possibility. . . .
>
> The problem of cohesion would arise because decisions have to be ratified by the member states in the 113 Committee [a reference to Article 113 of the Rome Treaty]. That committee makes decisions by a qualified majority. On a serious issue like XXIV:6 [this issue], we realized that we might not get one. There would be nothing more serious for Community cohesion than having the member states refuse to ratify an agreement the Commission had negotiated.[30]

The American threat quickly convinced some leading actors that their true alternative to agreement with the United States was much worse than they had believed at the beginning of 1986, prior to this bargaining episode. "Dropping

[30] Interview, Brussels, 1988.

something on the table" for the interim might help convince even French constituents and officials, too, that the Community should make concessions sufficient to get American agreement.

These talks continued to be tense and difficult, as grain producers on both sides of the Atlantic heaped on unrelenting pressure. After both negotiating teams hailed the July interim settlement, farmers on each side angrily blasted their representatives for weakness. On the Fourth of July, the French Association of Maize Producers (AGPM), joined by other French farm groups, mounted vocal demonstrations in Paris and dumped two tons of corn onto the streets in protest. They demanded to know why they should be the only Europeans to pay for enlargement. They branded the truce settlement "a veritable Munich."[31] The Community-wide farm lobby supported them with its own denunciations. Rumors suggested that the French government yielded to this interim setback only after the EC had agreed to side payments in the form of restitutions to finance exports of French corn outside the EC that otherwise would have been sold in Spain.[32]

Meanwhile, other European special interests likely to be hurt by a trade war also made their voices heard, though usually behind closed doors. In France, when cognac producers made their quiet contacts, the Government assured them that in the end the Americans would not go through with their threats.[33] A Washington policy maker reported, "The British, the gin people and so forth, were working frantically to try to head off U.S. retaliation."[34] According to a Brussels participant, "some of the biggest pressures on the Commission to reach a settlement came from the industrial people, people like Volkswagen and whiskey, who were very afraid of a trade war."[35] Automobiles were not on the American retaliation list, but an EC-U.S. trade war of this scale might have serious long-term consequences for the world trading system. Industrialists also might have been attempting to counter pressure from French farmers on Brussels to offer greater market access for American industrial products instead of corn.

The German government vigorously pressed de Clercq and others for a settlement. A well-placed French participant reported that the French government's hard-line position against any permanent concessions softened significantly in October 1986. They "wanted to avoid a major break with Germany." The Germans had worked quite closely with the French at Punta del Este, supporting French demands concerning the agenda of the new Uruguay round. The French were grateful, and "a trade war with the United States would have upset the Germans very much."[36] The Chirac government had made close ties with West Germany a central policy principle.

[31] *Le Monde*, 5 July 1986.
[32] *Agra Europe*, 4 July 1986.
[33] Interview with a French official, Washington, D.C. 1988.
[34] Interview, Washington, D.C., 1988.
[35] Interview, Brussels, 1988.
[36] Interview in Europe, 1988.

As the December deadline approached, de Clercq's and Yeutter's moves began hinting at a serious search for agreement, but they did not bridge the wide gap between them. The U.S. reduced its claim for losses in Spain from an estimated $600 million to $400 million. The EC offered a proposal guaranteeing that Spain would import 1.6 million tons of corn and sorghum per year for four years, but the United States said it would not accept less than 4.4 million tons for an indefinite period.[37]

On 30 December, Reagan signed an order imposing 200 percent duties on about $400 million worth of European brandy, white wine, gin, cheeses, olives, and other goods. French brandy and wine would account for $250 million of the total. At the same time, it was noted that hearings would be held on the final product list, and that the penalties would not take effect until the end of January, thus actually providing still more time for bargaining. The EC repeated that it would impose countermeasures if Washington struck.[38]

The two sides settled in the early morning hours of 29 January 1987 after a classic all-night haggle, and after Washington had agreed for the first time to accept a small amount of its compensation in industrial sectors. The outcome, though it fell short of initial American demands, was a major setback from the EC's status quo ante and for its legal principle. The Community agreed to cancel its new quota reserving 15 percent of Portugal's market for EC suppliers. More important, the Community guaranteed that Spain would import at least 2 million metric tons of corn and 300,000 tons of sorghum from third parties each year for the next four years. U.S. negotiators valued the European concessions at about $400 million per year, and they suspended retaliatory measures. French corn growers received export-subsidy side payments, and for several reasons European corn exports increased subsequently. The United States claimed substantial commercial value from the European Community and made no concessions of its own. This was a clear win-lose agreement relative to the prior status quo.

One European participant summarizes his analysis of the outcome in these words:

> Once the EC realized that they had to pay a price for enlargement, then it came down to an internal struggle over who was going to pay. This is always the way it is in the EC At the outset, the Government of France took the position "to hell with the United States." But this was not realistic. France was the only country that had a problem. The British and the Germans were not going to be willing to go to trade war with the United States on behalf of French corn. Politically it was not possible to build up a big enough coalition in Europe to support this hard-line view.[39]

---

[37] *International Trade Reporter*, 17 December 1986; *Agra Europe*, 19 December 1986.
[38] *New York Times* and *Wall Street Journal*, 31 December 1986
[39] Interview in Washington, D.C., 1988.

In Brazil, weaker demands for making concessions

In Brazil, the U.S. threat evoked loud demands for standing firm that almost drowned support for making concessions. For the Brazilian negotiator, the net internal political costs of making the demanded concessions were clearly greater than was the case for de Clercq, especially for the first eight months. On 7 September, the day Washington chose for its threat, is Brazil's national Independence Day, its most patriotic occasion. Arthur Virgilio, majority whip in the Chamber of Deputies, reacted indignantly, "who does Reagan think he is threatening us?" . . . "The fight for the market reserve is as important today as was the struggle for state control over oil some years ago." Some educated Brazilians felt the message was "it's OK for us to produce shoes, but high-tech is for grown-ups."[40] The informatics dispute became front-page news in Brazil for months, the largest problem in relations with the United States in a decade. Later one U.S. diplomat decried "clumsy" American handling of the affair, sputtering we "played right into the hands of the Shiites"—Brazil's nationalists.[41]

The Executive Secretary of the Brazilian computer industry association ABI-COMP insisted that Brazil accounted for only 1 percent of the world computer market and declared, "it is ridiculous to suggest that the American industry is harmed because it is not exporting computers to Brazil." In fact, the United States had a huge surplus overall, not a deficit, in its informatics trade with Brazil. Foreign firms' sales in Brazil had been rising smartly despite the market reserve policy, which did not restrict sales of mainframes and their software, only lesser technologies. One minister threatened that if the U.S. struck, Brazil could respond by opening its market to Japanese automobiles.[42]

Even prior to the threat, the informatics program had enjoyed unusually wide domestic political support, stretching from the left to business to the military. Benefiting most directly from the status quo were the computer hardware and software producers that had started their businesses under the *reserva de mercado*. The government had launched the program in the early 1970s with the goal of developing an informatics capability independent of foreign firms. During the 1960s virtually all Brazil's technology had come from abroad, in the form of small and medium-sized mainframe computers, 80 percent of them from IBM.

The plan called for Brazilian production of the more modest technologies, learning by doing, and expansion up the technical ladder, displacing foreign firms as the country developed the capacity to do so. The tools included state investment in a joint venture to produce the country's first minicomputer in the early 1970s, bans on imports of mini- and microcomputers in the mid-1970s, and other measures. Some of Brazil's largest bank conglomerates invested in informatics production, establishing a half-dozen large firms to produce equipment for au-

---

[40] *Wall Street Journal*, 5 June 1986.
[41] Interview, Washington, D.C., 1987.
[42] *New York Times*, 16 September; *Veja*, 18 September; *O Estado de São Paulo*, 21 September 1985.

tomating banks and supermarkets as well as a wide range of other products. Meanwhile, the invention of the personal computer spawned many smaller firms as well. By 1983, 118 new companies were producing clones of the IBM PC and the Apple computer. Overall, foreign firms' market share in Brazil eroded from 77 percent to 49 percent during the period 1979 to 1986. Their own sales had increased 130 percent over the seven years, but in the protected sphere, national firms' revenues were multiplying from a low base by 700 percent.[43] Thus by 1985 producers in Brazil were grouped into three segments: the foreign multinational subsidiaries, who generally chafed against the program's restraints and intrusions; relatively large Brazilian firms benefiting from but probably having less permanent need for it; and the small firms, many of which would not have survived without it. The Brazilian computer market was rated the eighth largest in the world and was growing rapidly.

The military services, especially the Navy, had led the program's initiation, seeking to free themselves from foreign dependence for intelligence and weapon system controls. During the authoritarian period they created a special agency, the Secretaria Especial de Informática (SEI) or Special Informatics Agency, under the authority of the National Security Council, to make the regulatory decisions affecting foreign and national producers. In 1984, while the nation was preparing to return to democracy, the outgoing military government sought to make the program permanent and more legitimate by having the Congress approve it by statute. During the election campaign, the victorious presidential candidate, Tancredo Neves of the opposition PMDB party, and his running mate, José Sarney, also strongly endorsed the program. In 1984 the Chamber of Deputies passed a compromise bill extending the program until 1992 by a vote of 378 to 1.

Some business sectors had criticized SEI, and the political right had introduced its own bill to dismantle the agency. But they clearly lost and the rightist party declined badly after 1984. The São Paulo State Federation of Industry was a locus of possible support for concessions. In September 1985 a few dissenting domestic voices were heard, but only a few.

Facing this extreme imbalance in domestic politics, President Sarney studiously avoided any step that could be seen as bending to foreign pressure.[44] Brasília essentially refused to negotiate over this issue at all. Its position was that its market reserve was a domestic measure to promote an infant industry, and as such was consistent with the GATT and not subject to negotiation.

Talks did begin after May 1986, when the superpower, not the developing country, pulled back. The State Department used an official visit by Deputy Secretary John Whitehead to "break the hysteria, to cool things off," as one U.S. diplomat put it.[45] Just prior to meeting with him President Sarney said, "We are

---

[43] *Brazilian Informatics Industry Directory 87/88*, ABICOMP, Rio de Janeiro.

[44] Neves died suddenly after the election but before his inauguration, and Sarney took his place. Sarney disliked the informatics program and preferred to dismantle it, according to later evidence. See Odell and Dibble 1992.

[45] Interview, Washington, D.C., 1987.

not going to negotiate anything with the Americans—even flexibility in the law's application, like they want." While Whitehead was in town, Senator Severo Gomes, a former Minister of Commerce and Industry, submitted a bill calling for severe restrictions on multinational corporations whose countries adopt policies hindering the export of Brazilian goods and services. The Senator said it was a defensive weapon, "like a revolver you keep in the drawer and pray you'll never have to use."[46] Whitehead, reportedly carrying an invitation from Reagan to Sarney for a state visit, signaled that Washington would not attempt to change the informatics law after all. Its complaint was with the way SEI applied it. He also said the United States was no longer threatening sanctions or imposing deadlines. This tactical retreat presumably reduced the credibility of the earlier threat still further. All these new moves did not result from a coordinated decision in Washington to change course. Reportedly State relaxed the pressure more than USTR had approved, and some Washington officials were furious.[47] But Brazilian leaders regarded these statements as providing some room for maneuver, and they agreed to begin negotiations after all. [48]

By this time dissenting Brazilian voices also began to sound a bit louder. The week Whitehead was in Brasília, the magazine *Veja*, comparable to *Time* and *Newsweek*, charged that SEI was multiplying its powers beyond the law and invading areas where it did not belong. All manufacturing projects in the country involving electronics in any way were forced to pass through the hands of a group of only seventy persons to get approval. One industrialist was quoted complaining that he had had to travel to Brasília at least twelve times to get permission to import a machine for frying potatoes because it incorporated a microprocessor to regulate oil temperature. Eugenio Staub—the leading Brazilian producer of audio components, a maker of microcomputers, and a member of CONIN, a new official Council established to supervise the informatics program—said he did not see problems with allowing foreign firms play a larger role within the reserved market. "Competition is also part of the market system." The magazine also questioned the Foreign Minister's initial stand that "there is nothing to negotiate." "This denies the very essence of diplomacy," contended *Veja*. The article's title described Brasília's decision to talk to Washington as a "Return to the real world."[49]

Meanwhile, the threat was bearing down on Brazil's export industries, and some began calling on the government to soften its position. During the Brazilian winter Ozires Silva, the president of Petrobras and former chairman of Embraer, the state enterprise exporting small aircraft to America, spoke publicly in favor of a negotiated settlement. Silva reportedly met in private with Sarney several times to express these concerns. The computer industry itself did not export to the

---

[46] *South*, August 1986, 115.
[47] Interviews in Washington, D.C., 1987.
[48] Brazilian Foreign ministry statement published in *O Globo*, 28 May 1986; interviews in Brasília.
[49] *Veja*, 4 June 1986, 116–20 (translation by Anne Dibble).

United States, though it did rely heavily on imports of U.S. components whose flow could be interrupted.

Elements within the Brazilian government also questioned the status quo. The Foreign Minister publicly criticized SEI, whose most vocal official opponents were the Ministers of Commerce and of Communications. They too advocated a more flexible negotiating posture. The Ministry of Commerce and Industry was concerned about damage to export industries from retaliation, and about long-term costs to informatics user industries. Large companies in the telecommunications sector were having difficulties with SEI regulators. Most major industries not involved in computer production were paying higher prices for Brazilian computers than they would have to pay for equivalent imports, the best technology available worldwide. But counterpressures remained weaker politically than those of informatics defenders.

After Whitehead's visit, Sarney named as his chief negotiator Ambassador Paulo Tarso Flecha de Lima, the secretary-general of the Foreign Ministry and a career economic diplomat. During a bilateral meeting in August Flecha de Lima did indicate a willingness to undertake some measures that were consistent with the law, that were sought by Brazilian constituents, and that Washington might describe as small gains back home. These included trimming SEI's wings to the extent of issuing a list of products that were outside its authority at that time. They promised to set up a committee to investigate complaints from foreign investors, and reported that the Brazilian government was preparing a bill that would provide copyright protection to software.[50] None of these measures was yet in place, however; all were promises. And none guaranteed measurable commercial gain to U.S. firms even when implemented. At the end of twelve months, superpower threats had changed little in Brazil, in sharp contrast to the EC case. Yeutter recommended and Reagan decided to postpone the decision on sanctions until 31 December 1986.

U.S. CREDIBILITY RISES IN BRAZIL ROUND TWO

The second year of the informatics case provides interesting causal variation that further confirms the first proposition. Well into the negotiation process, U.S. electronics and software industries came together in support of implementing the threat for the first time. Brazil received this information, Yeutter's credibility increased, and the value of impasse for Brazil worsened. Only then did Brasília make a major concession.

Ironically it was a nationalist victory inside Brazil's domestic politics that triggered this hardening in U.S. politics. Late in 1986, Brazilian nationalists prevailed over internationalist rivals during the drafting of key provisions of the new

[50] Interviews with participating U.S. officials.

software bill. It proposed to create sui generis software rules rather than extending existing copyright law for literary works to software. Protection against piracy would have been guaranteed for a twenty-five-year period, to foreign as well as Brazilian software. In some cases, however, foreign authors also would be required to divulge the program's secret source code if they transferred technology into Brazil. Furthermore, the bill codified several restrictions that could prevent many foreign programs from entering Brazil legally in the first place. It authorized SEI to deny a license whenever a "functionally equivalent" Brazilian program could be found. That is, this bill codified the protectionist market reserve for software now as well as hardware, which had always been the intention of Brazilian nationalists and a red flag for U.S. negotiators. The growing software market could be closed to foreign inventors completely.

This internal victory by Brazilian nationalists subsequently backfired against them via U.S. politics. The bill alarmed American firms including IBM and unified them politically for the first time. As they were studying the bill, Reagan's December deadline was approaching. Again, the administration decided to postpone retaliation and to continue the negotiation. Washington declared victory with respect to two issues, but regarding two others—software protection and foreign investment regulation—the President directed a further "final effort" and set 1 July 1987 as yet another deadline for a sanctions decision.

Intended beneficiaries of the threat now united to reinforce it. CBEMA, earlier the more restrained organization, testified in March 1987 that the 301 results overall were "disappointing," saying there had been no acceptable movement on software protection or investment regulation. Regarding software, the United States had managed to push other countries into joining a worldwide trend toward a standardized approach under international copyright norms. Brazil was a major hold-out, planning on a sui generis approach that fell short of international norms. Not only that, CBEMA's President observed,

> if the proposed software legislation goes through as currently drafted, we would be worse off than we were at the opening of the 301 investigation, because there is a judicial basis for the interpretation of existing law such that computer software is protected under the copyright law. Failure to satisfactorily resolve this issue would, I fear, send a signal to the rest of the world that we are not really serious either about protecting such intellectual property as software under the international copyright regime, or about taking action against unfair trade practices.[51]

The position of the American Electronics Association, already more demanding, also hardened. The AEA laid down four minimum objectives for the last three months of bargaining. If sufficient progress were not made on these points before

---

[51] Statement of Vico E. Henriques, President, Computer and Business Equipment Manufacturers Association, before the Office of the USTR, 12 March 1987.

July, "we believe it would then be appropriate for the Administration to take the next step in the process of implementing the President's October decision."[52]

In May the AEA, CBEMA, and two other industry associations met jointly in Washington with the Brazilian Ambassador to communicate their vigorous opposition directly, something they had been reluctant to do. This was the first time in this dispute that American computer and software companies had mounted a joint policy protest to the Brazilian government. They gave him a three-page memorandum listing amendments to the software bill that would meet their minimum concerns and "avert escalation." They made clear that U.S. companies, including those with investment stakes in the country, were all agreed now to support retaliation if these terms were not met. The Ambassador scheduled an immediate personal meeting with President Sarney to convey what he had heard.[53] Yeutter's credibility in Brazil had just increased.

At the end of May, Brazilian negotiators made a significant concession. The Secretary General of SEI, a Foreign Ministry diplomat, a U.S. embassy officer, and the U.S. Commerce Department's specialist on copyright met in extreme secrecy in Brasília to discuss foreign suggestions for changing the software bill under consideration in the Congress. The Brazilians agreed to change Articles II and IV on copyright, dropping the sui generis regime and extending the prevailing intellectual property law to software. Brasília continued, however, to refuse concessions on the marketing regulations that would discriminate against imports. The Brazilians regarded this bill as implementing the 1984 law with respect to software and insisted the market reserve principle was untouchable. Also the bill would still require that owners divulge their source codes in any cases of technology transfer. The Brazilian executive then presented what were described as technical adjustments to the PMDB majority leader in Congress for inclusion in the final bill. In fact they were making a change that would not have been undertaken without U.S. pressure.

Meanwhile in Washington, the Cabinet's Economic Policy Council was united in a decision to retaliate at last, if at least one house of Brazil's Congress did not pass at least this modified software bill by the deadline. This consensus included even the Secretaries of State and Treasury—notwithstanding pending talks on debt problems, Brazilian counterthreats, and possible harm to the bilateral relationship. [54]

In June SEI announced several decisions on investment modernization projects and piracy complaints that were favorable to U.S. firms. On 24 June 1987 Brazil's lower house passed the software bill.[55] Approval in the Senate was still needed before it could take effect. The U.S. companies told the Reagan administration that

---

[52] William K. Krist, Vice President, International Trade Affairs, American Electronics Association, before the Office of the USTR, 12 March 1987.

[53] A copy of the memorandum supplied by, and an interview with, a participating business representative, Washington 1988.

[54] Interview with a participating American official, 1987.

[55] *Journal of Commerce*, 25 and 26 June 1987; *New York Times*, 26 June 1987.

in these circumstances they were not in favor of sanctions, but also not satisfied with these partial actions.[56] On 30 June President Reagan announced that he was suspending the part of the investigation concerned with intellectual property protection. The three parts suspended so far would remain suspended until terminated or reopened. He directed USTR Yeutter to continue the investigation of investment problems but did not set any new deadline.[57] Yeutter's staff raised glasses of champagne to celebrate what they hoped had been the last act of their long-running drama. The Brazilian concession of mid-1987 was only a partial move of uncertain commercial value, and was not acknowledged publicly as a concession to the United States at all. This settlement was a tacit rather than written agreement.

And it was still not quite over. In September 1987, before the new law had been enacted, SEI denied a joint request from Microsoft and six Brazilian firms to sell MS-DOS software in Brazil. Many pirated copies were circulating, and this was Microsoft's effort to replace them with sales. Infuriated, the U.S. software industry demanded sanctions. In November Reagan finally did announce sanctions against Brazil and hearings were scheduled. But in December the Brazilian software bill became law and in January 1988, before Washington had acted, a higher body in Brasília reversed SEI in part, licensing sale of the latest version of MS-DOS.[58] In February USTR announced that implementation of the sanctions was being postponed. Washington finally terminated this investigation in October 1989.[59]

OTHER INTERPRETATIONS

Different institutions in the targets?

Three counterarguments might be raised to explain this chapter's paradox, but none holds up well under scrutiny. The most prominent institutional difference here is that target B was a nation-state in one case and the European Community in the other. One might suppose that the negotiator for an international organization will enjoy less autonomy from member states than the average sovereign state negotiator has from her constituents. Robert Putnam proposes that:

> the greater the autonomy of central decision makers from their Level II constituents, the larger their win-set and thus the greater the likelihood of achieving international agreement. . . . However, two-level analysis also implies that, *ceteris paribus*, the stronger a state is in terms of autonomy from domestic pressures, the weaker its relative bargaining position internationally.[60]

---

[56] *Journal of Commerce*, 1 July 1987.
[57] Statement by the Assistant to the President for Press Relations, The White House, 30 June 1987.
[58] *International Trade Reporter*, 20 January 1988, 62.
[59] Odell and Dibble 1992; Bastos 1994.
[60] Putnam 1988, 449.

Lesser autonomy, then, should improve the EC external outcome. But de Clercq gave up more, not less, than Flecha de Lima.

The evidence suggests, actually, that their constitutions and their constituents constrained both negotiators substantially and perhaps equally so. EC rules designated the Commission as the Community's agent dealing with third parties on matters relating to the Common Commercial Policy, as well as on certain other issues. Under the Treaty of Rome's Article 113, the Commission made recommendations to the European Council, consisting of member-state delegates. The Council authorized the Commission to open negotiations with third countries, and Articles 114 and 228 empowered the Council to ratify such agreements. At the end of the Tokyo round in 1978, the Council rejected final deals presented to it by the Commission twice, forcing further external negotiations.[61] The Commission also was required to consult during the negotiation process with a special advisory committee appointed by the Council, known as the Article 113 Committee. Thus EC institutions did give level two players continual access to the process as well as a veto over the outcome. The Council ratified the January 1987 Yuppie War settlement.[62]

Brazil's negotiator was also constrained, especially since at this time Brazil was shedding authoritarianism. In early 1985 a new civilian president had taken office as the result of an election for the first time since 1961. Any formal agreement with the United States to change the informatics law would have required ratification by Brazil's Congress. Sarney could have made lesser changes without formal Congressional approval, but the Congress could have overturned them if he had failed to achieve substantial political support. The negotiator's internal autonomy was not clearly greater in either Brazil or the European Community, yet their outcomes differed substantially.[63]

Different international institutions?

Could the greater EC concessions be due to differences between the international rules relevant to these two cases? All three parties were members of the GATT, but its 1985 rules gave the United States only weak leverage in each case, and equivalently weak, especially compared with the rules of the World Trade Organization adopted in 1994 (discussed in chap. 8). Thus this interpretation adds little here.

At the heart of the Yuppie War was GATT's Article XXIV, which authorized signatories to form a discriminatory customs union, provided that the resulting duties "shall not on the whole be higher or more restrictive than" those applicable

---

[61] Taylor 1983, 132–35.

[62] *Official Journal of the European Communities* 30 (April 10, 1987), L98, 1–6.

[63] Evans 1993 (399) also concludes from eleven sets of negotiations over security and economic issues that "the relative autonomy of international leaders decreases continuously and substantially over the course of most negotiations. State leaders are in the drivers' seat as international agendas are being formulated. The more clearly international options become defined, the more leaders are constrained by mobilized interest groups and trapped by personal investment in the on-going negotiations."

prior to the union (paragraph 5a). Article XXVIII provided procedures and remedies for a third party that felt injured. But Article XXIV:5a left open the question
over which the European Community and the United States disagreed: whether
compensation was due sector-by-sector or only on the whole. More generally,
agricultural trade had been largely exempted in practice when the GATT was negotiated and during its early years, especially at the insistence of Washington,
ironically. Furthermore, GATT's 1986 enforcement capacity was weak. It provided for appointment of an expert panel to rule on the merits, but any losing government could block GATT member states as a body from adopting a panel ruling
as binding. Both the EC and the U.S. availed themselves of this blocking option
more than once prior to 1994. In 1986 any of the three parties could have blocked
GATT from acting against it, had a panel ruled either way.[64]

GATT's 1986 rules placed very little discipline on the practices Washington
most wanted to challenge in Brazilian informatics. Although the General Agreement ruled out quantitative restrictions of the type Brazil used against many imports, Article XVIII granted a general exemption for developing countries when
these practices would advance their development. Brasília routinely claimed this
exemption when it reported its rigorous general protection regime. The 1986
GATT did not impose any requirements at all on treatment of intellectual property
rights or international investments.

In the 1990s the rules changed, and that change probably affected subsequent
negotiations. The Uruguay round did not clarify Article XXIV, and the inade-
quacy of this rule's application was a subject of continuing discussion, as more
and more new regional trade agreements were signed and reported but not found
to be either consistent or inconsistent with the Article.[65] Signatories did, however,
create a new set of international obligations to provide protection to intellectual
property rights, greater than those in existing accords and with more rigorous enforcement possible. Among other things, this pact extended fifty–year copyright
protection to computer software and databases on a non-discriminatory basis. The
1994 deal fused these new codes with the General Agreement on Tariffs and
Trade into a "single undertaking," so that gaining the benefits of any of the rules
now required a government to accept them all. This unification satisfied a major
U.S. negotiating objective and greatly expanded the international obligations of
many developing countries including Brazil.[66]

WTO members also agreed in 1994 to virtually eliminate the option to block

---

[64] The weakening of GATT's enforcement was hardly independent of U.S. behavior; in fact, it was
led by Washington more than any other capital. Judging from the period 1948–89, "the United States
appears to be the defendant that most frequently resists the legal rulings of the dispute settlement process," that is, in cases that are not blocked before they reach a formal GATT decision (Hudec 1993,
306). Canada was a close second and the European Community was next. Hudec adds that the European Community's measured record of compliance is improved by a legal style of seeking to circum-
vent GATT law without openly violating it (314).

[65] E.g., Lawrence 1996.

[66] The new rules are summarized in Schott 1994. Brasília allowed its 1984 informatics program to
expire on schedule in 1992, and it also undertook a substantial liberalization of imports in general.

findings of dispute-settlement panels. Today the World Trade Organization normally adopts these judgments as binding international law obligations. Thus all WTO members enjoy a much stronger mechanism for enforcing their agreements. Had the 1994 institution been in place in 1985, it would have offered a more attractive venue than the GATT, at least for gaining Washington's objectives on Brazilian software. In its first two years this stronger mechanism attracted two to three times as many disputes, including some in which developing countries were the only parties.[67]

International security differences?

All three negotiators were careful to isolate these disputes from other issue areas. None linked his proposals to developments in the Uruguay round or debt rescheduling talks or to security arrangements, as far as is known.

EC member states faced a more powerful external military threat in the Warsaw pact than Brazil faced. Might this difference account for greater EC concessions to the Americans, the leaders of their security alliance? While this reasoning seems appealing as far as it goes, it is incomplete. Any European negotiator would have known that the United States too feared the Soviet threat to western Europe, and of course more than it feared the Soviet threat to South America. After all, Washington had stationed its own army permanently in Western Europe and not in South America. Thus if military threats affect economic bargaining at all, Soviet forces should have lowered Washington's own resistance point in dealings with European allies. The European negotiator, knowing Washington's security fears as well, therefore would not have been more likely to concede for these reasons.

CAUSES OF THREAT CREDIBILITY

This pair of episodes suggests two possible sources of variation in the first causal variable itself, sources that should operate generally. The computer market was multinational in structure and some interested U.S. producers had substantial assets at risk in Brazil, while the feedgrains market was not dominated by multinational producers and corn farmers were not significant investors in the EC The hypothesis is that the more an interested industry in the threatening country is multinational, and the more its assets are exposed in a foreign country, ceteris paribus the more that industry will oppose making or executing threats toward that country, and the lower the credibility of a threat made on behalf of that industry.[68] If globalization spreads further, this bargaining advantage of the host country will presumably become ever more important.

---

[67] For an early assessment, see Jackson 1996. Schoppa 1999 finds that Japan's responsiveness to U.S. bilateral pressure fell sharply once the WTO was in operation.

[68] This point parallels other research on the effects of international markets on companies' political behavior such as Destler and Odell 1987, Milner 1988, Milner and Yoffie 1989, Goodman, Spar, and Yoffie 1996, and Keohane and Milner 1996.

Second, threat credibility may diminish with the openness of the domestic political institutions in the threatening country, which did not vary here. U.S. rules required the threatening negotiator to conduct public hearings before proceeding, at which time businesses affected by sanctions could plead that their products be exempted. These procedures could affect threat credibility through two mechanisms. They call constituents' attention to the possible consequences of Washington decisions earlier and more than otherwise, and thus probably increase public expression of opposition. They also make it easier for the target government to learn about opposing internal preferences than in countries where such decisions are taken behind closed doors and implemented without advance public discussion. Thus a negotiator for a more opaque or closed system, where the same fraction of domestic constituents is privately opposed to carrying out the threat, will suffer less loss in credibility abroad, in this view.

This second idea may seem to contradict others in the literature. North and Weingast 1989 contend that constitutional restraints on a government increase its credibility. But they are concerned with credibility of a different commitment—its promises to respect its own citizens' property rights. When a government borrows money, it promises not to renege on the terms and confiscate the lender's wealth. A monarch under no institutionalized restraints has difficulty making that promise credible. Institutions that subject the ruler to more domestic vetoes, giving wealth holders a say in subsequent government decisions, give lenders assurance they will be able to protect themselves. The resulting greater credibility of property rights, in this argument, will induce them to lend more than they would to a tyrant, as well as investing more in the economy and stimulating growth. Whether true or not, this claim does not contradict mine. A more restrained executive could be more credible when making such promises to its own citizens, and simultaneously have greater difficulty than an opaque or authoritarian society in making other governments believe threats to harm them. There is no reason why a more opaque government could not enjoy greater short-run threat credibility abroad while also having more trouble borrowing money from its citizens and a slower long-run growth rate.

Fearon 1994 argues for a different credibility advantage of democracies. Thinking about the escalation of military disputes, he theorizes that democracies should be better able than nondemocracies to send a convincing signal that they are willing to fight over the issue in dispute. This is because escalating and then backing down will have domestic "audience costs"; the citizenry will punish such behavior. A democratic leader can jeopardize her own tenure more credibly than an authoritarian by escalating; threats from the latter are closer to "cheap talk." Escalation by the democrat should therefore be a more credible signal and a bargaining advantage in a war of nerves. But this reasoning overlooks the possibility that backing down will generate "audience benefits" as well. Suppose some constituents will reward the leader who backs away from the brink, or who exempts their products when imposing trade sanctions. To that extent, backing down will not be so bad for the leader or even a political gain, and so her credibility edge shrinks or becomes a disadvantage. The authoritarian negotiator may lack the advantage Fearon imagines, but she benefits from less visible internal opposition. Perhaps future empirical work can clarify these alternative views.

Tough bargaining will gain more in some cases than others. Presumably many factors could influence the results.[69] But several analytical ideas that have been proposed for bargaining in general do not help us understand the paradoxical difference between these two outcomes. The same government used the same strategy during the same period. Greater U.S. gain from the European Community could not have been due to a greater U.S. power advantage there. The difference was not due to differences in relevant international institutions or security conditions or greater negotiator autonomy in the EC.

The negotiation processes did make a clear difference to the outcomes. If we had assumed away the processes, we would have missed critical reasons for the outcomes. Consider the American strategy choice, to use overt threats and offensive claiming. Could Washington have gained as much from the EC without rough tactics? European participants were asked this question in 1988. One, promised confidentiality, replied, "They absolutely would not have gotten another ton of corn without having made such a threat."[70] A second European added:

> You'll never get the EC to move in a bilateral situation without them. Now perhaps if you could get an improved GATT dispute settlement procedure, then you might get somewhere. But under the present system, it can take years, and you never get any results.[71]

Once Washington had threatened Brazil and the EC, different subsequent domestic processes in the United States conditioned the responses of Brasília's and Brussels's negotiators, and hence the diverging outcomes. The more credible threat toward Europe had its effect on behavior by changing beliefs there about the cost of no deal with Washington, moving their resistance point up, more so than in Brazil. The threats also touched off different domestic processes in the target parties, with powerful pressure for accommodation on de Clercq and nearly universal pressure against accommodation on Sarney. This contrast provides empirical grounding for two hypotheses for explaining economic bargaining outcomes, which also identify two practical pitfalls that might frustrate future claiming attempts if they were present again.

These cases also generated three supplementary hypotheses that could be investigated further. Threat credibility in economic bargaining may fall additionally if the market in dispute is structured by multinational producers in the threatening

---

[69] For other comparative, empirical studies that are also relevant (in diverse ways and sometimes less directly) for conditions that increase gains or losses from value claiming, sample Curran 1983, Kirshner 1995, Krauss 1993, Li 1993, Martin 1992, Noland 1997, Odell 1980, Odell 1985 and Ryan 1991. The most directly relevant companion study is Bayard and Elliott 1994, which evaluates the American use of section 301 in seventy-two trade negotiations between 1975 and 1992.

[70] Interview, Brussels, 1988.

[71] Interview, Washington, D.C., 1988.

country who have stakes invested in the target country. Threat credibility may also fall with the openness of domestic political institutions, which make it easier for domestic opposition to organize and for foreign negotiators to learn about this opposition. Finally, we have a hint that strengthening an international institution for settling disputes may shift states' subsequent strategy choices, encouraging them to forego bilateral offensive claiming.

Was Reagan's threat toward Brazil simply a blunder of incomplete information? Would the administration have acted otherwise if it had consulted more thoroughly with the interested industry first? Surely more accurate advance information about industry preferences would have been useful to the U.S. negotiators, but this case may have been more complicated than that. At least one participating U.S. policy maker did advise against targeting the informatics issue, precisely on the grounds that it was not as winnable as other Brazil issues. These choices may have stemmed in part from the simultaneous administration effort to launch a new multilateral negotiation and influence its agenda. The same officials who picked Brazilian informatics also were responsible for the latter. As one of them suggested, even failing in Brazil might help produce a U.S. gain in Geneva. By engaging in a bilateral fight over new issues they wanted to add to the GATT—intellectual property rights and high technology industry—Washington signaled a worsened no-deal alternative for the rest of GATT. These issues were in fact added to the 1994 multilateral agreement. Multilateral cooperation may increase bilateral conflict in some circumstances.

This chapter has dwelled exclusively on the pure claiming strategy. Yet strict adherence to this polar extreme will sometimes gain less than a mixed strategy. The next chapter illustrates two such situations.

CHAPTER 7

Mixed Strategies and Outcomes

Many laymen think of bargaining as an exclusively fixed-sum process in which each party tries to take something from the other. The previous chapter recognized that side of the picture and isolated the offensive value-claiming strategy. Yet as many experienced bargainers know, a mixed strategy is likely to gain more or lose less than a pure distributive strategy under some conditions, even when both negotiators believe their main objectives are in conflict.[1] This chapter turns back to the mixed strategy, and concentrates more on strategy and tactics themselves as influences on the outcome. It documents two such conditions that have practical importance. First, when A is defending against claiming, he may lose less if he can create a counteroffer that will satisfy B at lower cost than simply accepting B's demand. Second, when A is attempting to claim offensively, adding an integrative tactic may improve his outcome when strong domestic opposition in the other country is likely to block B's assent, but the added tactic will help B convince his constituents to ratify it.

This chapter provides empirical support for each of these arguments from international economic relations. Unlike other chapters in parts 2 and 3, this one does not contrast two matched episodes. It compares observations made over time during a single episode and draws inferences from within-episode contrasts. This technique is used twice, with two different episodes. Drawing an inference requires counterfactual reasoning, which is necessarily speculative.[2] But the technique brings to light variations over time that have analytical value when a matching second independent episode has not been found. Additionally, when the contrast is limited to a single episode, many potentially significant omitted variables are effectively constant.

INTEGRATIVE TACTICS AND THE MIXED STRATEGY

Before examining the first argument and its evidence, it might be helpful to elaborate a bit on what integrative tactics are added to make a strategy mixed.

---

[1] Walton, Cutcher-Gerschenfeld, and McKersie 1994 studied thirteen local cases of U.S. labor-management interaction during the 1980s, and found that neither pure claiming (which they call "forcing" change) nor pure value creating (termed "fostering" change) produced outcomes as good for managers as those yielded by mixed strategies.

[2] Counterfactual arguments and thought experiments are widely used and well known as a useful method (Fearon 1991, Tetlock and Belkin 1996).

Chapter 2 defined the integrative strategy in its pure form as a set of actions or tactics that are

> instrumental to the attainment of objectives which are not in fundamental conflict with those of the other party and which can therefore be integrated to some degree. Such objectives are said to define an area of common concern, a *problem*. . . . Integrative potential exists when the nature of a problem permits solutions that benefit both parties, or at least when the gains of one party do not represent equal sacrifices by the other.[3]

When integrative tactics achieve gains, they do so in one of two broad ways.[4] The first (not emphasized in this chapter) is by discovering and exploiting similarities—common threats or problems whose solution would benefit both parties, or issues on which their partially unknown objectives overlap. Two international creditors with exposure in Indonesia in 1997, for instance, shared the goals of promoting Indonesian government policies that would preserve or raise their assets' values and blocking moves that would undermine them. In other cases, governments' true objectives are not so obvious before talks begin.

A second broad way is by uncovering differences that can be exploited for mutual benefit. The most straightforward technique is to attempt to find two or more issues on which the parties' preference orders differ, and then offer to exchange concessions on those issues. This pattern is familiar in ordinary commercial exchange and legislative logrolling. Legislator A seeking votes for a measure he favors looks for another legislator who wants something different. If A and B value their votes on two measures differently—if A values B's vote on measure L more than giving up his own vote on measure M, and B values his own vote on L less than getting A's vote on M—then a deal to trade these votes will benefit both, even when the two bills have no substantive relation to each other outside this bilateral negotiation.[5] Linking the two issues can create or enlarge a zone of agreement between A and B when none would exist otherwise.[6] Analogously, a bargainer seeking a mutually beneficial deal could explore for trades not of actual concessions but of reduced demands for gain on issues where they differ. That is, agent A, in addition to offering to give up something he possesses, could offer to settle for less future gain on issue C than he had requested if B will fall back from

---

[3] Walton and McKersie 1965, 9. This classic study did not characterize negotiating "strategies" as distributive or integrative, but instead used these headings to describe collective processes. The choice inevitably facing the individual party, however, is what to do itself; the resulting process depends on how others act. The present theory focuses on the party's choice alternatives and does not assume that a decision to attempt an integrative strategy will be reciprocated. The opposite possibility is in fact taken into account in the mixed strategy.

[4] Lax and Sebenius 1986, chapter 5. Their third route is best understood as a special case of the first.

[5] Integrative bargainers dovetail differences not only in preferences but also sometimes in risk propensity or time preference.

[6] Side payments through issue linkage in diverse international settings have been discussed by Keohane and Nye 1977, Tollison and Willett 1979, Haas 1980, Sebenius 1983, Oye 1992, Martin 1992, Friman 1993, and Cameron 1997 among others. In most IR examinations, however, issue link-

what he had wanted on issue D, as part of a deal that would make both better off on balance.

A more fundamental tactic for discovering differences to dovetail, as well as common objectives for that matter, is to redefine the issues themselves. Rather than taking the parties' demands and the issue space as given and looking for agenda items to link and trade, they imagine a new conception of the joint problem, a new formulation of one's own demand, or a new arrangement that might fit the contours of both parties' unknown priorities better, and raise it for comment.[7] Negotiation texts illustrate redefining the problem with the tale of two sisters who each demanded the same orange. They could agree to split it down the middle and each gain fifty percent—a solution that would create some joint value relative to the prior status quo. Thérèse, however, thought to ask Yvonne what she wanted to do with the orange. Yvonne wanted to use the rind to make icing for a cake. She did not want the meat, and Thérèse wanted only the meat. Thérèse then proposed the obvious solution. By exploring Yvonne's true priorities, which her bargaining position had not revealed, Thérèse discovered a way to redefine the question from one issue, the orange, into two issues, the rind and the meat. Then she then offered to give up her demand for the rind, since she cared much less about it than about what she might get from Yvonne by giving it up, and Yvonne fell back from her demand for the meat for the same reason. The two dovetailed differences in preference, but not by linking a second issue (an apple?) to the orange as a side payment. By negotiating they created value for the pair relative to no deal, to the status quo ante, and even to the mutually beneficial 50:50 deal. Thérèse's improved gain was not achieved by wily deception or a threat to punch Yvonne in the nose. What each truly wanted was not apparent to the other at the outset, and the negotiation process had something to do with the discovery.

Single agenda items involving parties' qualitative rights and obligations often have proved to have more integrative potential than quantitative items such as wages and other prices. For example, the manager and the unionized engineers of an American firm were negotiating a new employment contract. One item concerned how future layoffs would be conducted, should they be needed. The manager wanted discretion to lay off the least productive employees regardless of seniority, and the engineers insisted layoffs would have to follow reverse seniority regardless of productivity. The talks were at an impasse on this issue.[8]

Then during a process of relatively open discussion the manager discovered that many engineers (who may have felt reasonably productive) were concerned that layoffs might be unfair—for instance, that personal favoritism might creep into supervisors' decisions—and were concerned about the uncertainty of not knowing how the pain would be distributed, more than about the seniority rule. Their true priorities evidently were a fair and predictable process that would protect most engineers as

---

age has been viewed in isolation rather than as one element in a full conception of the negotiation process.

[7] Fisher and Ury 1981 is the best known statement of this idea.

[8] Walton and McKersie 1965, 131–32. The book does not attempt to show what values the parties placed on their alternatives to agreement.

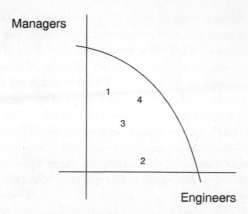

Fig. 8. Creating value on layoffs

long as possible. With this discovery in hand, the negotiator wondered whether there was a way to redesign his own demand that would cost the engineers less in terms of their true priorities yet not give up much on his own side's goals either.

Eventually, like the sisters, these negotiators baked a new pie. They fashioned a creative new layoff system that provided that supervisors would assign a "retention rating" to each engineer twice a year, based on merit and subject to a grievance procedure. Supervisors would be required to discuss the rating with each employee, eliminating much uncertainty. The firm would create a list of all employees for each job classification, rank them according to these ratings, and give the union the list after each rating, also reducing uncertainty. The only employees eligible for layoff would be those in the bottom twenty percent. For each of those, seniority points would be added to the average merit rating over the last two periods, producing a "modified" rating. These names would then be re-ranked and the first to be laid off would be the one at the bottom of the bottom twenty percent. This imaginative provision did involve some compromise, but each side got much of what it wanted, and probably more of what they wanted jointly than would have been achieved by simply splitting the difference between their openers. Again value was created but not by linking this item with a different agenda item.

Figure 8 provides a simple image of this last example of value creation (as perceived by both negotiators). The origin represents the status quo ante. Point 1 is the manager's initial position, a rule giving the manager unlimited discretion over layoffs. At point 2 we have the engineers' initial position, the rule that workers would be laid off in reverse seniority order regardless of productivity. One way to resolve such disagreements is for one negotiator to compel the other to retreat tactically to his own position, partly or wholly—both operating within claiming strategies. Management could decide to accept point 2, giving up most of what it sought on this item, or the engineers could move to point 1, allowing management to claim this value. Or they could split the orange evenly, each claiming half of this fixed pie (point 3). Any of these settlements would entail a movement from openers parallel to the possibility frontier.

In this process, though, none of these things happened. Instead, one side proposed a new arrangement that neither had conceived before, but which gave most of the engineers nearly all of what, it turned out, they wanted most—without a strict seniority rule—and the manager virtually all of what he actually wanted as well. This scheme moved the joint outcome northeast, toward the frontier rather than parallel to it. It created value for the pair, relative to no deal and also relative to the 50:50 solution. (If either party also attempted to claim value on other contract items, such as wage rates, then its strategy as a whole would be considered mixed.)

In chapter 5, the Mexican solution to the vegetable dumping case was an international illustration of this tactic of studying the other's priorities seriously and counteroffering with a new arrangement that might fit both side's priorities better than the demand by B.

A last tactical idea for creating value comes from Zartman and Berman (1982), who contend that a "deductive" sequence—first offering a general formula to guide the negotiating process, and only after reaching agreement on some formula, turning to settle details—often is responsible for diplomatic agreements that create joint value. Some formulas function by combining diverse particular issues into a grand exchange. The famous 1967 U.N. Security Council Resolution 242 embodied the principle that captured land would be traded for assurances of Israeli security. In 1974 U.S. negotiator Ellsworth Bunker restarted what had been acrimonious bilateral talks between Panama and the United States over the Panama Canal, by proposing that the two sides first try to reach agreement on a set of principles to guide subsequent detailed talks. They did agree on the formula that the hated 1903 treaty then in force would be abrogated; that they would work toward a new bilateral canal treaty with a finite term, not referring to "perpetuity"; that the United States would return to Panamanian jurisdiction the territory surrounding the canal; and that Panama would grant the United States rights to use land and water needed to defend and operate the canal.[9] Important issues still significantly divided the parties, who did, however, manage by 1977 to negotiate an agreement settling those details as well.

Another classic example comes from the multiparty process that launched the European Community between 1950 and 1952. There, states that had seemed jealous of their authority nevertheless agreed to transfer some of it, concerning coal and steel, to a new supranational regional entity, the High Authority, the ancestor of today's European Commission. How did these six states negotiate such an unprecedented new arrangement that each regarded as a gain? According to Ernst Haas, citing Robert Schuman, prior acceptance of the formula of supranationalism was a condition for participating in these talks. Furthermore, governments gave their agents only general instructions or none at all, allowing great leeway for flexible exploration by their agents. Third, tight secrecy isolated the delegates from national parliaments, the press, and the public, also freeing them to be more open. The negotiators were expert civil servants rather than diplomats

[9] U.S. *Department of State Bulletin*, v. 70, 25 February 1974, 184–85.

or politicians, and all these features together reduced the proportion of hard bargaining, according to Haas.[10] Value claiming was not absent. Schuman's and Monnet's most ambitious federal provisions were not accepted fully by the others, especially the three smallest states. Yet claiming did not block an unprecedented deal to pool sovereignty over the steel sector. This negotiation process and outcome created value for the group as they viewed it.[11]

If the deductive sequence does yield a mutual gain solution, the discussion of formulas may do so by uncovering and spotlighting shared objectives, building some trust between the parties, and simplifying the often complex thicket of issues and decisions that must be managed. A risk of following this sequence, though, is that if parties feel strong commitments to principles that are inconsistent, opening the discussion at the level of principle will highlight the conflicts between their objectives, strengthen the "war party" back in each capital, and perhaps even make political relations worse than they would have been with no negotiation at all.

A prominent risk of pure value creating in general is that B will not reciprocate and instead will attempt to turn A's relative openness into opportunities to claim from him. Revealing one's true priorities, for instance, creates an opportunity for B to take a prime value hostage. After learning this information, B could refuse doggedly to do anything to contribute to that value unless A gives up substantial value on some other issue. International negotiators always have some true conflicts of interest and significant, well-known incentives to withhold, manipulate or take advantage of information. Thus international negotiators, at least, are unlikely to abandon value claiming entirely for very long—which brings us to the mixed strategy.

DEFENSIVE CLAIMING PLUS A CREATIVE ELEMENT: BRAZIL, THE UNITED STATES, AND TRADE IN INSTANT COFFEE, 1966–71

The strategy ideas illustrated by the fictional sister and the corporate manager can now be extended to bilateral international economic bargaining. When A is defending against claiming, one way to make the strategy mixed is to design a counteroffer intended to satisfy B but at lower cost than A would pay by simply accepting B's demand. Rather than limiting himself to adamant rejections and efforts to worsen B's batna and form a blocking coalition, A also explores B's priorities seriously and looks for ways to reformulate B's position to reduce the cost of agreement to A. Whether attempting a mixed strategy in this sense will gain more than strict claiming naturally will depend on whether B accepts the counteroffer, which presumably will depend on many particulars. Still, the cost of attempting may be low, especially when trust prevails.

---

[10] Haas 1958, 251, citing Schuman 1953, 13–18.
[11] This is meant to be a brief illustration of mixed tactics and not, of course, a complete account of the reasons for this agreement.

Before: Brazilian defensive claiming, early 1966 through early 1967

In a case involving trade between Brazil (A) and the United States (B), such a mixed strategy by Brazil's negotiator helped Brazil lose less than it would have lost with a strict claiming strategy. In the mid-1960s, Brazilian exports of soluble (instant) coffee to the United States increased dramatically, from 33,000 pounds in 1964, to 6 million pounds in 1966, to 22 million pounds in 1967.[12] This market shift caused the dominant U.S. firm, General Foods, to become concerned about a threat to its dominance. The ensuing controversy (which an observer unfortunately dubbed a tempest in a teapot[13]) was indeed one of those commercial disputes that eventually received far more high-level political and press attention than would have been predicted from its small commercial size relative to the national economies, even that of Brazil.

General Foods—which sold the Maxwell House, Sanka, Maxim, and Yuban brands—operated several soluble coffee plants in the United States and supplied over half the instant coffee sold there. The Brazilian powder was entering for a price just half the cost of turning imported green coffee into soluble coffee, which seemed a powerful inducement to draw new competitors into the instant coffee market against General Foods, undermining the value of its processing investments.

In 1966, Washington—after hearing from General Foods and the National Coffee Association, the U.S. industry lobby[14]—protested to Brasília that its policies regarding soluble coffee were inconsistent with the prevailing International Coffee Agreement (ICA), to which both states were parties. The Department of State reasoned that the United States supported this agreement, which held up prices of green coffee at some sacrifice to itself and its coffee processing industry, in order to help Brazil and other developing countries. This agreement was what permitted Brazil's government to tax away about half the export revenue from its green coffee, they said. Brazil had long imposed a tax on its green coffee exports in order to raise finance for industrial development and other purposes, but it did not impose a tax on exported soluble coffee. The status quo meant that new Brazilian soluble makers could buy green coffee free of the export tax, then sell instant coffee abroad without paying the export tax, while their American competitors would have to pay the export tax to get the same green coffee. Brazil was using the International Coffee Agreement to permit discrimination that was a violation of the spirit, if not the letter, of the ICA, Washington maintained. The United States demanded that Brazil's government impose an equivalent tax on soluble coffee exports, to make their practices nondiscriminatory. The U.S. strategy, then,

---

[12] Cordell 1969, 32.

[13] Quoted by Bloomfield 1972, 13. This monograph provides the most complete description of this negotiation available, to my knowledge. The author participated in the episode as U.S. Economic Counselor in Brazil. Also see Krasner 1971, 270–81.

[14] J. McKiernan letter to E. Fried, Department of State, 31 May 1966, exhibit 6, Ganitsky and Burnham 1971.

was to attempt to claim value from Brazil, pure and simple, compared with the status quo. Washington did not offer any concessions in exchange.

Brazil's initial response was reciprocal—pure defensive value claiming. It flatly rejected Washington's demand and offered nothing in its place, effectively insisting on the status quo. "Conversations between the two governments in 1966 and early 1967 got nowhere."[15] Their negotiators were at impasse.

After: Brazilian integrative tactic, September 1967–April 1971

Accepting this demand would have made Brazil worse off than it was prior to this negotiation. Imposing a stiff export tax would have discouraged these exports, of course, worldwide, not only to the United States. In addition, Brazil maintained that soluble coffee was a manufactured product, and that all developing countries needed to increase in-country processing of their raw materials if they were ever to industrialize and raise their incomes. Thus yielding to this demand would have cost some additional value as a possible unfavorable precedent. Would the rich countries next try to use this same "nondiscrimination" rationale to snuff out other emerging industries in the South, just as developing countries are negotiating to establish the principle that we deserve "special and differential treatment" in trade?[16] Figure 9 graphically represents the U.S.-proposed value-claiming outcome as point 1. Brazil's opening position is represented as point 2. The origin depicts the prior status quo and the graph represents the situation as perceived by both negotiators.

Simply standing firm was risky, however, when state B was the world's superpower, in general and in the coffee market. Washington might, for instance, unilaterally impose a corresponding import duty on Brazilian soluble at the U.S. border, which meant roughly half the world's market at one fell swoop. Early in the dispute, a bill to do exactly that was introduced in the U.S. Congress. In the summer of 1970 the American government came close to imposing a countervailing duty. The evidence to be presented next strongly suggests that if Brazil had simply held firm without qualification, Washington probably would have taken unilateral action, yielding an outcome for Brazil worse than the actual outcome and worse than the prior status quo—something like point 1.

An adjustment in Brazil's negotiating position proved decisive. After an initial period of standing firm, party A added a value-creating element to its strategy— something like the manager talking to the engineers' union. A offered an ad hoc counterproposal intended to satisfy the commercial interests behind B's demand but in a different way that would not impose any new direct burden on Brazilian soluble coffee earnings. If U.S. soluble processors really want tax-free access to Brazilian green coffee, Brazil said in effect, then let them have it, up to the quantity of Brazil's soluble sales in the United States. In September 1967, Brasília of-

[15] Bloomfield 1972, 19.
[16] Ibid., 25.

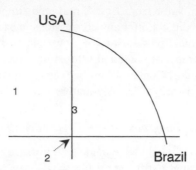

Fig. 9. Soluble coffee trade, 1966–71

fered to exempt from its export tax a certain annual quantity of green coffee suitable for soluble processing if sold to the United States. The tax-free quantity would not be greater than the equivalent of Brazilian soluble coffee purchased by the United States in some base period, and it would be subject to verification as to its use in the soluble industry.[17] This solution would forego some limited tax revenue for the Brazilian Treasury. But depending on how American firms acted, it also might generate greater sales of green coffee exports at the expense of Brazil's international competitors. On balance, this outcome therefore might even put Brazil's coffee trade as a whole ahead of the status quo ante, or at least not much behind (point 3). Most important, it would avoid any new direct disincentive to Brazilian soluble exports.

Brazil continued firmly to reject the idea of adding an export tax on soluble coffee. They did not accept the argument that the International Coffee Agreement required imposing it. That agreement concerned raw materials; soluble coffee was a manufactured product, they contended. The United States and other countries had recognized developing countries' needs to take measures to nurture new industries, and precedent was involved. Furthermore, General Foods was able to get less expensive green coffee from Africa; in practice U.S. soluble makers were not using Brazilian green, for the most part.[18]

Outcome: Agreement, 1971

In the end, Brazil came out of this dispute no worse off commercially than when it entered. Eventually Washington accepted its counterproposal and ended the dispute on roughly those terms, though not until after four more years of mutual public criticism and tortuous domestic U.S. bargaining. In Rio de Janeiro in late March 1971, negotiators from the two states agreed that Brazil's government

[17] Article by Edmundo de Macedo Soares, Minister of Industry and Commerce, in *O Globo*, 6 December 1968, cited by Bloomfield 1972, 20.
[18] Bloomfield 1972, 18.

would make available for purchase a special allotment of 560,000 bags of green coffee annually to U.S. soluble makers free of any export tax. This quota would be allocated to U.S. firms in proportion to their shares of total American soluble output during the previous two years. The pact would remain in effect as long as both parties implemented the 1968 International Coffee Agreement.[19]

Analysis

Brazil's trade negotiator in this case did what the corporate manager of the engineering firm did with the layoff item. He redesigned his opening position to offer some satisfaction to the other at much less cost to Brazil than the U.S. opening demand. A chief reason for the long U.S. resistance to this ad hoc solution, according to Richard Bloomfield,[20] was that the Department of State attached significant weight to the principle of nondiscrimination and to arms-length dealings with business. As with other trade issues, Washington negotiators favored general rules designed to preserve market competition, leaving the commercial results to be determined by actual competition, and shunned ad hoc rules formalizing special treatment for particular companies and industries. This deeply-rooted preference reflected the view that ad hoc business arrangements discriminate unfairly in favor of the politically privileged and too often come at the expense of the public interest. They also tend to become embedded and difficult to terminate even after the conditions that led to them have disappeared.

But why, then, did the U.S. executive finally accept this offer rather than act unilaterally? Why did Brasília come out better than if it had simply accepted the American demand or triggered the equivalent by unilateral action? First, Brazil's agents continued to refuse Washington's first choice with remarkable persistence, and they had proposed this alternative that would allow the State Department to satisfy its loudest internal constituency demand, if not its preferred policy principles. Second, the State Department finally settled because General Foods was able in 1971 to persuade a major congressional committee chairman to hold the entire International Coffee Agreement hostage to some substantial Brazilian concession.

Along the way the bargaining took several twists and turns, of which a summary will be sufficient here. Throughout, the Brazilian press gave substantial publicity to attacks on the U.S. position, keeping up the pressure on its negotiator. In January 1968 Washington, for its part, persuaded the member states of the International Coffee Agreement to enact a new rule against governmental measures which, taken as a whole, "amount to discriminatory treatment in favor of processed coffee as compared with green coffee" (Article 44). The members compromised this new rule's significance, however. When authorizing a member to impose countermeasures in case of a violation, the Article called on the member

---

[19] U.S. Department of State *Bulletin*, 10 May 1971, 627–28, and *Coffee Annual 1976*, 99.
[20] Bloomfield 1972, 99–103.

to "have due regard to the need of developing countries to practice policies designed to broaden the base of their economies through, inter alia, industrialization and the export of manufactured products . . ."[21] With this rule in hand, added to the leverage of its superior alternative to agreement, Washington did extract from Brasília a small 13 percent export tax on soluble coffee in 1969. The United States agreed not to retaliate for one year, reserving the right to insist on an increase in its magnitude.[22]

Meanwhile, General Foods persuaded Congressman Wilbur Mills, the chairman of the House Committee on Ways and Means, to take up its claims for additional concessions.[23] This committee was responsible for all tax and trade legislation passing through the Congress, including bills authorizing U.S. participation in the International Coffee Organization. Mills delayed renewal, or extended ICO authority only for short periods, repeatedly in order to harden the U.S. negotiating position on soluble coffee imports. During 1969 those imports from Brazil increased further.[24] During the summer of 1970 as one Mills deadline approached, government lawyers began drafting an order imposing a unilateral countervailing duty. With signs of possible Brazilian concessions, Mills granted an extension.

After Mills credibly threatened to take the United States out of the International Coffee Organization altogether, the President's true alternative to the Brazilian ad hoc proposal was not perfect adherence to nondiscriminatory international rules, but loss of the multilateral regime itself. Having already spent considerable public resources on a commercially-small issue, Washington decided in 1971 to accept Brazil's 1967 scheme. Accepting some offsetting cost in terms of principle, it gained some satisfaction for the complainant and ended this dispute with an agreement. Brazil ended its 13 cents per pound export tax on soluble coffee.

Many other causes cited as relevant for negotiation in general could not have been responsible for this particular outcome—an escape for Brazil's government rather than the significant loss that appeared likely in mid-1967. There had been no material change in the structure of the two nations' commercial coffee interests or in the value either placed on their bilateral political relationship. Nor did any significant change in the countries' political cultures, their national political institutions, or the international security situation account for the Brazilian success on soluble coffee relative to what almost certainly would have happened under Brazilian pure claiming.

Did international institutions or changes therein shape this outcome? The two states were parties to two international agreements, the GATT and the ICA, whose rules could be considered relevant for this episode. Neither party cited GATT rules or procedures, however, and they disagreed whether the ICA was relevant. Washington did persuade the member states to pass Article 44. But what

---

[21] United Nations, *Treaty Series*, vol. 647, 1968, I, no. 9262, International Coffee Agreement 1968 with annexes, 56.
[22] U.S. Department of State, press release 97, 30 August 1969.
[23] Bloomfield 1972, 33.
[24] Exhibit 11, Ganitsky and Burnham 1971.

Washington received for this multilateral effort was meager and temporary. It was superseded by the 1971 outcome, which had been available since 1967, before Article 44 had been adopted.

Would this dispute have occurred at all, in the absence of the International Coffee Agreement? It is true that Washington used the ICA as the rationale for its complaint, and each government placed some value on that agreement. But what would the world coffee system have been like without the ICA? Presumably world coffee prices would have been somewhat lower, yet the distribution of coffee trees and coffee drinkers across the globe would have been similar. Many of the same firms would have populated the industry, exporting and importing governments would have taken similar stands, and the United States would still have had a superior batna in general. Suppose that, in that world, Brazilian investors had launched new exports of soluble coffee toward the American market, threatening General Foods' dominance, and that General Foods had been equally concerned and its political access similar. With no ICA, the State Department would not have been the most likely point of access. But giant U.S. companies supported by industry associations in other sectors have certainly found ways to gain official action against competitive imports, despite the absence of sectoral international organizations. During the 1970s, U.S. firms turned to the general countervailing duty law more and more often as a means of blunting low-priced imports from developing countries, or discouraging potential competitors abroad from entering the business in the first place. (That American law predated the GATT by several decades.) Special sectoral deals were negotiated for other industries too, often by the USTR, Commerce, Transportation, or the Treasury Department rather than the State Department. These special agreements too were not always perfectly consistent with norms of nondiscrimination and free trade. It is hardly far-fetched to imagine General Foods using the countervailing duty law or new bills in Congress to pressure Brazil in a similar way in the absence of the ICA. Nor was either the ICA or the GATT necessary for Brasília's counteroffer. This bilateral outcome probably did not depend on the existence of either regime.

To summarize, Brazil's government attempted to fend off a demand that would have harmed itself and benefited the United States. Brazil's strategy was a sequential mix, falling nearer the distributive end of the spectrum on balance. After the initial phase, the strategy departed from pure defensive claiming by adding an element of value creation that proved decisive. The new arrangement, the tax-free quota counterproposal, was responsive to U.S. arguments at least partly; its effect was not to exploit or simply frustrate an adversary. However, it responded by means that would cost Brazil far less than the U.S. demand. Thus, this counterproposal eventually moved the outcome closer to the possibility frontier, like the tactics of the manager negotiating with the engineers' union. Had Brazil adhered to pure value claiming, it almost certainly would have lost more than it did. Note too that value was not created in this case by linking a new issue to the deal so as to transfer value to the other side, as in legislative logrolling. The integrative element here was to create a new arrangement as a substitute for the other's demand, as with the engineers' demand for a seniority rule.

OFFENSIVE CLAIMING PLUS A CREATIVE ELEMENT:
THE UNITED STATES, JAPAN, AND TRADE IN BEEF, 1988

Pure offensive claiming may gain less than a mixed strategy under certain conditions, such as when A, the offensive claimer, will not back down from his original demands, and B's constituents will not ratify the demanded package of concessions, or not without a conflict that would be costly to A. If a concession in the opposite direction on another issue, shifting value from A to B, will tip B's constituents to accept the amended deal without such a conflict, then A might regard the demanded deal plus the "sweetener" as a superior outcome, even though A's concession reduces his own net gain. The sweetener functions by helping negotiator B persuade his constituents to accept a painful win-lose deal, raising its value above B's resistance point. Party A will gain from adding a costly sweetener as long the value of the package minus the reverse concession is still better for A than impasse, which may include penalties imposed on the economies and political relationships of A as well as B. Whether the outcome turns out better for A in a given case will again depend on how B responds, which presumably will vary with numerous particulars. Making a pure claiming strategy mixed by adding a new item may not move the outcome much closer to the possibility frontier, even if it permits an outcome better than impasse. But this issue linkage is conceptually analogous to the process that, if expanded, could lead to a more balanced logroll for joint gain.

In some situations, offensive claimer A, rather than shifting to a mixed strategy, might be able to tip B to agreement by making a tactical retreat within the claiming strategy—reducing the concessions demanded. If the two moves are equivalent to A, the mixed strategy will not gain more for A. But the two are not equivalent in all situations. If, for example, negotiator A has made a commitment on the original issues before audiences at home and abroad, such that he will view a tactical retreat as costly to his future negotiating credibility or even his tenure in office, then adding a different, creative element that achieves the same net result for B without this disadvantage to A will indeed win A greater net gain. A will be able to claim that he refused to settle until his demands were met.

Before: U.S. offensive claiming, 1987–88

In a case arising from trade between the United States and Japan, such a mixed strategy by the U.S. negotiator helped his country gain more than he would have gained with a pure distributive strategy. In a 1987–88 negotiation concerning access to Japan's markets for beef, oranges, and orange juice, the U.S. government (A) opened with pure offensive claiming. Tokyo (B) opened with pure defensive claiming. For years Washington had been demanding one-way concessions regarding Japan's small quotas that sharply limited beef imports.[25] In 1977–78, the

[25] Background information and analysis can be found in Sato and Curran 1982 and Reich, Endo, and Timmer 1986. Porges 1994 is the most thorough published account of this episode, based on

Carter administration sought to eliminate remaining agricultural quotas and to increase the size of any remaining quotas. This first episode ended in an agreement not to end the quotas but to increase the amounts slightly through 1984. In 1982, Washington began a second push to eliminate beef quotas, but the Japanese side resisted until the previous deal expired on 31 March 1984. As USTR William Brock was preparing to file a complaint with the GATT, Japan's Agriculture Minister Shinjiro Yamamura offered a larger annual quota increase. Brock accepted, for a period to expire on 31 March 1988, but insisted this was the last time Washington would agree to continued beef quotas of any size.[26]

In 1987, USTR Clayton Yeutter repeatedly pledged in public to end Japan's beef quotas once and for all, through a third bilateral negotiation that began that year. This time the U.S. side said it would not negotiate over beef and citrus again unless Tokyo agreed to eliminate quotas on some specified date,[27] and that it would expect compensation if quotas continued beyond 1 April 1988. Washington did not offer Japan's government any compensation for beef quota removal; this was not an effort to make both governments better off. Washington maintained that these restrictions violated the international rules, and of course advanced the argument that market opening would benefit Japan's consumers.[28] But the other party was the government of Japan, and for the Liberal Democratic Party (LDP), ending these quotas would be a clear loss of something it valued highly, not a gain. The U.S. government attempted, once again, to claim value from the Japanese government. The Deputy USTR, Michael B. Smith, was the chief American negotiator, and his counterpart was Hidero Maki, Vice Minister for International Affairs reporting to Agriculture Minister Takashi Sato.

Events unfolding concurrently in the GATT context proved to be relevant. GATT states had launched their multilateral Uruguay round in September 1986, and worldwide agricultural policy reform was a centerpiece of the U.S. position in Geneva. Japan was a leading food importer yet had proposed to retain barriers against sensitive products, insisting on the importance of food security. Every political party in Japan was on record opposing liberalization of beef and citrus. These products were important substitutes for rice farming, which also faced strong pressure to accept market opening.[29] For each government, then, to concede the bilateral battle on beef might encourage the other side to dig in even more firmly on additional agricultural issues in the multilateral round.

On 30 October 1987, a GATT panel of experts ruled on an earlier U.S. complaint against Japan's treatment of twelve small agricultural products other than beef and citrus. The Geneva panel found that Japan's restrictions were contrary to

sources in Japanese as well as English. Porges had been associate general counsel in the office of the U.S. Trade Representative.

[26] Interview with Michael B. Smith, Los Angeles, 17 February 1998.
[27] *International Trade Reporter (ITR)*, 16 March 1988.
[28] Meanwhile, Washington imposed protection against its own consumers at home. The Meat Import Act required restrictions on imports of beef if they reached specified levels. During 1988 Washington insisted that Australia restrain its beef shipments to the U.S. (*ITR*, 14 September 1988, 1241).
[29] Porges 1994, 237, 239.

GATT rules. Japanese farmer organizations responded by threatening to retaliate against U.S. feedgrain exports if they lost their protection.[30] They complained bitterly that the United States itself maintained quotas against agricultural imports, including even meat. But the LDP leadership told Diet members representing farmers that Japan could not afford to defy world opinion, and the government decided to eliminate quotas protecting eight of the twelve small items.[31] At a summit meeting with President Reagan, Prime Minister Noboru Takeshita promised appropriate action. Soon thereafter, on 3 February 1988, Yeutter announced that if Japan did not accept his demands on beef and citrus, he would file a new GATT complaint against those barriers as well.[32]

During the 1980s, as America's trade deficit and Japan's surplus expanded to unprecedented levels, bilateral tensions between the two had become progressively more intense. The most severe conflict concerned semiconductors. In April 1987, President Reagan imposed an economic sanction on Japan for the first time since the occupation. Washington complained angrily that Tokyo had reneged on its 1986 agreement to prevent chip dumping and to help U.S. firms increase sales in Japan. Furthermore, Congress was writing new trade legislation in 1988, and Yeutter was negotiating with Congress's leaders while talking to Japan's diplomats. The mood in Congress was increasingly hostile to Japan and it was a presidential election year. Pressures from Congress for more tough action, as well as an unusual degree of unity in the bureaucracy on beef and citrus, enhanced the credibility of Yeutter's threat in 1988. Naturally the U.S. demands and sanctions generated Japanese hostility toward the United States.

Early in March, Japanese Dietmen who were extreme opponents of farm concessions were sent to Washington to experience American pressure first hand.[33] Nevertheless, another 31 March deadline passed without Japanese acquiescence. Throughout two Washington visits by Maki and one by Minister Sato, Tokyo's negotiators remained firm, pointing to the strong forces in the Diet and the public constraining them. There was no sign of a positive zone of agreement. Yeutter immediately asked the GATT Council in Geneva to establish a panel to rule on Japan's beef and citrus barriers.[34] Japan blocked the formation of this panel at the April Council meeting.[35] In Tokyo, the Liberal Democratic Party's farm committee repeated that it rejected the U.S. demand to remove import quotas.[36]

On 27 April, a Japanese delegation flew to Washington and offered for the first time to eliminate the quotas. Back home, ministry officials had cited the "GATT 12" ruling in arguing to Dietmen that the world would certainly condemn the beef quotas as well. The GATT ruling seemed to worsen the batna the LDP perceived,

---

[30] *ITR*, 24 February 1988, 238.

[31] *Japan Times*, 7 January 1988, cited by Porges 1994, 247–48.

[32] *Journal of Commerce*, 4 February 1988, 5A.

[33] This level-two tactic had softened domestic opposition in past negotiations (Kusano 1983, cited by Porges 1994, 249).

[34] *ITR*, 6 April 1988, 491.

[35] *ITR*, 13 April 1988.

[36] *Japan Economic Newswire* (Kyodo News Service), 12 April 1988.

or at least its external value. Some reasoned that bilateral negotiations with the United States, before GATT had handed down a specific beef ruling, offered a greater chance of substituting another form of protection. Others argued that a positive domestic adjustment policy would be better for Japan's farmers in the long run.[37]

What Sato and Maki offered Washington, however, was to replace the quotas with a variable duty, one that would rise or fall with the government's domestic stabilization price. Japan's beef duty was 25 percent and was not bound (Japan had not pledged not to increase it). While the details of this proposal are not known, it would have been a more GATT-defensible technique for achieving the same commercial protection. But to say "variable levy" to a U.S. trade negotiator in 1988 was like waving a red flag in the face of a Spanish bull. For years American farmers had been attacking the European Community's highly protective variable levy, and the last thing USTR was likely to do now was sign an agreement creating a new levy in another huge market. Yeutter and Smith refused even to discuss a variable tariff.[38] On 4 May Yeutter angrily threatened unspecified retaliation if Japan refused to open its market, declaring, "My patience as a negotiator has come to an end."[39] That day the GATT Council established panels to rule on Japanese beef and citrus measures.

Prime Minister Takeshita reportedly gave his agents a deadline of 20 June for finding a solution. Takeshita did not want to meet Reagan in Toronto that day at the next G7 summit meeting without a beef-citrus agreement in hand.[40]

After: U.S. concession, May–June 1988

Maki and Smith met next in Tokyo, and again in Washington in late May and early June, still without reaching agreement. The U.S. side remained adamant that quotas must end and must not be replaced by a variable duty. But the U.S. negotiator also indicated a willingness to allow Japan to extend the quotas for a final two years, if the deal guaranteed their elimination at that time. Japan would have to enlarge the quotas in the meantime and to "pay" for this extension by expanding market access for other agricultural imports. Yeutter and Smith indicated that their opposition to the variable tariff did not necessarily mean they would rule out any one-time increase in the beef tariff. The media cited a U.S. official commenting that the United States could live with a "substantially high" but not variable tariff for some period of time,[41] to help his counterpart sell the deal at home. Meanwhile, a key LDP Diet leader of the farm caucus threatened to resign an-

---

[37] *Asahi Shimbun*, 7 April 1998, 2; 9 April, 3; 11 April, 1 and 3; *Nihon Keizai Shimbun*, 17 April 1988, 2; cited by Porges 1994, 250–51.

[38] Porges 1994, 252.

[39] *Los Angeles Times*, 5 May 1988, IV-1.

[40] *Japan Economic Journal*, 21 May 1988; *New York Times*, 18 June 1988, 33.

[41] *Japan Economic Journal*, 21 May 1988, *Japan Economic Newswire*, 24 May 1988; and Porges 1994, 252–53.

other post concerned with tax reform, which was also highly salient to Takeshita, if the prime minister gave ground on beef.[42]

At the Washington round from 31 May through 5 June, the Japanese side maintained its position. Minister Sato said on 7 June that he was not bound by any specific deadline for solving this problem.[43] Smith continued to reject that position, but he also offered to fall back to a transition period of three rather than two years.[44] There were press reports that Washington now also was willing to discuss a safeguard provision that would allow Japan to raise special restrictions temporarily in response to a rapid import surge after quotas were removed.[45]

In mid-June Smith went to Tokyo for another round, but back in Washington Yeutter was telling the press his delegation was "somewhat pessimistic at this point" in view of Japanese resistance.[46] At one stage, Maki and Smith stared at each other in silence for more than an hour—each insisting that the other blink.[47]

Then on 18 June came a critical turning point, according to Smith. During a recess, Smith called Tsutomu Hata and asked for a meeting alone. Hata had negotiated with Smith on other issues but was not a member of this delegation. He was a prominent LDP Diet member and strong Takeshita supporter. He had served as Agriculture Minister in 1985–86 and now chaired the LDP's key committee on agricultural policy. Meanwhile, Smith had asked the U.S. Embassy staff to come up with a number estimating the aggregate protective effect of all Japan's barriers to beef imports, in terms of the equivalent tariff rate. Smith told Hata that according to U.S. calculations, Japan's total protection of beef amounted to no less than 371 percent—an astronomical figure not found even in the least developed countries of the world. Smith hoped that seeing their stand framed this way, the Japanese delegation would feel especially ashamed of having to defend it. He proposed that if Tokyo agreed to wipe out 300 percent of the total (quota elimination), Washington would agree to its *raising* its beef tariff from 25 to 70 percent for 1991—the U.S. concession. This tariff would have to fall to 60 percent in 1992 and 50 percent in 1993. Its level for subsequent years would be subject to negotiation within the Uruguay round.[48]

When official negotiations resumed, Maki told Smith his team had received Smith's idea. They had made their own calculations but found they could not agree with the figure of 371 percent. With Smith fearing the deal was lost, Maki went on to say that actually the correct figure was 376 percent.[49] The Japanese side accepted these new terms including the sweetener, and the deadlock over the

[42] Porges 1994, 253.
[43] *Journal of Commerce*, 8 June 1988, 7A.
[44] *Asahi Shimbun*, 14 June 1988, 3; *Yomiuri Shimbun*, 20 June 1988, evening ed., 3, cited by Porges 1994, 253–54.
[45] *Journal of Commerce*, 9 June 1988, 5A.
[46] *Los Angeles Times*, 17 June 1988, Business 8.
[47] Interviews with Michael B. Smith, Los Angeles, 8 and 9 March 1990 and 17 February 1998.
[48] Interview with Smith, 17 February 1998.
[49] Ibid.

main beef issues had been broken. Yeutter flew to Tokyo and the two cabinet ministers resolved several remaining issues at the eleventh hour.

Outcome: June 1988

On the eve of the summit conference, then, the Japanese government surprised observers and accepted a bilateral beef deal that gave up substantial value to Washington on balance. The U.S. negotiator made a tactical retreat on the main quota issue and added a concession. The net effect was still a remarkable gain for the U.S. government and an unwelcome brew that all Japanese political parties had strenuously objected to swallowing, particularly only a year after Washington's semiconductor slap. The beef quota limit would rise from the 1987 level of 214,000 metric tons by 60,000 tons annually for three years and then the lid would come off entirely[50] Tariffs would jump up then, but tariffs can still allow a foreign competitor with sufficiently low costs to undercut the home producer. Furthermore, Tokyo agreed to phase out the involvement of the quasi-governmental Livestock Industry Promotion Corporation in distribution of beef imports, permitting foreign suppliers to deal directly with Japanese buyers.[51] The bilateral agreement did not earmark any of the market for U.S., at the expense of other, exporters. Yeutter forecast that U.S. exports of beef and oranges to Japan could double thanks to this official deal.[52] The Japanese Ministry of Agriculture announced spending plans to help farmers adjust to the new competition.[53] The day the final text was signed, 5 July 1988, the United States withdrew its GATT complaint on beef and citrus. Japan's government implemented this agreement. In response to a survey conducted later by the American Chamber of Commerce in Japan, asking U.S. firms to rate bilateral Japan-U.S. market-opening agreements on a subjective scale of 1 to 10, beef exporters gave the beef provisions of this agreement the highest possible grade of 10.[54]

Analysis

A year earlier, hardly anyone would have believed a forecast that Japan's government would agree to eliminate beef and citrus quotas, given the seemingly airtight domestic politics in Japan. This U.S. demand is depicted in figure 10 as point 1 (as perceived by both negotiators, with the origin standing for the status

---

[50] U.S. Department of State *Bulletin*, September 1988, 16; *International Legal Materials* 27 (1988): 1539–95; GATT document L/6370, 8 July 1988, "Japan: Market-Opening Measures on Beef, Citrus and other Products."

[51] *Japan Economic Journal*, 2 July 1988, 3.

[52] Associated Press, 20 June 1988, via Lexis-Nexis.

[53] *Japan Economic Journal*, 2 July 1988, 3.

[54] The American Chamber of Commerce in Japan 1997, 115–16. As a component of the Uruguay round package, Japan in 1994 promised to lower its beef tariff further by steps to 38.5 percent in the year 2000 (Japan's tariff schedule, supplied by the Embassy of Japan, Washington, 1998).

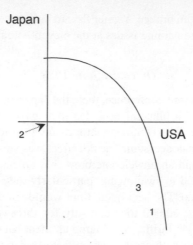

Fig. 10. Beef trade, 1988

quo ante). Japan began by resisting all concessions (point 2). Yet in the end Tokyo retreated quite substantially, and the two settled on a substantial shift in favor of the United States, point 3.

How, then, is this surprising win-lose outcome best understood? Conditions besides the negotiator's tactics surely contributed. Of course the United States was more powerful overall and this inequality certainly aided U.S. claiming. But America has not gained nearly as much in other trade negotiations with Japan. U.S. business is less thrilled with outcomes, for example, on telecommunications 1980 (score 2), leather and leather footwear 1985 (score 4), construction 1988 and 1991 (5), supercomputers 1990 (6), computer products and services 1992 (7), apples 1993 (4), and insurance 1994 (3). And the United States had an even greater power superiority over Brazil in 1985–88. An unequal power relationship leaves open a wide range of bargaining possibilities.

Nor is it likely that beef was far superior in commercial qualities to the other potential U.S. exports to Japan; U.S. firms are world leaders in many of those other sectors. Market analysis would not be sufficient either.

U.S. government credibility was probably higher here than in some cases. The Americans committed themselves publicly and repeatedly to elimination of quotas. They felt that backing down and accepting Japan's insistence on maintaining quotas indefinitely—a third time—would cost them dearly in credibility, at home and abroad, including in the Uruguay round where the stakes were larger.[55] In other cases the executive branch was less unified. Here even the Department of State rebuffed Japanese pleas for more time or an exemption.[56] The U.S. beef in-

---

[55] Interviews with Smith.
[56] Interview with Smith.

dustry also was unified regarding U.S. negotiating positions, unlike some cases in Japan as well as Brazilian informatics.

In this case the international organization context seems to have affected a bilateral negotiation, by worsening Maki's perceived batna and helping Smith claim more. The 1987 GATT-12 decision seems to have made a significant difference in the Japanese government's beliefs and behavior, and the United States launched an additional GATT inquiry on the beef issues in April. Still, GATT norms alone and even a panel ruling do not guarantee a given outcome. The same GATT articles had been in force during the earlier bilateral beef negotiations, when Tokyo had insisted on continuing the quotas and Washington had agreed. The United States also won a GATT panel ruling against Japanese leather quotas in 1983, and yet the subsequent bilateral agreement in that case left binding quantitative restrictions in effect. Note too that the effect of the international organization here was not to facilitate a win-win outcome, if gains are defined over governments and relative to the status quo ante.

Thus on 18 June—despite the GATT and its panels, U.S. power superiority, domestic unity, the passing of the 31 March deadline, and the threat of retaliation—the two negotiators were still deadlocked. The internal political pressures on the Takeshita government were still intensely against concessions. If the U.S. diplomat had insisted strictly on his original demands, rather than offering a tactical retreat and adding the sweetener, Tokyo's political leadership probably would have chosen no agreement, or perhaps a nominal agreement followed by behavior contrary to Washington's expectations. Negotiator A believed this was a real possibility, considering B's firm behavior and the obvious constituent pressures on him, and that if so, agreement with this sweetener would be better for A than impasse and conflict.[57] The mixed negotiation strategy gave Sato and Maki at least something to show their government for their efforts, and helped it grudgingly to accept and implement the deal without further international friction.

In this case markets later behaved much as negotiators had expected. In 1995 Japan's beef imports totaled 658,000 metric tons, about half of them coming from Australia. The market share of imports rose from 31 percent under quotas to 55 percent.[58]

In international economic bargaining, a mixed strategy will gain more than a strict distributive strategy under some conditions. Brazil's response concerning trade in instant coffee exemplified a departure from pure defensive claiming. There party A was faced with unwelcome claiming by the United States. The integrative tactic was a counteroffer designed to address most of B's objectives while costing A much less than B's opening demand. In this case Washington, like the unionized engineers, finally accepted the counteroffer and the two settled.

A mixed strategy also can prove superior to pure offensive claiming under cer-

---

[57] Interview with Smith.
[58] The American Chamber of Commerce in Japan 1997.

tain conditions. In the Japan-U.S. beef negotiation, negotiator A was not willing to back down from his original demand for quota elimination, yet B's constituents fiercely opposed making concessions, producing an extended stalemate. When the offensive claimer added a concession as well as a tactical retreat, B accepted, ratified, and implemented the unwelcome win-lose deal.

Here we have more evidence of ways in which variations in the economic negotiation process make a difference to outcomes. For Brazil in 1967, a plausible case could have been made for more than one strategy choice at the outset. Some governments of developing countries facing Washington's demands simply comply, however contrary to their interests.[59] As usual, objective background conditions and "interests" are an ambiguous guide. If Brasília had not used a mixed strategy in 1967, if it had stood firm on its strict refusal and taken no initiative, or if U.S. negotiators had not finally accepted the Brazilian counteroffer, strong forces in Washington were pressing toward imposing a countervailing duty and keeping the revenue. In the 1988 Japan beef case, had the U.S. government clung strictly to offensive claiming, there was a good chance the outcome would have been worse for Washington as U.S. negotiators saw it, considering the intense feelings inside both countries. Had the economic negotiation process been different, the outcomes probably would have been significantly worse for Brazil on coffee and the United States on beef.

---

[59] See the contrast between responses of Argentina and Brazil to countervailing duty investigations in 1974 in Odell 1980. This article advances the idea of a technocratic strategy that overlaps with the mixed strategy discussed here.

PART THREE

AN EXTENSION

CHAPTER 8

Changing Domestic Institutions and Ratifying Regime Agreements

with Barry Eichengreen

To this point we have analyzed negotiation outcomes by abstracting from the ratification process. Yet principals do not always approve international economic agreements without a political struggle, and occasionally they fail to ratify. To this point we also have compared only two-party interactions where domestic political institutions were basically fixed. Governments also negotiate in groups over international regimes, and occasionally nations change the domestic institutions that govern their economic bargaining.

This chapter extends economic negotiation analysis to the ratification phase and to multiparty regime cases. It also relaxes the assumption that national institutions are fixed. The central claim is that the greater the slack between the negotiating agent and her principals at home during bargaining, the greater the chance of ratification failure. "Slack" refers to the looseness or tautness of domestic rules requiring consultation, accountability, and approval by the principal during the negotiating itself, prior to the ratification phase.[1]

Delegating authority to an agent entails at least some level of ex ante agent discretion. Government chief executives and legislators delegate to negotiators because principals lack the specialized expertise to conduct complex talks themselves, because doing so would not be the most productive use of their own time, and probably for tactical and other reasons as well. They also provide the economic negotiator, like their other executive officers, with at least some slack in recognition of the uncertainty inherent in the process. If they kept their agent on an extremely short tether, these principals would deny themselves scope to discover unanticipated risks and opportunities, and to shift their positions efficiently as conditions evolve. While they could eliminate potential ratification problems, they could also wipe out the chance of reaching any agreement at all.

Yet an agent under looser requirements to consult will receive less exact information about the principals' preferences concerning demands and offers that turn up and other changes that evolve during the process. Thus the agent will be more likely to accept terms that will be rejected at home, other things equal. Tighter institutional requirements to hear changing constituent demands and interim reactions will calibrate the agent more exactly as the negotiation evolves. Further-

---

[1] Principals may influence or constrain agents in other ways as well, such as through selection of office holders and by imposing the requirement of legislative approval after they act. For related analysis see Calvert, McCubbins, and Weingast 1989, Epstein and O'Halloran 1994, and Martin 2000.

more, tighter requirements give the agent more opportunities to persuade her principals, by beginning the persuasion before the ratification phase. Prior to negotiations themselves, when principals give agents their marching orders, national interests often have not been formed in specific terms. Domestic firms and industries have high expectations that often are unrealistic abroad, even when viewed individually. Constituents sometimes pay less attention to what other fellow citizens are demanding at the same time and how the combined demands will look to other governments. They shy away from facing trade-offs that imply less gain for their sector or company. An agent in a more constraining institution will have earlier opportunities to report how other governments reacted to high opening demands, to educate constituents on what can be achieved and on the trade-offs that may need to be faced, and to build support for her package.

In the late 1940s, to take an example, U.S. agents proposed and negotiated agreement on a multilateral treaty creating an International Trade Organization (ITO). They signed the charter with other diplomats at a Havana ceremony on 23 March 1948. Congress failed to ratify the charter, however, and the ITO never came into being. In contrast, Washington ratified and implemented an agreement to create a World Trade Organization (WTO) in 1994, after its agents had again played a leading role in negotiating the Uruguay round. Washington acted quite differently in the end regarding two of the most ambitious international economic regime agreements of the twentieth century.

Why would a government propose, negotiate and sign an agreement and then reject what it had created? This experience confirmed America's reputation for moodiness in other countries, who well remembered the Senate's repudiation of Wilson's 1919 peace treaty. But then why did Washington not do the same thing again in the nineties?

Several prominent possible explanations come to mind but do not survive scrutiny. First, the hegemony hypothesis has received much attention.[2] Its more benevolent version treats international organizations as suppliers of global public goods, which facilitate the internalization of externalities that spill across borders. Trade is a case in point. At least some of the benefits of a country's decision to liberalize accrue to its trading partners, and a trade organization that promotes the exchange of commercial concessions can be thought of as internalizing such externalities. Large countries, like dominant firms in imperfectly competitive markets, should have the strongest incentive to invest in arrangements capable of internalizing such externalities. Trade liberalization thus should proceed smoothly when there exists a dominant power but slow in periods of hegemonic decline. But the United States was more dominant in international markets soon after World War II than in the 1990s by almost any measure. The hegemony hypothesis surely implies that the United States would have been more likely to ratify the ITO than the WTO.

A second familiar argument emphasizes that the security context colors foreign

---

[2] See Kindleberger 1973, Gilpin 1975, and Krasner 1976 for seminal statements of this hypothesis and related ideas, and Kindleberger 1981, McKeown 1983, Snidal 1985, Eichengreen 1989, and Lake 1993 for critiques.

economic policy decisions, and specifically that fear of a new war against communism after 1946 led the United States to pay a higher price to support the security of allied countries for military-political reasons—by lowering its own import barriers to their goods, among other things. But if this is so, then should the decline of security threats and fear especially after 1989 not have made the United States *less* inclined to ratify the WTO?

Third, the U.S. economy was somewhat more open in the 1990s than in the late 1940s. More U.S. companies were oriented toward export markets, this argument might go, so lobbying for trade liberalization must have been stronger. But greater openness cuts both ways in domestic politics; it stimulates losers as well as winners (chap. 3). Pro-trade groups including multinational corporations did push U.S. policymakers toward liberalization and away from protection.[3] But producers exposed to international competition at home pushed in the opposite direction. In fact, during these decades greater openness coincided with a shift from a postwar U.S. trade surplus to a sizable persisting deficit. Greater openness with a trade deficit would seem to imply, if anything, stronger net constituent opposition to ratification in the 1990s than the 1940s.

Histories of the ITO debate emphasize that the Congress was overloaded with other international issues at that particular time, straining the capacity of internationalists in the Senate and the House. These included the Marshall Plan, NATO, and the Korean conflict, which shifted the ITO to the back burner. But when is the Congress not overloaded? It is not clear that this problem was any less severe in the early 1990s, when the Congress dealt with both Operations Desert Storm and Provide Cover, the collapse of the Soviet Union, NAFTA, China's trade and human rights practices, the federal budget, health care, "reinventing government," and campaign finance, among other domestic issues.

Many argue that memories of trade conflict in the 1930s lent powerful impetus to the campaign for multilateral trade liberalization after World War II. The collapse of trade was associated with the Great Depression in the minds of both politicians and the public, legitimizing the campaign for liberalization. But these memories were fresher in the 1940s, when Congress refused to charter a multilateral organization, than in the 1990s, when it agreed. This explanation too works in the wrong direction. Several shifts in prevailing conditions over that half century seem to have made the 1990s result *more* difficult to achieve politically, making it even more interesting.

Three key differences will nevertheless help make sense of this historical puzzle. Between the two episodes the United States changed its domestic institutions to tighten the slack between agents and principals during trade negotiations. The domestic rules of the 1940s did not require the negotiator to remain in close touch with principals and build domestic support during the bargaining, whereas the post-1974 rules kept the two quite close together throughout. Two additional factors will help complete this picture. In 1949 American businesses and legisla-

---

[3] Destler and Odell 1987 and Milner 1988.

tors who favored trade liberalization perceived a better alternative to ratifying the multilateral deal than did corresponding 1994 principals, in terms of each's goals. And President Truman also spent much less political capital to win votes for ITO ratification than did President Clinton for the WTO.

THE TWO NEGOTIATIONS IN BRIEF

The two negotiations shared three common features. The United States provided the strongest push to initiate each round; other governments induced the U.S. negotiator to accept compromises that added issues; and in neither case was U.S. ratification guaranteed.

The ITO

From the start, the ITO was an American idea. A set of interdepartmental committees that met in Washington from the spring of 1943 through the summer of 1945 developed the proposal for a postwar trade organization. Its four foundations were (1) generalized most-favored-nation treatment, with exceptions only for long-standing preferences, (2) no increases in existing preferences, (3) a commitment to negotiate reductions in existing trade barriers, and (4) a ban on the use of quantitative restrictions except under exceptional conditions. It emerged from the wartime planning that also produced the Bretton Woods institutions and the United Nations.

As a condition for the 1945 Anglo-American loan, Britain committed to the restoration of current account convertibility and nondiscriminatory trade. In notes exchanged with the United States in 1945–46, Belgium, Czechoslovakia, France, Greece, the Netherlands, Poland, and Turkey, all current or prospective recipients of U.S. aid, committed to similar goals.

The first trade round took place in London in 1946. Participants agreed that quantitative restrictions should be removed and that all trade barriers should be applied in nondiscriminatory fashion. But the British and French emphasized the need for import controls to support their fragile balances of payments. The British further stressed the importance they attached to trade with the Commonwealth and Empire. The Australians insisted that controls were needed to facilitate industrialization and the pursuit of full employment. The U.K., Belgium, and the Netherlands opposed U.S. proposals for sanctions against state trading and cartels.

The key issue in the next round in Geneva in 1947 remained the use of controls for balance-of-payments and development purposes.[4] The U.K. and France succeeded in adding to the draft a clause specifying conditions under which their use would be permitted, but conceded to the United States an amendment requiring the trade organization, in deciding whether such measures were warranted, to ac-

---

[4] At American insistence, delegates also discussed discrimination against foreign motion pictures and the treatment of private foreign investment.

cept the determination of the IMF (in which the United States had dominant voting power).

Negotiators covered the same ground again in Havana in early 1948. Dispute over the use of controls for balance-of-payments purposes was settled by allowing countries to choose between the London and Geneva provisions while limiting their discriminatory application to a transitional postwar period, as specified by the IMF Articles of Agreement. The diplomats elaborated alternative methods of obtaining permission to use import quotas to promote the development of new industries, but the principle of prior approval was preserved. In return for what were considered significant compromises by the Europeans and Latin Americans, the U.S. negotiator eventually accepted a one-country, one-vote procedure for ITO decision-making.

As Michael Heilperin emphasizes, other governments placed less weight on trade liberalization than the United States did, giving priority to other economic policy goals.[5] The British were worried about their balance of payments and consequently sought exceptions and exemptions from free trade. Primary producers like Australia were preoccupied by the instability of their commodity prices. Developing nations were primarily interested in the right to use import quotas to protect their infant industries. India and Latin America were prepared to accept only a weak liberalization regime riddled with exceptions. The U.S. negotiator offered compromises as he attempted to assemble a coalition on behalf of the new organization.

The negotiations over foreign investment rules showed the same dynamics. These clauses were of value mainly to investors in the principal international creditor country, the United States. Facing resistance, Washington's agent again agreed to a compromise. The draft charter asserted that governments could not expropriate or nationalize such assets except under conditions that were "just," "reasonable," or "appropriate." Such terminology implied that the United States was prepared to recognize circumstances under which expropriation or nationalization was justified, something it had never done before.[6]

This discussion omits what turned out to be the negotiators' most significant achievement: the conclusion of General Agreement on Tariffs and Trade (GATT). The parties began negotiations to cut particular tariffs at the 1947 Geneva conference. Twenty-three countries bargained bilaterally on a product-by-product basis, talking about products for which one country was the other's principal supplier. They conducted 123 bilateral negotiations covering 50,000 items, and all concessions obtained were generalized to every member of this group. The parties cov-

---

[5] Heilperin 1949. Heilperin was an advisor to the International Chamber of Commerce and attended both the Geneva and Havana Conferences.

[6] In late December 1947, the deputy U.S. negotiator in Havana, Clair Wilcox, facing strong opposition in other countries to a charter fully consistent with U.S. principles, recommended accepting no agreement rather than falling back to accepting a purely advisory "skeleton ITO." His superior, Will Clayton, however, had identified himself with the Charter and overrode Wilcox's doubts about continuing to talk. During January through March 1948 Clayton made several additional concessions on the use of import quotas and on voting rules to get a deal (Dryden 1995, 21ff).

ered half of world trade and cut the average tariff by 35 percent. Eleven more countries signed the GATT in 1949 at the Annecy round, and concessions that had been negotiated at Geneva were generalized to their economies.

What is most relevant here is that the original parties concluded this narrower agreement early—in 1947 before the full ITO negotiations had concluded—and that they did not make the GATT contingent on ITO ratification. The General Agreement was based directly on the chapter of the proposed ITO charter concerned with tariff cuts. The GATT's "general clauses" prevented countries from using quotas and domestic impediments to trade to reduce the value of the agreed tariff cuts. Otherwise the GATT did not address import controls, cartels, foreign investment, commodity-price stabilization, or industrialization. The Department of State was anxious to begin cutting tariffs and had authority to do so under existing U.S. legislation.[7] Implementing the full ITO would require new authority from Congress. In contrast, all the major 1994 agreements were linked together in a huge "single undertaking."

The WTO

The protectionism associated with the oil shocks and international economic imbalances of the 1970s provided the impetus for the Uruguay round, the GATT parties' eighth.[8] Again the United States provided the earliest and strongest initiative. It sought to enhance U.S. suppliers' access to foreign markets. But more fundamentally, it sought to extend the rules' coverage to agriculture and services and to remedy perceived shortcomings in areas like intellectual property and foreign investment. The first U.S. proposal met with little support, however, at the 1982 GATT ministerial. Europeans were leery about agricultural liberalization. Developing countries firmly objected that industrial countries should finish implementing the old rules, lowering their own remaining barriers to exports from the south, especially in apparel and textiles, before expecting developing states to take on additional new obligations.

The Reagan administration therefore negotiated bilateral liberalizing agreements with Israel and Canada, and used offensive claiming bilaterally as we have seen, to gain additional market access and put new issues on the agenda, while also imposing new barriers against some of its own imports. In 1986, at Punta del Este, Uruguay, Washington and other advocates overcame the lingering opposition of Paris and leading developing countries and launched the round, whose expected concluding date was 1990.

William Diebold once said that the ITO had been squeezed between the protec-

---

[7] The Trade Agreements Act was scheduled to expire in June 1948. While Congress did renew it in 1948 for a single year, this required a major battle and victory could not have seemed certain in 1947 (see below).
[8] More information on this round can be found in Oxley 1990, Stewart 1994, Schott 1994, Paemen and Bensch 1995, Preeg 1995, Weiner 1995, and Hoekman and Kostecki 1995.

tionists and the perfectionists.[9] The same was true of the Uruguay round in the second half of the 1980s. The United States insisted on the elimination of all agricultural protection and subsidies, something to which the Europeans could not agree; they countered with a proposal for limited cuts. Other agricultural exporters (the Cairns group of states) insisted on reductions in farm subsidies and refused to accede to U.S. demands for the liberalization of services, in which they had relatively little interest, unless such reductions were forthcoming. The result was impasse at the December 1990 GATT ministerial conference in Brussels.

John Crosbie, Canada's Trade Minister, had proposed the creation of a "Multilateral Trade Organization" in April 1990,[10] and in 1991 GATT Director General Arthur Dunkel incorporated the suggestion into his comprehensive compendium of interim agreements (the Draft Final Act, or Dunkel draft).[11] In part, this initiative can be understood as an effort to bundle together the various issues and facilitate logrolling. By obtaining a credible commitment on services and intellectual property, the United States might be willing to compromise on agriculture. By obtaining concessions from Europe on agricultural trade, the Cairns Group might be willing to compromise on services. The "single undertaking" provision linked treaties on these diverse issues under the WTO umbrella.

A key problem was that it was not clear that Europe stood to gain significantly. The E.C. sought to reduce U.S. offensive claiming outside the multilateral rules and to raise the cost to America of ignoring panel rulings. Europe stood to benefit from protection for intellectual property and from liberalization of services trade, albeit less than the United States. But there was also significant resistance to a negotiated agreement. European farmers continued to block agricultural liberalization. The French government's concerns over cultural imperialism led it to oppose the liberalization of services if this left its domestic market vulnerable to Hollywood films. Thus, concessions by the Europeans were essential to bring the round to a successful conclusion.

Most accounts suggest that two factors combined to bring about this result. First, resistance was disproportionately concentrated in France, where the agricultural and cultural issues had special resonance. But France also had a particularly strong desire for monetary unification, negotiations over which were proceeding in parallel. The turmoil in the European Monetary System in 1992–93 underscored the extent to which reaching this goal was contingent on German support, strengthening the hand of German and other European governments that preferred concessions on trade issues from France. Second, the Clinton administration signaled its readiness, like that of Bush, to walk away from the table if concessions on agriculture were not forthcoming. It committed to a binding deadline by requesting that Congress renew its negotiating authority only through 1994. It showed its willingness to pursue the regional option by negotiating

---

[9] Diebold 1952.
[10] Preeg 1995, 113.
[11] Jackson 1990 had provided important intellectual support for this approach.

NAFTA, bringing Mexico into the North American pact, and giving increasing prominence to Asia Pacific Economic Cooperation (APEC) meetings. The final WTO deals were cut at the end of 1993 and the formal signing took place in April 1994.

A BETTER BATNA IN THE FORTIES

One reason why Washington did not ratify the ITO but did join the WTO is largely overlooked in histories of these episodes but is brought to the surface by negotiation analysis (chap. 2). The batna for U.S. business and the President was more attractive in the first instance than the second (in terms of their primary objectives in each case), which led them to resist the deal more in the 1940s than in the 1990s.

The decline in the perceived value of the alternative was not found primarily in regional opportunities, however. A regional trade pact was not objectively a better alternative for America in either period. In the 1980s the United States did try to get tactical leverage in Geneva by this means. In part because the GATT contracting parties refused to initiate a multilateral negotiation in 1982,[12] Washington used bilateral North American free trade to worsen the no-deal alternative perceived by reluctant countries. The Canada-United States FTA, signed in 1986, "provided the USTR with a credible threat to warn its trade partners that it could be forced by Congress to abandon the GATT system," and not coincidentally gave an impulse to the Uruguay round.[13] In 1990 U.S. Trade Representative Carla Hills warned that NAFTA might be extended into a hemisphere-wide free trade area.[14]

Reportedly APEC also alarmed some European policymakers sufficiently to squeeze new concessions from them in Geneva in 1993.[15] By then, the Uruguay round was running aground again over agriculture. President Clinton upgraded the November 1993 Seattle meeting of APEC ministers, adding a high-profile leaders' meeting. APEC accounted for a much larger share of world trade (40 percent) and had the most rapidly growing share of the world total at that time, but excluded Europe. Clinton flew to Seattle the day after the key House vote approving NAFTA and posed for pictures with thirteen other APEC leaders. Soon Germany pressed the French and the European Community made additional concessions on agriculture in Geneva. Thus regional moves could affect the terms of a WTO agreement at the margin.

NAFTA, however, never was a truly credible substitute for the global agreement. Exports to Canada and Mexico—indeed exports to the entire Western

---

[12] As argued by Schott 1989.

[13] Weiner 1995, 10.

[14] Ibid., 183. A participating U.S. official observed, in response to an earlier draft, that James Baker—successively President Reagan's chief of staff, Treasury Secretary, and President Bush's Secretary of State—did act in private as though he believed that regional economic deals were a serious alternative for the United States. Private communication with the authors.

[15] Destler 1995, 231–32, and Frankel 1996.

Hemisphere—accounted for too small a fraction of the U.S. total to provide an attractive alternative to multilateral liberalization. Nor was it obvious that extending NAFTA into South America would have been politically straightforward. The value of APEC as an alternative vehicle for trade liberalization was far more symbolic than real. Achieving serious multilateral agreements among countries as diverse as China, Japan, the United States, and Mexico would be difficult. Moreover, U.S. negotiating objectives in the Uruguay round were to stem creeping protectionism, roll back agricultural protection in Europe, and bring services trade and intellectual property rights into the multilateral system, goals which could be achieved only in multilateral negotiations with the leading industrial countries.

The United States lacked a credible regional alternative in the 1940s as well. As the Cold War came to a boil, Washington sought to rebuild the trade and economies of Western Europe, Japan, and other parts of the world perceived as vulnerable to communist threats, as well as to benefit the U.S. economy through trade. No one or two regional arrangements could have accomplished these goals in the relevant regions. From the standpoint of U.S. objectives, the GATT was a more efficient solution.

To the extent that a regional alternative existed in the 1940s, it belonged to the Europeans. The British had established an extensive set of imperial preferences starting with the Ottawa Conference in 1932. Trade with the Commonwealth and Empire accounted for nearly half of Britain's merchandise trade in the second half of the 1940s. If Britain failed to obtain acceptable terms in the ITO negotiation, it could credibly threaten to walk away and fall back on trade with the Commonwealth. The British obtained a GATT clause that grandfathered pre-World War II preferences, allowing them to hold out against their removal. While other European countries did not possess equally extensive imperial ties, they could look to the possibility of European integration. Much of continental countries' trade was with one another. Additionally there was a strongly-felt desire to lock a peaceful Germany into Europe by strengthening its trade links with its neighbors. This process commenced with a proposal in July 1947 for a Franco-Italian customs union, and led to the formation of the European Payments Union of 1950 and the European Coal and Steel Community of 1951. The European Payments Union ultimately incorporated not only Britain but its overseas dependencies as well. While EPU members committed to freeing their trade with other EPU members, this agreement allowed them to continue restricting imports from other countries.[16]

The difference between regional options helps explain the terms of the two multilateral deals. In the 1940s the Europeans managed to extract concessions on such ITO matters as the use of trade restrictions in the event of unemployment or payments problems. In 1993 the coincidence of NAFTA ratification, an APEC summit meeting, and the Uruguay round's last deadline evidently helped Wash-

---

[16] Triffin 1957, 203.

ington to extract some final agriculture concessions from the Europeans. In both periods, however, the value of the regional option was significantly lower in reality than that of a multilateral deal for the United States.

Americans seeking more trade did have a more attractive *institutional* alternative in the 1940s, however. The GATT was available as a fallback in both periods, and it looked more attractive in the 1940s than in the 1990s. When ITO ratification became a live question, the General Agreement was already in place. The president went ahead with the GATT by itself first because of urgent concerns about European recovery and security. In 1947 Europe's economy was worsening and the Cold War with the Soviet Union was beginning. Shortages were pervasive and the European economy threatened to grind to a halt that winter. The reconstruction of intra-European trade was lagging behind the recovery of trade elsewhere. While the Marshall Plan was one response to these problems, widening commercial access to the enormous but highly protected U.S. import market was another. While the Truman administration's bargaining position with constituents and Congress might have been strengthened by delaying the effort to operationalize the GATT, U.S. policymakers felt that conditions abroad were too risky. State decided to proceed quickly with tariff cuts through familiar reciprocal negotiations under existing authority. The President would base his adherence to a General Agreement on Tariffs and Trade on the established Act, and then later the GATT could be folded into a completed ITO, which would require fresh legislative authority.[17]

Because of this combination of circumstances, when American principals were then asked for their opinions about the full ITO charter in 1949 and 1950, those who favored trade liberalization already had some or most of what they wanted in U.S. policy. Two GATT rounds established the viability of the limited strategy of generalizing bilateral tariff cuts to all contracting parties. The 1947 Geneva round had reduced the tariffs applied by the contracting parties to one another's exports by more than a third, and the 1949 Annecy round expanded the number of GATT signatories by nearly half. U.S. business and congressional critics of the ITO could invoke the GATT as a proven alternative to an ITO charter, which some saw as a threat to American sovereignty and others complained was riddled with loopholes and exceptions. Voting "no" did not mean blocking all trade liberalization.

The case should not be overstated. In 1950 there was ample evidence of opposition to future import liberalization in other countries. Latin America was pursuing import-substituting industrialization. Other primary-commodity producers sought to support their export prices through the use of marketing boards and other trade restrictions. France and other European countries saw trade liberalization as incompatible with their programs of state-led investment in industrial modernization. Many countries had displayed their reservations about tariff reduction during the ITO talks, extracting a variety of concessions in return for agreeing to tariff cuts. It was possible to discount the 35 percent cuts adopted in

---

[17] Aaronson 1996, 115–24.

Geneva and Annecy as nothing more than the removal of the most onerous wartime restrictions, and to question whether they would have real economic effects in a Europe still blanketed by quantitative barriers. Contemporaries dismissed the results of GATT's 1950–51 third round and the 1956 fourth round as "meager," "modest," and "not . . . a success."[18] While hindsight shows that the post–World War II GATT system proved remarkably successful for industrial countries, this could not have been known for sure in 1950.

In 1994 the GATT remained the obvious institutional fallback were the WTO package to be rejected. But by then the GATT had run its course. Average duties in the industrial states were quite low, and it was easy to foresee the day when tariff cutting—its bread and butter—would reduce them to zero. The GATT had proven less adequate as a device for removing the nontariff barriers that remained.

Most important, more ambitious new objectives were at the top of U.S. negotiating priorities—combating piracy of intellectual property and restrictions on services companies and on foreign investment. An agreement designed to reduce border measures was of limited effectiveness when the goal was deep integration, when further equalizing of market access meant modifying a variety of domestic practices. These were not covered by the GATT but by major new Uruguay round pacts like the General Agreement on Trade in Services and another on intellectual property. Participation in the GATT alone would not oblige another state to accept these new obligations. It would be free to opt out if no WTO linked all these pacts into a single undertaking. Thus American business in the 1990s, concerned especially with these new issues, stood to lose substantially if Washington fell back to the GATT. The perceived worsening of U.S. principals' institutional batna weakened their opposition to WTO ratification, compared with that of their predecessors in the 1940s.

This first point clearly is insufficient to solve the puzzle, however. If some key U.S. principals were going to oppose this ITO charter because they had a superior alternative, then why did the agent arrange and agree to it? And why did his successors in the 1980s and 1990s bring home a pact that proved to be closer to constituent preferences at the end? Two additional points will help.

GREATER AGENT SLACK AND WEAKER PRESIDENTIAL LEADERSHIP IN THE FORTIES

In early 1948 U.S. negotiator William Clayton probably did not anticipate the full extent of the domestic business opposition the Havana compromise would generate.[19] His successors during the Uruguay round had far more precise knowl-

---

[18] Irwin 1995, 135–37.

[19] Gardner 1956, 371–72, says Clayton was aware of some ratification dangers but was optimistic that another domestic campaign would be successful. Such campaigns had won congressional passage of Bretton Woods and the 1946 loan to Britain despite serious opposition.

edge about what domestic support and opposition their provisional deals would stimulate—thanks to a significant intervening change in domestic institutions governing the conduct of trade negotiations. In the 1990s (and in the 1970s and 1980s) U.S. principals instructed their agents much more frequently, at more levels of government, and in much finer detail throughout the bargaining, and agents negotiated accordingly while also adjusting home expectations and methodically lining up political supporters for ratification. Thus the final multilateral deal and final congressional opinion were much closer together in 1994.

Still, some internal opposition to virtually every proposal is normal in politics. In the 1940s, was it really impossible for the presidency, with its ample means of persuading members of Congress, to generate sufficient support for the ITO, even given complaints from some influential constituents, their batna, and domestic institutions? President Truman in fact expended little domestic political capital to win votes for the ITO, far less than Presidents Bush and Clinton spent for NAFTA and the WTO in 1993 and 1994. This third variable also helps account for the difference.

The counterfactual proposition that a sophisticated political campaign by the Truman administration could have won ITO ratification is not far-fetched. When President Roosevelt submitted the Bretton Woods Agreements bill of 1945 to Congress, the banking community opposed ratification and prospects in the relevant committees were quite bleak.[20] Yet vigorous executive leadership helped turn that situation around. The same could be said of the Marshall Plan, when circumstances were still less favorable. At the time few thought an unpopular Democratic administration could push such an ambitious plan through an increasingly isolationist Republican congress. But Truman, like Roosevelt in 1945, launched a "full-court press." Over the fall and winter of 1947 and into the spring of 1948, Truman used messages and speeches to drive the need for congressional action. He accommodated the desire of the senior Republican senator from Michigan, Arthur H. Vandenberg, to depoliticize the issue and separate it from the 1948 election. He authorized giving Vandenberg continuous advice and support, including weekly briefings by Marshall, as well as providing other legislators with different things they wanted.[21] The American presidency, representing the entire electorate, typically supplies the most forceful institutional voice at home on behalf of trade liberalization as well.[22]

What might account, in turn, for variations in presidential campaigns for ratification of these trade pacts? Trade is only one of many issues on which presidents are asked to provide statesman-like leadership. International trade accounts for a relatively small proportion of the U.S. economy. When will a president choose to

---

[20] Eckes 1975.

[21] As Neustadt 1980, 41–42, puts it in a discussion of presidential leadership in support of the Marshall Plan, "Truman himself had sufficient hold on presidential messages and speeches, on budget policy, on high-level appointments and on his own time and temper" to "deliver [what his political allies and opponents] wanted in return."

[22] Goldstein 1993 and Goldstein 1996.

expend her scarce political capital defending the general interest in trade liberalization against hostile lobbies, rather than on other projects? A superficial answer might be when she is not preoccupied by more pressing issues, but this would only beg the question. Social psychology contends that in general, people will take larger risks to avoid a loss than to realize a gain of the same magnitude.[23] In the late 1940s, U.S. leaders framed "world communism" as a military threat of possibly catastrophic significance. Faced with a difficult choice, Truman and Marshall chose to allocate the bulk of their scarce political capital to ratification of the Marshall Plan and NATO rather than the ITO, even though they agreed that the latter was also worthwhile. In 1994, no one in Washington perceived any security policy danger as comparable in severity. Thus not having spent his domestic political capital as Truman had done, Clinton retained enough to push more vigorously for U.S. participation in the WTO.

U.S. institutions, the President, and the ITO

In the 1940s agent slack was quite loose. The President delegated most international negotiations, including those concerned with trade barriers, to the Department of State, and the degree and form of consultation with constituents and Congress was left to the Department's discretion. From 1941 through 1948, during the planning and negotiation of the GATT and the ITO, especially before 1947, U.S. agents distanced themselves from their principals. Trade planners made a deliberate decision between 1943 and 1945 to give top priority to building international support rather than domestic support for trade liberalization.[24] In the 1934 Reciprocal Trade Agreements Act, Congress had delegated tariff-setting to the executive branch precisely in order to insulate the process to a greater extent from constituency pressures that were difficult to resist. Recall too the hypothesis concerning the particular culture of the Foreign Service when dealing with business, mentioned in chapter 7.

Secretary of State Cordell Hull, his assistant Leo Pasvolsky, and Harry C. Hawkins envisioned the ITO as a critical component of a radically new U.S. foreign policy that would stand as a more hopeful legacy left by the generation that had fought a terrible world war. Professor Clair Wilcox, economist and chief trade planner who with William Clayton succeeded Pasvolsky and Hawkins in 1946, wrote:

> The logic of our position allows us no alternative. We must go on, in international cooperation, from politics to economics, from finance to trade. World organization for security is essential; but if it is to succeed, it must rest upon continuous international participation in economic affairs. . . . If political and economic order is to be rebuilt,

[23] Levy 1992 and Levy 1997 review this literature.
[24] Aaronson 1993, chapter 3. Aaronson 1993 and 1996 provide by far the most thorough available evidence on this process, going well beyond William Diebold's early and still valuable essay (1952).

we must provide, in our trade relationships, the solid foundation upon which the superstructure of international cooperation is to stand.[25]

At home, State Department negotiators operated differently from Henry Morgenthau's Treasury, which had planned the 1944 Bretton Woods conference and secured passage of the implementing legislation,[26] and differently from the way United Nations planners involved members of Congress and the general public to gain support for the U.N. ITO planners kept Congress in the dark as to the essential details until 1946. They did not include representatives from either Congress or the public on their interagency planning committees, let alone delegations. In 1944 some officials advocated creating a formal channel for business opinion, but after extensive internal debate, senior State officials explicitly rejected the idea.[27] They made only vague public statements about plans for trade liberalization. During 1945 while they sought renewal of the Trade Agreements Act, their testimony never discussed plans for an International Trade Organization or spelled out how they would use this authority in multilateral rather than in bilateral negotiations as before. This reticence was not attributable to lack of interest on Capitol Hill. Expressed industry opposition to further liberalization was as plentiful as support. Members had been sending signals that support for further liberalization would need to be cultivated.[28] Hearings in 1946 on the loan to the United Kingdom can be seen as providing further warnings. However, they could also be interpreted as warnings that if we open a public discussion before we have a beneficial deal to point to, the domestic beneficiaries might remain silent and the usual opponents might manage to strangle the babe in the cradle.

In 1946 William Clayton and Clair Wilcox continued to concentrate on the international level. Clayton rejected Wilcox's and Hawkins's suggestions to involve the Congress and the public at home.[29] After publishing the first version of their proposals in December 1945, they did not publish the first complete suggested charter until 20 September 1946, just before the opening of the first multilateral conference on the proposal at London.

The strategic decision to keep the home front in the dark during these years would prove costly. By 1946 American public enthusiasm for new civilian multilateral organizations had subsided from its high water mark. Strikes and inflation agitated the home economy, and just before that year's congressional elections a meat shortage drove President Truman to lift price controls on meat. Citizens were frustrated by higher taxes and insufficient housing and employment for returning veterans. Voters punished Democrats and gave control of both houses of

---

[25] Wilcox 1949, xvii.

[26] On forming the Bretton Woods delegation and ratifying this agreement, see Eckes 1975 and Odell 1988. Vernon 1995 detects a common pattern in all U.S. economic negotiations during the 1940s—executive officials launch bold institutional initiatives but in the end the United States rejects significant constraints on its own future policy choices.

[27] Aaronson 1993, 96.

[28] Ibid., 69.

[29] Ibid., 65–67.

Congress to the Republican party that year. Republican leaders, foreshadowing 1994, announced enthusiastically that voters must want fundamental change from the New Deal path. Some Republican leaders concentrated greater fire on the trade agreements program thereafter. That fall and winter State's trade planners privately voiced fears that they had missed their chance by largely disregarding congressional and other domestic opinion for so long.[30] While polls showed no strong mass opposition to a new trade organization, neither did ordinary people care much about it.

In response to Republican and particular industry concerns, in February 1947 Truman modified the trade agreements program through an executive order that guaranteed an escape clause to any sector that might be affected by the coming GATT negotiations. During 1947 and 1948 State held public hearings to collect views on the ITO, and they made some changes in their negotiating positions as a result. They invited private-sector and congressional representatives to advise the delegation at Havana. At the same time, however, they overestimated public support for their general plans and held to their earlier domestic tactics in some ways.[31] At the Geneva conference in 1947, negotiators settled on the General Agreement and a provisional draft of an ITO, and the Havana conference completed the Charter late that year and in early 1948.

After the negotiations, constituent reaction proved to be mixed at best. The administration made some efforts to mobilize domestic support for ratification, but these efforts were delayed and only lukewarm even then. Truman and Secretary of State Marshall decided to spend most of their scarce Washington political resources on other issues. By 1948, well-known post-war frictions between the USSR and the West had escalated dramatically to proxy wars and even the brink of superpower war. After 1946, trade negotiations had to compete for U.S. official and media attention with subversion and violence overseas and pleas for new foreign commitments to avoid World War Three. In 1947 the European emergency especially seemed to demand measures that could make a difference quickly. Top leaders at State—the new Secretary George Marshall supported by Robert Lovett and others—decided to give priority in Congress to winning ratification of their own expensive European recovery program and the North Atlantic Treaty signed in 1949. Facing this new international competition, efforts by Clayton and Wilcox to convince their new superiors of the ITO's continuing centrality and its need for greater support proved unsuccessful.[32]

As for trade, Truman and Marshall evidently found the old Trade Agreements Act (TAA) plus GATT a useful second best. Early in 1948 the Democratic administration, facing a Republican Congress and a general election, decided to postpone submitting the more ambitious ITO Charter for ratification until the next Congress. The TAA was also due to expire in June 1948, and achieving another extension, the safer course, looked like quite a challenge in itself. The TAA hear-

[30] Ibid., 70–71.
[31] Ibid., 71–78.
[32] Ibid., 86, 93–96.

ings turned out to be a platform for hostile Republican attacks on the State Department, revealing how much distrust its largely closed process had planted, as well as Republican general determination to take charge of trade policy. A vigorous effort to round up supportive industries did bear some fruit and Congress did extend the Act—but for only one year.[33]

On 28 April 1949 the second Truman administration finally proposed the charter to Congress,[34] after Democrats had taken back control of both houses in the 1948 elections. (Divided government could not have caused this ratification failure.[35]) The administration sought ratification by both houses through joint resolution rather than by the treaty procedure.[36] The House of Representatives held hearings in April and May 1950. Domestic politics were not one-sided. The League of Women Voters, the Farm Bureau—the largest farmer organization in the country—as well as organized labor and several business organizations—the Committee for Economic Development, the National Planning Association, and the Committee for the ITO—all called for approval. The chairman of General Electric was one of the advocates.[37]

On the other side, along with predictable protectionists, the Chamber of Commerce of the United States, the National Association of Manufacturers (NAM), the National Foreign Trade Council (NFTC), and the U.S. Council of the International Chamber of Commerce opposed ratification. The U.S. Chamber and the NAM were the largest business organizations in the country, and the NFTC had been at the heart of earlier coalitions for liberalization.

These business critics, whom Diebold dubs the perfectionists, objected mainly that the Charter as it came back from Havana failed to sufficiently implement its liberalizing principles. Many critics concentrated on the exceptions that allowed continued use of quotas during balance-of-payments difficulties. Some objected that the Charter might sanction government commodity cartels, even though its provisions provided tighter controls on the use of commodity management than had ever been agreed before.

The investment provisions provoked some of the loudest corporate cries. Investors complained that once passages on compensation for expropriation had been qualified with adjectives such as "just" and "appropriate," investors could actually end up with less protection than they had under the status quo.[38] Ironically it was these same business lobbies that had insisted that a reluctant State De-

---

[33] In 1949 State assigned some officials to monitor and influence elite opinion through speeches to and private lunches with representatives of the American Farm Bureau Federation, the National Association of Manufacturers, the U.S. Chamber of Commerce, and narrower interest groups. Junior staffers drafted articles for business journals. William Batt, president of SKF Industries, a manufacturer of ball bearings, agreed to head a private-sector Committee for the International Trade Organization, after two more prominent business leaders had declined. Batt secured endorsements from some one hundred leaders in business, unions, civic organizations, and universities (Aaronson 1996, 103).

[34] *Public Papers of the Presidents of the United States: Harry S. Truman 1949*, 233–35.

[35] The interpretation in Milner 1977, chapter 5, differs in this respect but is similar in others.

[36] Campbell 1949, 218.

[37] Aaronson 1993, 2.

[38] Diebold 1952, 18.

partment add the investment issue to the negotiations in the first place. The diplomats had warned that other countries might not accept a provision that would satisfy U.S. business. Only after business representatives had told Clayton they would "strongly support the ITO charter in toto in Congress," . . . and "will swallow all other provisions" if it covered investment, did Clayton agree to add the issue.[39] The NAM's paid adviser to Clayton, who was present in Havana, did support ratification of the final Charter, and he labored, unsuccessfully, to persuade his employers to endorse it. Business disapproval of this particular provision cannot be attributed to an absence of advance consultation.

The critics felt that the ITO did not add much value, because the United States would live up to its obligations but most other countries would use the Charter's loopholes. But rather than saying that the Charter was a package of compromises that fell short on balance, some chose to denounce it as "a dangerous document" sanctifying principles utterly contrary to the American way, that "in effect commits all members of the ITO to state planning for full employment."[40] As the Cold War and Joseph McCarthy were heating up the body politic, some opponents depicted the ITO as posing a choice between "socialism" and "freedom."

Facing divided domestic politics, the Truman administration did not pull out all the stops to generate grassroots support for ratification in 1949 and 1950, as Morgenthau's Treasury had done for Bretton Woods four years earlier, nor do as much as Clinton would do for the WTO. In fact, Winthrop Brown, an administration spokesman facing complaints about the ITO during the 1949 Senate Finance Committee hearings on TAA Extension, even hinted that there could be an alternative to the ITO.

> The general agreement [the GATT] is so set up that it can stand on its own feet . . . If the ITO does not come into being there will be consultation to see what should be done with the general agreement. . . . We would ask the Congress to make changes to permit us to make this agreement definitely effective.[41]

This is not the sound of an administration driving its congressional allies to take risks to support a new measure.

During this debate, the NATO treaty was signed and Congress was investigating possible treason in the State Department. On 25 June 1950 North Korea suddenly attacked across the thirty-eighth parallel, and soon American soldiers were dying in another hot war. The President sent troops back to Europe as well and quietly abandoned the ITO.

[39] Aaronson 1996, 85.
[40] The Executive Committee of the United States Council of the International Chamber of Commerce, quoted by Diebold 1952, 414–15.
[41] U.S. Senate Committee on Finance, *Hearings on HR 1211*, 1071 and 1083–94, quoted by Aaronson 1996, 121.

U.S. institutions, the President, and the WTO

Between these two episodes the United States changed its domestic rules for negotiating and ratifying trade agreements, greatly diminishing slack between agent and principals. The changes came in two steps. In 1962, perhaps partly as a delayed reaction to the ITO as well as later GATT experiences, Congress took chief authority for trade negotiations away from the Department of State and created a new position, the Special Trade Representative (STR). These were conditions Congress attached to the authority President Kennedy sought for making concessions in what became known as the Kennedy round.[42] The STR was now the chief agent abroad as well as the chief manager of the related domestic politics. After 1962 the lead agency in trade diplomacy no longer had any responsibilities for other foreign policies. If military or political objectives came into conflict with trade guidelines, only the President could overrule the latter. This at least freed trade policy from compromises inside the State Department like those that had weakened trade's domestic position between 1947 and 1950. After 1962, commercial objectives were likely to dominate daily decisions to a greater extent on average.

The Trade Act of 1974, which authorized the President to participate in the Tokyo round, greatly tightened negotiator slack. Congress mandated quasi-corporatist consultations with the private sector and reports to the key congressional committees throughout the bargaining process. It established an Advisory Committee for Trade Negotiations: forty-five citizens appointed by the President to represent all social sectors including labor and consumers, and to meet frequently with American negotiators in Washington and Geneva. In practice, corporate executives dominated overwhelmingly. The act created three advisory committees at a secondary level covering industry, labor, and agriculture, respectively. In turn, reporting to these would be no fewer than twenty-seven single-industry advisory committees. Negotiators were required to provide these constituents and congressional staffers with access to confidential information. Little opportunity was left for incomplete information about constituency demands or concerns. The law directed the private-sector advisors to publish an advisory opinion—a report card, in effect—on the final agreement.[43]

Planners in 1974 were concerned about the risk that Congress would simply delay the bill indefinitely or would enact inconsistent conditions that would be impossible to renegotiate. Such problems had dogged the Kennedy round's outcome. Thus came additional new rules creating a sui generis "fast track" for ratifying the expected agreement. The Act stipulated that once the President presents the results to Congress, Congress must approve or disapprove the package within sixty days. No amendments or delays would be in order once the President formally submitted his bill. These rules created a strong incentive for the administration to involve key congressional leaders informally in drafting the implementing

---

[42] Rightor-Thornton 1975.
[43] Winham 1986, 133–37.

legislation as well as the negotiation. Equally, the lobbyist seeking changes after the negotiation was left with only the possibility of entering the private process of crafting the President's bill, where negotiators have greater autonomy to block entry. In 1979, following these new rules the House of Representatives and Senate did ratify the Tokyo round's complex set of deals by the remarkable margins of 395 to 7 and 90 to 4, respectively.[44]

The same internal rules were in effect during the Uruguay round, and this institutional change helps make sense of much U.S. government behavior. Negotiators located in this dense domestic consultation process, far from keeping their principals in the dark about details, presented them directly and frequently and heard constituents' demands and complaints many times during the bargaining. The executive had many opportunities to temper expectations about what could be achieved, and worked throughout to build support for ratification. As one close Washington observer noted just after the round concluded, "what [USTR Mickey] Kantor sought above all in Geneva was an agreement that could pass Congress."[45] In February 1994 William T. Archey, vice president of the U.S. Chamber of Commerce, added: "The genius of the negotiation was that those who would have made the gravest problems [on Capitol Hill] were to some degree taken care of. There are a number of people who do not love this agreement but are not disposed to oppose it."[46]

For example, the agenda established in Punta del Este in 1986 bore the clear fingerprints of a huge coalition of U.S. industries seeking better protection of intellectual property rights abroad that had been meeting in Washington for a year under U.S. Chamber of Commerce auspices. During the round American negotiators built support methodically via many bilateral negotiations, some of which have appeared in earlier chapters. The long list of constituents benefiting included California and Florida citrus farmers, from agreements with the EC and Japan; corn farmers from the 1986 Yuppie War; cattle ranchers in Japan's market; and lumber producers regarding Canadian softwood. USTR levered doors open in lucrative Asian markets for cigarette makers. Boeing and McDonnell-Douglas enjoyed Washington backing for years in their rivalry with the European Airbus. The automobile industry got President Bush to push their interests to the top of his list during his first overseas trip after the Soviet Union's collapse—to Tokyo in January 1992. NAFTA was even dearer to Detroit's heart. The semiconductor industry achieved the most impressive Washington trade leverage, pound for pound.

The beleaguered steel industry affected negotiations especially on multilateral dumping rules. USTR Mickey Kantor managed in 1993 to negotiate some weakening of the pact designed to discipline antidumping measures, though some serious limits remained in the final agreements. The Clinton administration then found technical ways in its implementing legislation to mute the new disciplines,

---

[44] Winham 1986, 308; Winham 1980.
[45] Dryden 1995, 389.
[46] *National Journal,* 12 February 1994, 353.

to keep steel on board for ratification.[47] After failing to win any commercially significant concessions for Wall Street securities firms, Kantor neutralized their possible opposition with an agreement to continue financial services talks for an additional eighteen months. One of the last high-profile struggles took place on behalf of Hollywood's film exporters against European Community protection.

The addition of the umbrella World Trade Organization itself to the package would engage the Presidency directly. U.S. diplomats had taken a lead in efforts to strengthen the GATT as an institution for exposing one nation's violation of another's rights. Their proposals attempted to limit the convention under which an accused state could prevent the parties from endorsing an unwelcome GATT expert panel report.[48] But American negotiators had resisted creation of a World Trade Organization, partly because of fears of domestic opposition. Washington did not agree, in fact, until the morning of the very last day of the round—15 December 1993. Because this institutional issue had been added near the end of the process, Congress and U.S. constituents heard little about it. This relative lack of consultation would come back to haunt advocates, just as it had in the 1940s.[49]

On 12 January 1994 the President's Advisory Committee for Trade Policy and Negotiations commended the negotiators for their gains, and concluded, after balancing these against disappointments, that the President and Congress should ratify and implement the package. Only one member of thirty-seven, representing the AFL-CIO, dissented.[50]

Even after all the close consultation, however, there was serious opposition and the Clinton administration, including Clinton himself in contrast to Truman, spent much time and effort rounding up votes. In May 1994 the *Financial Times* reported a warning from House Speaker Thomas Foley that Congress faced "a very real crisis" over ratification. Said the *Times*:

> Although President Clinton's power to pull off more victories ought not to be underestimated, passage this year of the implementing legislation for the GATT agreement now seems almost as improbable as did the NAFTA victory last year. Mr. Foley and his colleagues see as the chief impediment the need to raise $10 billion to $14 billion over the next five years and perhaps as much as $40 billion over the next decade to compensate for the tariff revenue lost under the Uruguay Round deal. Budget rules require this to be done either by programme cuts or taxes.[51]

A second prominent criticism was that creation of a World Trade Organization, together with its virtually automatic enforcement mechanism, would infringe

---

[47] Destler 1995, 240–44.
[48] Preeg 1995, 77–78 and 103.
[49] Destler 1995, 232.
[50] U.S. Advisory Committee for Trade Policy and Negotiations 1994.
[51] *Financial Times*, 25 May 1994, 5.

U.S. sovereignty, including the authority to regulate pollution and consumer safety at home. Here the threat came from political rather than commercial entrepreneurs. Senator Bob Dole, the Republican Minority Leader, cited many constituency concerns about sovereignty as a reason to delay consideration.[52]

Consumer advocate Ralph Nader and Patrick J. Buchanan were the most vocal opponents.[53] The Citizens Trade Campaign, which had worked against NAFTA the year before, also ran advertisements against GATT. On the other side, twenty corporate chief executives lobbied Congress together on behalf of the pact in June. Their "Alliance for GATT NOW" also bought $2 million worth of advertising and mounted grassroots campaigns. The main organizations behind this Alliance were the Business Roundtable, the National Association of Manufacturers, and the U.S. Chamber of Commerce.[54]

The process of writing implementing legislation lasted until 27 September 1994, when the Clinton bill finally entered the Capitol's fast track. "As it shopped for Congressional support for the pact, the Clinton administration agreed to do favors for a host of industries: steel, cars, wheat, lumber, cement, ball bearings, cellular telephones, civil aircraft, and apparel."[55]

After the bill was finished, there was more for the President to do. Senator Bob Dole, despite his long history of advocating trade liberalization, held out until Thanksgiving before announcing that he would support WTO ratification. Dole was to become Majority Leader and was contemplating a run for Clinton's job in 1996. He eventually said he had extracted from the President an agreement to support later legislation that would create a "WTO Dispute Settlement Review Commission." This group of five federal appellate judges would review all final WTO panel judgments adverse to the United States. If the commission found, during any five-year period, three such decisions in which a WTO panel "demonstrably exceeded its authority" or "acted arbitrarily or capriciously," then any member of Congress could introduce a joint resolution pulling the United States out of the organization.[56] This last deal was additional to a provision for a congressional vote again every five years, which Representative Newt Gingrich had negotiated earlier to provide his own political cover. With Dole now on board, and after further personal meetings and telephone calls by Clinton, the Senate voted its approval by a margin of 76 to 24 and the House ratified by 288 to 146—with majorities of each party in each house voting in favor.[57]

---

[52] *New York Times*, 31 August 1994, A12.
[53] *National Journal*, 2 July 1994, 1571–75; *New York Times,* 3 October 1994, C1. The definitive account of the NAFTA negotiation and ratification struggle is Mayer 1998.
[54] *National Journal*, 2 July 1994, 1571.
[55] *New York Times*, 30 September 1994, C1.
[56] *Inside US Trade*, 25 November 1994, 23–24, quoted by Destler 1995, 253.
[57] *Washington Post*, 30 November 1994, 1; 1 December 1994, A40; and 2 December 1994, 1. A bill to enact the Dole reservation was introduced in Congress in November 1995 and reintroduced in January 1997 (H.R.78), but no votes had been taken on it by the time of writing. U.S. Library of Congress World Wide Web service, <http://thomas.loc.gov>.

In summary, three arguments, when combined, make sense of this historical puzzle. Between the 1940s and the 1990s the United States greatly tightened the institutionalized slack between principals and their bargaining agents, so the agents' deal and the principals' preferences were closer together at the end of the WTO negotiation. In addition, the GATT was a better institutional alternative to the ITO than to the WTO for Americans who favored trade liberalization. The President also spent fewer political resources to win votes for ITO ratification than for the WTO.

This contrast provides evidence for three corresponding hypotheses about the ratification phase. In general, the risk of failure will rise with the degree of slack the domestic institutions permit between negotiator and principals during bargaining—an element of the context that was constant in earlier chapters. The basic batna principle extends to the behavior of principals during ratification: the worse their perceived alternative at that time, the more likely they are to support a given agreement, other things equal. And the more a nation's leader frames another issue as posing a larger potential loss, the more she will shift scarce domestic political assets to that other issue, reducing the odds of ratification.

This analysis raises other interesting implications for scholarship. As noted at the outset, several logical hypotheses from international relations theory, including those relying on the international power structure and market openness, seemed inadequate to account for this significant historical puzzle. Advocates of these perspectives need to dig deeper, identifying the limits of their ideas.

Connections between economics and security may not be as clear as we have been told. We hear that the two are tightly intertwined, and specifically that during the early Cold War, security threats led the U.S. government to act like a world leader on economic issues. This specific claim needs to be amended inasmuch as it overlooks the fate of the ITO in U.S. politics. There the Cold War had, if anything, the opposite effect. In the absence of the perceived need to respond to communist threats, which led to the North Atlantic Treaty and the need to ratify it at home, the Truman administration would probably have mounted a larger domestic effort to ratify the ITO, to complete a project in which it had already invested several years of effort. The WTO success despite the Cold War's disappearance raises a question of how sensitive economic negotiations are to the rise and fall of security threats.

This brings us to the end of the empirical analysis. Part 4, after summarizing the main points, steps back and highlights other key implications for research and for negotiation performance.

PART FOUR

IMPLICATIONS

CHAPTER 9

Improving Knowledge

Scholars can improve knowledge of international economic negotiation in a number of exciting ways. This book, and negotiation theory more generally, point toward many unexploited research opportunities, as well as helping us integrate earlier findings not seen now as parts of a common whole. More broadly, I believe scholars of international relations should rethink some widespread conventions. This chapter highlights these key implications for basic and applied research, after first recalling the main points up to this stage.

How monetary and trade negotiators interact with each other and with markets can make a significant difference to the process and its outcome, contrary to the impression left by much scholarship. If we had attempted to analyze these cases while abstracting from the negotiation process, we would have missed decisive elements in every case. Actual negotiators use different behavioral strategies in different situations. Washington exemplified the range from pure offensive value claiming (regarding the Japanese yen 1971, Brazilian informatics 1985, the EC 1986), to a mixed strategy dominated by claiming (Japanese beef 1988), to a roughly balanced one (Mexican gas 1977), to a mixed strategy dominated by value creation (regarding currency stability 1942–44 and the Japanese yen 1985). Reducing Brasília's behavior on soluble coffee, or Mexico's contrasting actions in two trade cases, to either "defection" or "cooperation" would have concealed as much as it revealed about behavior, and we would have been puzzled by the outcome differences. Our resulting theory would be crippled both for generating new hypotheses and aiding practice. Studies of negotiations over security, environment, and other issues also might be enriched by applying this strategy continuum. We have seen that actual strategies are not fully determined by international or domestic structures, and that negotiators achieve greater gain in some cases than in others even when using the same strategy.

Parts two and three developed and documented specific hypotheses emphasizing market conditions, negotiator beliefs, and domestic politics as influences on strategies and outcomes. All are ceteris paribus.

From variable market conditions to strategies and outcomes:

• The worse the alternative the relevant market (outside the official talks) presents to the government negotiator, the lower his resistance point inside the talks, hence the softer his claiming tactics and the smaller his gains and vice versa. This process seemed to influence the Carter administration's tactics toward Mexico during the late 1970s, for example (chaps. 3 and 5).

- The contrast between two U.S. attempts at offensive claiming against Brazil and the European Community (chap. 6) generated the idea that when the market in question is structured by multinational producers who have stakes invested in the target country, the credibility of threats by their home government, and hence its gains from offensive claiming, will be lower on average.

From negotiator beliefs to strategies and outcomes:

- Negotiator A, operating with bounded rationality, is less likely to choose the value-creating strategy the more he believes B will resist and exploit that strategy, among other things. U.S. monetary negotiators used markedly different strategies toward Japan in 1971 and 1985—to achieve the same objective toward the same country when the context was largely the same. Ignoring the difference in this key belief about feasibility would have obscured a key reason for this notable strategy difference (chap. 4).
- If negotiators are subject, like the rest of us, to cognitive judgment biases, then gains and losses from a strategy will vary directly with the extent to which the negotiator uses tactics designed to compensate for his own biases. Mexico's agents dealing with the same U.S. administration used basically the same mixed strategy in two cases, but used debiasing tactics less in the 1977 natural gas case than in 1979 with winter vegetables, and Mexico clearly gained less in the earlier case (chap. 5). If Díaz Serrano had used debiasing tactics to a greater extent, he almost certainly would have gained more for Mexico in 1977, even if all else had been the same.

From domestic politics and institutions to outcomes:

- The more that constituents inside a threatening country express opposition to implementing the threat, the more they will diminish overseas gains from the offensive distributive strategy. American constituents voiced more opposition in informatics than in feed grains, which undermined the U.S. diplomat's credibility and hence reduced his gains from Brazil, compared with the more powerful European Community, paradoxically (chap. 6).
- As constituents in a target country raise the political cost of compliance for their government, gains from the offensive claiming strategy will diminish (chap. 6).
- As institutionalized slack between the agent and his principals at home is reduced, the risk of ratification failure will fall, even though some discretion has other advantages (chap. 8).

From strategy to outcome:

- Choosing a mixed strategy rather than strict claiming may gain more or lose less under some circumstances, even when bargainers believe their main objectives are in conflict. In chapter 7, Brazil, defending against claiming by a stronger party, probably would have come out worse in the case of instant coffee had it held firm to its initial stance of strict defensive claiming. Brazil's counterproposal proved to be a way out with less loss and possibly even some gain for Brazil.

• Ambassador Smith in Tokyo was trying to claim offensively from Ambassador Maki and Japan. Smith's supplementary integrative tactic, adding a new sweetener that would help his counterpart achieve ratification at home, helped break a deadlock in the 1988 beef trade case. The evidence indicated that holding to strict claiming would not have produced a meaningful commercial agreement, and thus the U.S. negotiator would have returned home without the gains that American producers found so satisfying (chap. 7).

The two-case method of difference provided more thorough evidence with more rigorous analysis for these hypotheses than we have from many earlier case studies and other works on international economic negotiation. Naturally this method cannot demonstrate how far these ideas will generalize, but it does establish a strong warrant for testing over a larger domain.

NEGOTIATING BILATERALLY

One approach for improving economic negotiation theory further is to concentrate on other bilateral economic negotiations around the world, recent and historical—a substantial share of the total. This book's main hypotheses, among others, could be checked in other two-party cases to establish how widely they apply. One can easily imagine many analogous two-case contrasts centering on experience not of Washington but of Ottawa, Brussels, Cairo, Canberra, Beijing, Seoul, Tokyo, Buenos Aires, and many other capitals. These studies could include a negotiation with a multinational firm or international organization. They would surely generate many new ideas as well.

Statistical analyses with large numbers of observations could test hypotheses including those on markets in chapter 3, assess case studies' representativeness, and disentangle multiple causes. Two observations are never sufficient for the latter purpose. The pair of Mexico-U.S. trade episodes in chapter 5 presented variation in an effect—Mexico's gain from bargaining—and in two possible causes—the changing value of the American market alternative to agreement, and differential Mexican use of debiasing techniques. In chapter 8, more than one thing changed between the demise of the ITO and WTO ratification. But developing indicators that would be valid over multiple negotiations is a complex task in its own right. Few large studies such as the one on Japan-U.S. trade outcomes by the American Chamber of Commerce Japan have been attempted. Far more resources could be devoted to such efforts at uniform classification of bargaining strategies, outcomes, and other important variables.

We could tease out additional logical implications of these main ideas, in mathematical or verbal form or both. For instance, if negotiator A will avoid choosing the mixed-integrative strategy to the extent A believes B will exploit it, then a rational B may attempt, earlier, to send signals to influence A's later strategy choices. This particular line of reasoning disregards the two-level complexities facing negotiator B, which often complicate neat manipulations of signals that nations send, even in an authoritarian polity such as China today. But those complexities too are interesting research challenges. Another possibility: will A's strategy and tactics depend on his belief as to how far the status quo or a provisional AB agreement is from the frontier? One might conjecture that if A believes the current joint position is far from it, A will use more value creation, but the closer he believes they are to the frontier, the more he will lean toward strict claiming.[1] What other beliefs might be key to the bargaining process? Analysts could generate many additional hypotheses and investigate them empirically.

Furthermore, we could investigate interaction effects, looking for conditions that will amplify or mute the effects found here. For example, does one of these causes condition the effects of another? Do extreme market conditions—like a run on a currency or a near-default—dampen the effects of uncorrected judgment biases? Or do extreme conditions increase stress on the average individual and thereby amplify biases' effects? Or are the two mostly independent? Do governments' responses to market changes vary with the development doctrine that dominates their policy thinking?

NEGOTIATING INTERNATIONAL ECONOMIC INSTITUTIONS

We could improve our understanding of how economic institutions change (or fail to change) by investing greater effort in observing and generalizing about the negotiation process in those settings. Pioneering case studies and other works on multiparty[2] institutional bargaining give us promising foundations to build on.[3] This book deliberately concentrated on simpler two-party interactions, until chapter 8 began to show that the approach is relevant beyond them as well. This section illustrates further.

Pairs within groups

Regime studies could undertake similar investigations of key two-party interactions that shape multiparty talks. Many prominent institutional negotiations have been either organized by two-state relationships or polarized basically into two

[1] I am grateful to James Morrow for suggesting a form of this idea.
[2] The term *multilateral* is often reserved for very large numbers of parties, while other terms such as *plurilateral* and *minilateral* are used for smaller numbers greater than two.
[3] Beyond cooperation research discussed in chapter 1 and works cited below, see Zartman 1971, Winham 1977, Winham 1979, and Winham 1986 on trade bargaining, and Sebenius 1984, Young 1994, and Friedheim 1993 on environmental bargaining. The latter also cites the extensive literature on U.N. parliamentary diplomacy (373). Zartman 1994 introduces six analytical approaches to multilateral negotiation. Related, from formal theory, are Bueno de Mesquita 1990 and Martin 1992.

camps. The U.K. and the United States dominated preparations for Bretton Woods. Tariff negotiations under the 1947 GATT were conducted as sets of overlapping bilateral talks among major suppliers.[4] The 1963 partial nuclear test ban treaty emerged from a process that "remained essentially a bilateral East-West dialogue"[5] even after it became formally multilateral in 1962. In the 1970s bargaining over a proposed New International Economic Order, governments became polarized into two large coalitions.[6] In the 1985 monetary case, the United States and Japan proceeded bilaterally before calling the G5 together in one place. Chapters 6 and 7 reported bilateral trade negotiations concerning informatics in Brazil and beef in Japan that overlapped the Uruguay round. These bilaterals probably influenced the priorities, resistance points, and tactics of the parties themselves and possibly third parties in the round as well. An E.C.-U.S. standoff over agriculture delayed agreement on the entire package for the last three of the round's eight years.[7] Governments responded to the 1997–98 Asian financial crisis in part through bilateral negotiations outside the IMF, for instance between the U.S. Treasury and Jakarta, as well as through bargaining between the Fund and borrowing countries.

Strategy variations

What strategies do governments use most often when negotiating economic institutions, in either pairs or groups? A common strategy taxonomy might aid in describing and comparing institutional bargaining processes. Chapter 2 gave examples. When a player mixes claiming and creating value, is it more common to sequence the two or to blend them concurrently? Is one mix more effective than the other in general? We have little standardized evidence for answering such questions.

With a baseline description of strategy variations in hand, comparative research could investigate what determines strategies used in regime bargaining. As an illustration, consider the contrast between the Roosevelt administration's behavior in 1933 in connection with the London monetary conference, and in 1942–44. Its strategy in the earlier case was mixed but marked most by distributive moves, while in 1942–44 Roosevelt attempted a mixed strategy clearly from the integrative side of the spectrum. In 1933 Washington did not take the initiative to propose a negotiation or a plan for the collective welfare. The British and French took the initiative, and attempted to claim substantial value from the United States as well as to benefit everyone, as they saw it. When Roosevelt took office in March, he agreed to negotiate. In April, however, before the conference, he halted gold exports and allowed the dollar to float downward somewhat. This boosted

---

[4] On the Kennedy round, see Preeg 1970, 184ff.

[5] Hopmann 1996, 284.

[6] Rothstein 1979, Krasner 1985.

[7] We could also benefit from formal and informal analysis of what difference it makes whether a bilateral negotiation is embedded in, or independent of, a concurrent multiparty round.

U.S. producers and beggared neighbors at a time when America did not have a trade deficit. During the June conference France pressed Washington to stabilize the dollar immediately, and France and the U.K. effectively defaulted on their June debt payment to the United States.[8] For a few days U.S. representatives discussed others' proposals to stabilize currencies. But later Roosevelt sent his delegation his "bombshell" telegram indicating he was unlikely to support any international agreement to stabilize exchange rates, even a loose one his delegates thought was harmless, even for the length of the conference.[9] The meeting disbanded without agreement.

In sharp contrast, in August 1942 Washington opened with a complex proposal designed to benefit the entire community of allied countries, including the United States of course, but requiring contributions from Washington, not just one-way concessions. The administration offered in effect to provide official loans to other countries by joining and contributing to a permanent international organization that would be run partly by other countries, if the others agreed to rules that would open their financial markets and prevent competitive devaluations.[10]

Why such different strategies by the same president? A prominent interpretation has pointed to American hegemony in the world power structure to explain creation of the Bretton Woods regime.[11] Yet the United States had already attained as much world economic hegemony by the late 1920s as it would enjoy two decades later.[12] It already had as much to gain, in this relative power sense, from an international monetary regime. Why did Washington not use more integrative tactics in 1933, or why not mostly value-claiming again in the 1940s? Arguably, U.S. claiming was even more likely then, considering how badly allied countries now needed military support as well. Why did Washington not withhold government monetary concessions and direct others to American banks, encouraging them to get their payments financing there and adopt the U.S. dollar as the world's international money? Winthrop Aldrich, chairman of the Chase National Bank, proposed an alternative approach close to a dollar standard.[13] Why did the Treasury propose instead to turn U.S. money over to an international organization, especially one where, by the end of the negotiation, the debtors held most of the votes? American bankers and members of Congress angrily asked exactly this question. The power structure clearly left room for more than one U.S. negotiat-

---

[8] Feis 1966, 182.

[9] Ibid., chapters 19 and 20.

[10] The U.K. and Canada also made mixed-integrative proposals that shaped the outcome, as explained below.

[11] Keohane and Nye 1977, 135–36, finds that an overall structure model accounts best for the monetary regime from 1944 through 1958, while also giving some credit to an economic process model. No attention is given to the negotiation process.

[12] The United States already accounted for 35 percent of world manufacturing production (League of Nations 1945, 13). It supplied 43 percent of all international investment and 17 percent of world trade (Kuznets 1966, 308, 323).

[13] *New York Herald Tribune*, 30 April 1943, quoted in Van Dormael 1978, 95.

ing strategy. Once again, structures do not fully determine strategies. Further investigation is needed.[14]

Specific hypotheses

This book's specific hypotheses could be applied to illuminate strategies and outcomes. One could inquire how objective changes in market conditions tend to shift the economic regime negotiator's strategy, perceived batna, tactics, and gains achieved. Chapter 3 illustrated how coffee price increases during the 1960s toughened claiming tactics inside the International Coffee Organization, and how the oil market shift in the late 1970s pulled the plug on talks underway in the International Monetary Fund. What other market properties, such as varying lags, might help make sense of contrasts such as that between trade and finance negotiations?

If negotiators' beliefs about a strategy's feasibility shape their choices in two-party talks, they should shape institutional negotiators' strategies as well, though obviously things become much more complex. If debiasing tactics improve gains from two-party bargaining, should they not do so in regime talks as well? If domestic opposition to implementing a threat limits the threatener's credibility and his gain in bilaterals, will it have a like effect in multiparty bargaining over economic rules? What tactics for managing internal differences are deployed, and do they help account for regime failures and successes? How have domestic institutions in countries other than the United States affected regime talks? Would domestic changes elsewhere make ratification defeats less likely, or more so?

Process and outcome

In brief, promising projects could ask what difference the negotiation process makes to economic regime outcomes, and seek to generalize about conditions or tactics that make each strategy more or less effective. Contrast the 1933 and 1944 monetary outcomes. In the 1940s London, Ottawa, and Washington invested heavily in the diagnostic phase of the negotiation process—studying technical information about the problem, producing thorough plans for a new financial organization, and first vetting them internally. Not all regime negotiators invest so heavily in the diagnostic phase. Washington did much less in 1933. This tactical variation has been identified as a key general reason for multiparty impasses and agreements that capture only minimal gain, for the parties separately as well as jointly.[15]

---

[14] Odell 1988 emphasizes the recovery in the home market and hence lower policy discount rate, and changing policy ideas in Washington due to the discrediting of old beliefs by vivid, extreme experience—the depression and the war.

[15] Zartman 1987, concluding chapter. Another key reason for minimal results from the 1970s North-South talks was a much greater divergence of goals than characterized the parties at Bretton Woods.

Offering a thoroughly prepared integrative plan does not guarantee agreement. In the early 1940s, after John Maynard Keynes and Harry D. White offered their plans, had either stuck to pure defense of his plan and claiming from the other thereafter, they probably would not have reached an agreement, or not anything like the actual IMF charter. The two plans were inconsistent in fundamental design and they embodied conflicting national objectives. A counterfactual scenario of strict tactical claiming would certainly not have been implausible at the time, in view of the domestic pressures on each delegation. For his part, Keynes secretly recorded his understanding of congressional hostility to internationalism, and his fundamental concern that in the end "the U.S.A. would do nothing."[16] Washington had used strict claiming in the past, and as we know, has done the same many times since then. Keynes faced his own strong domestic pressures against making concessions that Washington demanded.[17] Anything looking like the discredited gold standard was sure to provoke heated attacks, which was a key reason the British Treasury wanted to create and name a brand-new international money.

As it happened, neither main delegation stuck purely to distributive tactics after the outset. These partially-informed negotiators also engaged in a discovery process, debating what effects this or that rule would have in practice after the war ended, under a complex institution that had never existed, and economic and political conditions that could not be forecast with precision. There certainly was strong pushing and pulling,[18] but White and Keynes eventually searched for ways to dovetail their differences. Specifically, by the time of their provisional two-party deal in April 1944, Keynes had fallen back from the cherished British overdraft scheme that would have created a new international money.[19] He had accepted much more limited U.S. financial exposure via the new institution, and most difficult of all, had finally agreed to IMF authority to approve a large devaluation.

The hegemonic American delegation also had fallen back from significant initial positions. To get Keynes to accept the U.S. design principle, White agreed to double the Fund's size (and maximum American exposure) compared with the U.S. plan, to reduce the role of gold in subscriptions, to add a clause authorizing restrictions against American exports if the dollar became "scarce," and to give up the initial demand that Washington must have a veto over most IMF decisions.[20] The United States did retain an effective veto on any change in its quota. On the extremely sensitive issue of how to control competitive devaluations, the American delegation eventually decided that if the U.K. would accept IMF authority on large devaluations, Washington could accept a rule authorizing a member to de-

---

[16] Quoted in Van Dormael 1978, 75.

[17] Gardner 1956 elaborates.

[18] Van Dormael 1978 provides detailed archival information about this process that was not available to Gardner 1956.

[19] Horsefield 1969, vol. III, 3–36; Van Dormael 1978, chapters 10–12.

[20] Horsefield 1969, vol. III, 37–96; Van Dormael 1978, chapters 10–12.

value up to 10 percent without consulting the Fund in a case of "fundamental disequilibrium."[21] They evidently preferred this famously ambiguous term over no deal, at least after eighteen months of strenuous effort. Each delegation retreated on some issues to get the other to retreat on others. The IMF as we know it resulted from a process of negotiation.

Generally, studying strategy variation might also greatly improve our understanding of the distribution of gains between parties, in multilateral as well as bilateral economic cooperation. One logical hypothesis, for example, would predict that when a relatively integrative strategy goes up against a relatively distributive one, the latter side will claim a larger piece of the pie, by exploiting the relative openness of the value creator, even when parties' power assets are roughly equal. Again, we lack evidence whether this conjecture is valid in international economic negotiations.

Coalitions

The most obvious difference between the two-party and the multiparty process is coalition formation. A strategy for any multiparty negotiation needs some tactical plan for forming a winning coalition and breaking up blocking coalitions. Coalition tactics will shape the distribution of gains as well as chances of reaching any deal. Although we have little grounded theory on coalition formation in international economic negotiation, James Sebenius and David Lax have suggested interesting ways to classify alternative tactical sequences for approaching potential partners.[22] Additional research could theorize this area more fully, and investigate which paths are chosen and which ones have worked best under what conditions.

The simplest conceivable path is to call a simultaneous meeting of all potential parties as the first and only step. "Everybody first" might be worthwhile when the goal is modest, such as exchanging information and ideas about the problem, current policies, and possible new ones. But it could be a recipe for disappointment if the goal is more ambitious and some parties are likely to engage mostly in pure claiming or blocking maneuvers, as occurred for instance during much of the 1970s North-South international bargaining. Well-known difficulties with large numbers often seem to drive ambitious coalition builders to smaller numbers first, or along some path leading through one potential partner at a time.[23]

When contemplating "bilateral first," the next question is whom to talk to in which order. The path taken probably will be decisive for the outcome in some cases. A natural instinct is to start with the easiest and postpone dealing with the parties least likely to agree. Building on Sebenius's ideas, in some situations "easiest first" could also prove the most valuable path in the end, say, if most participants are deeply skeptical that any agreement is possible and a break in the ice

---

[21] Van Dormael 1978, 104–107, from British government sources.
[22] This section draws from Sebenius 1996 and Lax and Sebenius 1991.
[23] Kahler 1993 discusses these issues.

would undermine this skepticism. But in other situations it could waste an opportunity or even defeat the larger purpose. In 1990 the Bush administration, assembling a military coalition against Iraq, did not turn first to Israel, at least not publicly. That sequence might have killed the prospect of signing up many Arab governments later.

In some cases the greatest eventual payoff may come from "most influential first," even if the biggest will be difficult. This path goes first to those whose joining will most worsen the alternative of staying out for the holdouts. If we begin with the least influential, they may resist making any costly commitment, thinking it would be wasted as long as the big players are blocking a multilateral deal. If so, they will reduce this path's expected value. White and Keynes each followed "most influential first" as the route to Bretton Woods.

Paul Volcker, as Chairman of the U.S. Federal Reserve, illustrated this path again in the 1980s. During the 1970s and early 1980s several multinational banks collapsed, raising the danger of a chain collapse rippling through many countries. A system that prevented this nightmare from occurring would have joint value, and multinational banks were not subject to much international regulation. But if one government unilaterally imposed more stringent prudential requirements on banks headquartered in its jurisdiction, it would raise costs for its own banks competing with those based in less demanding countries.

During the early 1980s the leading central banks first tried a large conference in Basel, Switzerland. This was a cutting-edge problem and national regulatory systems differed greatly. Regulators were less than certain whether any technical regime would work best in all countries. Here too diagnostic research, joint and separate, was undertaken to better understand it.[24] But these Basel talks bogged down as governments were unwilling to abandon their distinctive regulations. Germany and Switzerland were especially strong opponents of a Basel agreement, and the European Community discussed a new approach for their members that differed substantially from one toward which Washington was moving.

In 1986 the Federal Reserve settled on new requirements to make U.S. banks safer, modeling a technique used by the Bank of England. But U.S. bankers protested imposing them unilaterally. Volcker went to Britain, then Japan and the other Europeans.[25] He negotiated secretly with the Bank of England first because Britain satisfied three desiderata: it was still highly influential on this issue; London was one of the world's three top banking centers. It was also relatively easy—the two governments' technical preferences were close. And getting an EC member to commit to an international rule contrary to the EC approach would drive a wedge into that potential blocking coalition.[26] Thus Volcker's strategy was mixed-integrative, not purely integrative. In January 1987 the Bank of England and the Federal Reserve shocked the other central bankers with a separate bilateral deal.

Japan also was highly influential, as the home of eight of the ten largest banks

[24] Kapstein 1989.
[25] Ibid., 341.
[26] Sebenius 1996, 334.

in the world at that time, but it was not nearly as easy. Japanese negotiators objected to the Anglo-American standard and defended their own different banking regulations.[27] But Volcker had just worsened their batna, lowering their resistance point. Japanese banks were operating inside the other two leading markets and were applying for permission to expand. They had to worry about Washington and London, now a team, penalizing them if their home government did not accept this emerging rule. Soon Tokyo joined, after some modifications to the scheme.

This growing coalition of the Big Three now diminished the value of staying out even more sharply for remaining advocates of other rules. Even Germany and Switzerland quickly fell in line behind what came to be labeled the 1988 Basel Accord on bank capital adequacy. They too achieved some compromises. The main uniform rule was that any bank operating internationally from any signatory country must maintain a ratio of capital to assets of at least 8 percent by 1992 at the latest. Volcker's coalition tactics helped produce an agreement that strengthened the whole network while pulling the terms toward the preferred U.S. position.

A different bilateral path might be termed "information first." The sequence is modified so the earlier process will uncover information that will be helpful later, or perhaps so the process will conceal inconvenient information temporarily. Korean negotiators faced with U.S. demands for textile export restraints during the 1960s and 1970s preferred to delay their bilateral talks and "let Hong Kong go first." They hoped Hong Kong would uncover information about the true American resistance point, or counteroffer with arrangements less restrictive than Korea might invent. Hong Kong's negotiators were mostly native speakers of English who had longer experience negotiating the technicalities of textile restraints. Then Seoul would insist on terms no less favorable than Hong Kong and even try to do a bit better.[28]

Sebenius 1996 reports a fascinating example of sequencing two negotiations in order to delay the release of information that would be less harmful to the process later. In July 1992 France was negotiating with its EC partners over European monetary union, and simultaneously with all GATT governments in the Uruguay round. The French foreign minister wanted to delay settling the GATT trade deal, which meant French concessions in agriculture that he was willing to make, until after settling the EU monetary deal. He calculated that if Paris revealed its hand on trade to its own farmers first, they would explode and manage to block the EU accord, but the opposite sequence would not torpedo the GATT agreement.[29]

Our knowledge of institutionalized cooperation, then, might be improved by fresh comparative research on the process of coalition formation, modeling possible paths, describing actual practices uniformly, and documenting whether or

---

[27] Kapstein 1989, 341. Oatley and Nabors 1998, another case study of this negotiation, gives one-sided emphasis to the distributive aspect of the process.
[28] Interviews with former Korean negotiators, Seoul, 1981.
[29] Sebenius 1996, 339.

not and how the choice among paths has contributed to impasses, agreements, or particular payoff distributions.[30]

Recently governments have admitted nongovernmental actors into the business of certain international organizations and negotiations. How does this change affect the negotiation process? Does adding NGOs make official agreement more likely, or less? Do they regularly help certain governments claim from others? Do they move the official possibility frontier outward, or inward? Do they cancel each other out? Should additional international organizations open their doors, or should they resist?

VARYING CONTEXTS

We could greatly improve our knowledge of how the economic negotiation process interacts with its context. When parameters that did not vary in this book do change, does our understanding of either bilateral or multiparty bargaining need to be modified? Earlier isolated studies of bargaining contexts might achieve greater influence if viewed together as contributions to a broader theory of economic and other negotiation. Fresh inquiries could resolve inconsistencies and look for conditioning effects.

Domestic institutions

Domestic political institutions have received only slight attention here, mostly in connection with ratification. The chapter on offensive claiming reminded us that additional empirical work is needed to sort out the debate over whether authoritarian or democratic states have a systematic bargaining advantage. Earlier studies of institutions[31] can be read as suggesting the possibility of other links with the negotiation process, which could be tested in other domains and better integrated with each other. States differ as to bureaucratic structure, central bank independence, regulatory approaches, federalism, electoral rules, and number of political parties. We could investigate whether these variables have predictable effects on economic and other negotiations beyond selected cases. Do states with certain domestic institutions tend to favor characteristic international rules for economic regimes? Or if a country's institutions systematically afford special influence to the military, will that government trade off commercial for military gains more than average when facing a dilemma? Are some national institutions more sensitive to time pressure, or less likely to correct judgment biases, than

[30] A related project could investigate leadership in these settings. For a typology of leadership modes, see Young 1991. Sebenius 1992 illustrates mediation that draws multiparty integrative agreement out of division in an environmental case.

[31] Complementary contributions emphasizing this angle, though often missing elements emphasized here, include Cowhey 1993; Evans, Jacobson, and Putnam 1993; Simmons 1994; Henning 1994; Messerlin 1996; the February 1997 special issue of *Journal of Conflict Resolution*, edited by Robert Pahre and Paul Papayoanou; Raustiala 1997; and Milner 1997.

others? Would evidence show that some governments tend to claim greater value, regardless of the issue, because they are organized at home to facilitate a more unified bargaining position, or do gains and losses depend mostly on other things? Encarnation and Wells 1985 argue that the effectiveness of developing countries when bargaining with multinational firms varies partly with the country's domestic organization. Do domestic institutions make some countries more liable to ratification failure than others? Milner 1997 contends that more polyarchic government generally reduces the chances of cooperation through international organization. Can changes in domestic political institutions condition the effects of other variables, such as connections between market behavior and negotiator behavior?

Cultures

Are some cultures predisposed to value-claiming or value-creation tactics more than others, independent of market situations, security situations, and domestic government institutions? Do some cultures create joint gains more readily than others? Do Asian and European cultures approach institutional negotiations in systematically different ways, regardless of the market and power conditions and the issues? Is their difference about how formal the rules should be, or aspects of the negotiation process, or both? Do cultures condition the effects of other variables? Do different cultures respond differently to market changes? Are some cultures more prone to judgment biases or against debiasing than others? Are some particular biases more characteristic of certain cultures? Although some experimental studies provide tantalizing support for notions like these, we have little comparative empirical analysis outside the laboratory.[32]

Security

We have seen that economic negotiations have dynamics of their own, varying considerably even when security conditions do not.[33] We should question the bromide that economics and security are inextricably intertwined until further research can pin down these relationships more rigorously. No neutral test here has refuted any security hypothesis, however. Even if economic bargaining is driven mostly by other things, some security variations also could make a difference.

While a state is fighting a war, as in 1942–44, will its economic negotiators increase the weight they place on military-political objectives in their bargaining

---

[32] For experimental studies, sample Graham 1993 and Brett and others 1998. These recent nonexperimental offerings feed in here: Cohen 1991, Faure and Rubin 1993, Mingst and Warkentin 1996, Bonham, Sergeev, and Parshin 1997, Berton, Kimura, and Zartman 1999, and a spate of mostly particularistic field studies on Chinese negotiation practice, such as Tung 1982, Shenkar and Ronen 1987, Kirkbride and Tang 1990, Chang 1991, Tse, Francis, and Walls 1994, and Cohen 1996.

[33] Urban 1983 also shows how much Poland's economic negotiations and trade with Germany continued between 1925 and 1934 despite Germany's high-profile political demand for return of its Silesian territories and a so-called tariff war between the states.

over trade and finance issues? During wartime their estimates of the cost of no agreement may weight military conditions more heavily. If so, offers of military assistance and threats to withhold it, for instance, may have greater ceteris paribus effects on that economic diplomat's moves than in peacetime.

During peace as well as wartime, will weaker states place greater weight on security objectives in economic bargaining—at the expense of external commercial ones—than stronger states, on average? Military planners always anticipate the prospect of war, and their chief executives may also factor military needs into international economic bargaining. But a given increment to security might be worth more to a highly vulnerable state than to one that is already less likely to be conquered, on the principle of diminishing marginal returns. Thus a strong power like the United States may be less willing to sacrifice other goals to achieve that increment. Having less reason to worry about abandonment, it will tend to place greater weight on achieving commercial gains when the two are in conflict. In principle, such a cross-national variation in effective priorities could occur even if individual leaders were not consciously attempting to make it so.[34]

Joanne Gowa reasons that trade always has security externalities, potentially helping the partner country militarily, and that states concerned about their security should therefore discriminate against enemies and in favor of allies. While a state could take such actions unilaterally, this argument suggests the possibility that allied governments will negotiate over trade differently with each other— softening their claiming tactics, making more generous offers, exploring joint gains more openly, or some combination. Little research has studied negotiation behavior, as opposed to export data, with this hypothesis in mind.[35]

Exogenous military events could shift the market alternative for an economic negotiator, thus indirectly influencing the process. If the military-political situation worsens the commercial market alternative to agreement, we would expect the trade negotiator to soften his distributive tactics in trade bargaining with potential allies and neutrals but harden his claiming from likely enemies, except perhaps when the fear of imminent war is below some intensity threshold. In peacetime does a military alliance among certain parties cause their trade or monetary negotiators to form coalitions along military rather than commercial lines? Are bargaining linkages between economic and military issues more frequent between alliance members than between neutrals or enemies discussing the same economic issues? Is ratification of a trade or financial agreement by constituents more likely under certain security conditions, such as wartime or intense fear of war—presenting economic diplomats with exogenous opportunities? Again, we really do not know.

[34] Skalnes 1998 points to the case of Britain in the 1930s to support a form of this idea, namely that that the likelihood of a discriminatory policy favoring allies will increase the more a great power needs allies militarily.

[35] For her only case study Gowa 1994 selected a disconfirming case, the British-French entente of 1904 which did not lead to a discriminatory trade agreement, and even there the main focus is not on the negotiation process.

Do security conditions interact with other potential influences? Do some countries' security policies and circumstances bias their negotiators against deals that would open their economies to market forces, and make them less responsive to market changes during a particular negotiation? Or do security crises tend to amplify the effects of judgment biases, implying an even greater payoff from debiasing tactics in a concurrent economic negotiation? In wartime do porous domestic institutions and divided government make less difference to ratification of economic agreements than in peacetime?

This book has sampled from negotiations where economic issues are not mixed explicitly with military issues. Similar analysis could be extended to special mixed episodes concerned, for example, with exchanges of base rights for foreign aid,[36] joint construction of weapons systems,[37] and arms sales. Further, all this work might be brought under a common umbrella with the large literature on economic sanctions for political-military purposes.

International institutions

Scholars could investigate what difference it makes when bilateral negotiations take place in the context of different international organizations. Only isolated hints appeared in this book. Chapter 6 speculated that the existence of an International Coffee Agreement actually had not made much difference to the outcome of Brazil-U.S. coffee bargaining. On the other hand, a ruling by a GATT panel concerning Japan's small agricultural quotas worsened Tokyo's perceived batna in the larger 1988 beef case, helping the United States to claim more. The chapter on Brazil and the European Community raised the possibility that strengthening the GATT for dispute settlement shifted Washington's tactics after 1994, encouraging it to use the Geneva institution in place of claiming outside Geneva.

Along these lines, fresh research could examine the possible effects of pre-1994 GATT panel rulings on bilateral bargaining more systematically, and could compare strategies and tactics before and after the 1994 change. A few comparative studies already cast shafts of light into this area. Ryan 1995 finds that during the 1980s and early 1990s, international rules influenced Washington's choices among trade cases to take to the negotiation table. The U.S. Trade Representative initiated most section 301 negotiations with Japan, South Korea, and Taiwan when the other government's practice was regarded as relevant for GATT rules, either those on the books or rules under negotiation. Regarding outcomes, Noland 1997, using a different data set, finds evidence that USTR gains more when the other country's practices violate international norms. But we actually know little about institutional influences on U.S. bargaining choices and outcomes on other economic issues and in other times, and still less about those of other governments. We have few comparative studies investigating whether and how the economic bargaining process varies with the organizational context.

[36] E.g., Wriggins 1976, McDonough 1979.
[37] Tucker 1991, Chang 1991, Spar 1992.

Table 2. Multiparty Negotiations, Issues, and Context

	The Issues Are Regime Rules	Issues Other Than Regime Rules
Not all members of common organization	London conference 1933; talks that created the ITU, ILO, World Bank, IMF, United Nations, OPEC	Geneva conference 1954; settlement of Rhodesia civil war 1979
Members of a common organization	IMF talks over amendments to articles of agreement; GATT & WTO talks on new codes & decision making procedures	OPEC price & quota changes; summits of G7 & G8 states; G5 Plaza agreement 1985; LDC debt reschedulings; GATT members re tariff cuts; IMF & member state over loans and debtor policies

Do international regimes really govern subsequent bilateral bargaining among their members, as theorists assume? Suppose two bilateral economic negotiations over similar issues take place between similar countries, one pair members of a common international institution and the other, members of a different common institution or none at all. In what respects do the processes differ? Do regime properties change negotiators' priorities, their perceived batnas, the possibility frontier, their strategies, or their gains and losses? Do members of an organization make more issue linkages than similar parties outside, on average? Will a mixed-integrative strategy have the same effects or will they vary? We lack sufficient evidence to answer these questions today.

For multiparty bargaining too, a final aspect of the environment is organizational. Here it may be fruitful to separate two dimensions. The first is whether or not all parties are already members of a common international organization. The second is whether the multiple parties are negotiating over regime rules or other issues. The two dimensions do not correlate perfectly.[38] Consider some examples (table 2).

In the northwest cell, the states that created the International Telegraph Union in 1865, the International Labour Organization in 1919, and the IMF were not all members of a common organization at the respective times, but their negotiations were concerned centrally with writing regime rules. Other multiparty bargaining over regime rules, in the southwest cell, occurs among member states of a common organization.

Many multiparty negotiations—the right half of the table—concentrate on issues other than regime rules. In some, all parties are members of a common organization (the southeast cell). An IMF member state negotiates with its headquarters, a multinational board, over loans and borrowing-state policies,[39] not over the

---

[38] Contrast Zartman 1994, 6: "The outcomes of multilateral negotiations are mainly matters of rule making rather than the redistribution of tangible goods." In the same volume Kolb and Faure 1994 asserts flatly that international multilateral negotiations "actually take place in organizations" (114).

[39] Analyzed in Odell 1979 as well as sources cited earlier.

IMF's rules.[40] GATT signatories bargain over particular exchanges of tariff cuts, and members of commodity organizations like OPEC and the International Coffee Agreement negotiate changes in particular intervention prices.

On many other occasions, parties that are not all members of a common organization negotiate over issues other than regime rules. Many peace settlements, such as those in 1954 concerning Indochina and in 1979 concerning the Rhodesian civil war, are good examples.[41]

All except those in the upper right corner can be considered organizational negotiations in some sense, but these distinctions give rise to somewhat different research questions. It would be interesting to see empirical analysis comparing the left and right sides, to determine whether the multiparty process of negotiating rules differs on average from the process of negotiating over other issues.[42] Cases that do not change international regime rules are hardly trivial. In the late 1990s, IMF negotiations with Russia, Indonesia, Korea, and other states were prominent. At stake were incomes in the billions of dollars, a distribution of gains and losses, political as well as financial, across different sectors and states, incentives to be created for investors in later years, and sometimes political stability of borrowing governments. Yet while students of military conflict resolution have paid substantial attention to the right side of the table, the economic cases are underrepresented in scholarship.

In addition, we could compare the top and bottom halves—multiparty negotiations outside and inside a common organization. Are international organizations basically arenas in which governments manifest the same behavior they would display if the organization did not exist? Or would comparative evidence show, for instance, that governments outside a common regime make shallower commitments on average than member states make to one another, because a common institution promises to make subsequent cheating more transparent, as some theorists suggest?

Does the multiparty negotiation process unfold essentially the same inside and outside organizations? If not, how does it change? Does the same distributive strategy have different effects inside and outside organizations? What about mixed-integrative strategies? Are negotiators any less subject to partisan bias when operating inside organizations? Are the same coalition tactics relevant, or must they be modified? Does issue linkage take place less outside organizations than inside, as some theorists conjecture? When linkages are made, do they al-

---

[40] While the G5 and G7 were all IMF members, their private interactions after 1976 were little constrained by IMF rules, and in fact amounted to a competing decision-making forum. Summits are analyzed by Putnam and Bayne 1987, von Furstenberg and Daniels 1991, von Furstenberg and Daniels 1992, Iida 1993, and Bergsten and Henning 1996.

[41] The Hedley Bull tradition in international relations would probably argue that general international law and the United Nations system made some difference even in these cases. Also see related ideas from sociology in Meyer et al. 1997.

[42] Winham 1986 (367) reports trade negotiators' consensus that bargaining over numbers, such as tariff rates, with their greater precision, encourages stricter adherence to reciprocity and less flexible exploration than occurs in bargaining over words. But some regime rules include numbers, as in the Bretton Woods case, and some nonregime issues include words.

ways facilitate agreement or sometimes impede it or shift the distribution of gain? Does the presence of an international secretariat induce governments to identify more opportunities to create joint value than they identify in negotiations without a secretariat? We do not really know.

International organizations vary greatly among themselves. Which aspects of organizational structure or behavior make the most difference to the bargaining process? Do certain institutional settings make agents freer with information and more inclined toward value-creating moves.[43] Do some organizations facilitate the formation of coalitions more readily than others, or bias the parties toward certain coalitions and away from others? Do particular institutions establish specialized processes, such that negotiator behavior differs reliably from one organization to another even when the same governments are involved? For instance, one might compare the process of a typical IMF loan negotiation, the average GATT tariff negotiation, and the typical European Community enlargement negotiation—all as special variations on the general process of economic negotiation. Comparing organizations as to their effectiveness for facilitating gains might suggest innovations to organizations themselves.

Serious methodological problems obstruct efforts to disentangle these complexities. Scholars have made a significant start, mostly with diverse case studies, but past efforts have been designed separately, not under any one theoretical framework, and their findings are not yet commensurable. According to Blair 1993, for one, the OECD's norms and secretariat do not have much discernible effect on governments' negotiation behavior on trade issues or on multiparty outcomes, though more precise rules on one issue enjoy greater compliance than others. Aggarwal 1996 reports that the League of Nations did not affect outcomes of debt renegotiations, but that the IMF and the Brady Plan did. Rothstein 1979 and Susskind 1994 complain that the UN organizational context—UNCTAD for the former and formal universalism in environmental talks for the latter—has thwarted valuable settlements that might have been achieved. Winham 1986 sees in the GATT's Tokyo round a transition toward a new system for managing international trade by multilateral negotiation. Martin 1992 finds that when an international organization calls on its members to impose economic sanctions on a country, the level of cooperation among sanctioners increases. Finnemore 1996 reports three historical cases in which an international organization shaped states' very interests and hence their behavior in negotiations and elsewhere. Garrett and Weingast 1993 cite the case of the European Court of Justice and the 1987 European Community decision to complete the "internal market" to support an argument that international institutions can help states construct focal points that they might not have found by themselves. Other students of the European Union, however, contend that the national governments are much more important that the Brussels institutions in these matters.[44] The extent to which their findings generalize outside the European Union is also not clear.

[43] I am grateful to Thomas Heller for this point.
[44] For recent debates see Sandholtz and Zysman 1989, Wolf and Zangl 1996, Beyers and Dierickx 1997, Moravcsik 1998, Moravcsik 1999, and earlier works cited.

Do multiparty regime negotiations really incur smaller transaction costs on average than a set of bilateral negotiations aimed at the same objective, as some theorists assume? Other theory tells us that larger numbers should make it more difficult to supply a public good optimally. Extremely lengthy talks over disarmament, the law of the sea, and trade have left some veterans vowing "never again!" States do choose bilaterals on many occasions. How much does it really cost a government to complete the average bilateral international negotiation, relative to the aggregate economic and political outcomes produced? Will regime negotiations have lower costs under some circumstances but not all? This assumption too needs empirical investigation.

A last set of projects could explore effects of international norms, as opposed to formal rules and organizations, on negotiation behavior.[45] Katzenstein 1996 reports evidence for and critique of the emerging case for norms regarding national security policies. Schoppa 1999 finds that Japan's responsiveness to American bilateral claiming dropped abruptly after 1992 because the social context had changed. The Cold War that had legitimated deference to the United States had evaporated, U.S. behavior had undermined Japanese trust, and new WTO rules further delegitimated U.S. claiming outside these rules. More focused empirical work on norms and negotiation behavior might prove fruitful.

Admittedly, it is easier to identify opportunities for research than to complete this work. But when we design new studies, viewing all negotiations through a common framework and as parts of a related whole would enhance the contribution of each study to cumulative knowledge.

BROADER IMPLICATIONS

Finally, scholars can improve knowledge of international relations generally by reconsidering some widespread conventions. We need not assume that a researcher may work only within the rationalist research program or one emphasizing subjective meanings but not both. Rationality need not imply formal models, maximization, or complete information, and it need not exclude the subjective level. This book joins others in demonstrating that intellectual payoffs flow from the bounded rationality premise and studies of actors' beliefs. Such a theory integrates interests and policy ideas together, and it is consistent with some variants of constructivism. Bounded rationality explains why so many bargaining outcomes fall short of the efficient frontier, as well as the integrative tactics of those attempting to approach it. It helps explain why there is space for the process to make a difference, and why negotiated outcomes scatter widely while interests seem constant. Both formal and verbal theorists are contributing to the bounded rationality approach, in areas other than negotiation as well, but it can be pushed much further.

[45] Hasenclever, Mayer, and Rittberger 1997, chapter 5, reviews knowledge-based or cognitivist theories of international regimes.

The research community will advance more rapidly, in my view, if we avoid an overriding commitment to defend one grand theoretical "ism" against all others. This style of argument can be stimulating in the short run, but in the longer term it becomes a dead end. Had this book been confined to either realism or liberalism, it could not have explained the observed contrasts and would have missed valuable ideas.

Consider realism. No one denies that a gross power disparity—think of Côte d'Ivoire and the European Union, or Thailand and Japan—often bounds the distribution of gains from bargaining.[46] Power thinking certainly contributes something valuable. Yet we have seen three pairs of outcomes where greater power could not have accounted for greater gain because the power advantage was no different or even less in the case of greater gain. Elsewhere many examples of the so-called power of the weak have also been documented.[47]

We should replace *bargaining power* with *batna* if we wish to get to the heart of strategies and outcomes. Too often "bargaining power" is still only another label, not an explanation, for the outcome. *Batna* introduces a variable that really can do explanatory work for us. A claim that a party's no-deal alternative improved is easier to falsify than the slippery claim that interests changed. The batna claim also is more general, since the value of the bargainer's alternative depends on things other than a state's power assets. Many governments allocate some of their means to specific ends more or less permanently. Thus when the European Union has committed most of its power assets to other purposes and when reversing those decisions would be costly, its actual alternative to a given deal with Côte d'Ivoire in a particular month will be far less attractive than a count of power assets would suggest. Middle-range negotiation theory focuses more sharply on the decision the negotiator must make.

Joanne Gowa argues "that the division of international relations into two discrete subfields does not make a lot of sense. . . . The pursuit of power and of plenty are two sides of the same coin."[48] We have seen evidence to the contrary. Economic negotiations vary significantly when security does not. Outside of wartime, the dynamic of negotiators, market conditions, and domestic politics may be equally or more powerful than security in determining government economic bargaining. We do need better research sorting out whether models of security bargaining apply to economic bargaining, and when security and economics affect each other. But it is clear that strict power-and-security thinking alone is too simple.

Liberalism also contributes something valuable, certainly regarding international economic relations. It directs our attention to objective world market conditions and domestic divisions they introduce into national politics. But we also

---

[46] Odell 1985 documents a skewed distribution from thirteen trade conflicts between South Korea and the United States. Bayard and Elliott 1994 find that in section 301 trade bargaining, Washington gains more from countries whose economies are more dependent on United States.

[47] As one example, Odell 1985 finds significant deviations.

[48] Gowa 1994, 121–22.

have seen strategy choices vary when market conditions are similar, and outcome differences that are difficult to understand by analyzing markets alone. Economics is not enough. Neoliberal institutionalism concentrates on international institutions, but they leave much evidence unexplained. Liberalism is insufficient too, even in political economy.[49] Advocates of grand theories should attempt to specify their theories' boundaries, or conditions when their contributions will be greater and less.

Scholars collectively will advance general knowledge about international relations most rapidly over the long term, I believe, by aiming to deepen middle range theories, each representing the most valid ideas for a given problem. We could invest more in theoretically-guided empirical research. Theorists could turn their attention more often to variables that actors (and not only governments) can use. IR theory, by becoming more useful in a more direct sense, could arouse much greater interest and achieve wider impact in the societies in which we live.

[49] Contrast Moravcsik 1997.

CHAPTER 10

Improving Negotiations

We could and should improve our international economic negotiations before additional research is completed. Scholars in every country are citizens as well, and students of international relations care about policy and practice at least as much as theory. Some citizens give advice to their representatives, and some advise other governments, companies, nongovernmental organizations, and international organizations. This final chapter pulls together lessons for best practice today, based on what we do know, and expressed in the form of advice that could be given to one who will conduct or supervise negotiations on any economic issue.[1]

To improve management of the world economy by international action, it will not be enough to have solid economics, legal expertise, and an appealing blueprint. The successful proponent of a new agreement also needs an effective negotiation plan—a strategy for achieving other parties' assent in the face of opposition. Except when unilateral action will be sufficient or the parties have no relevant disagreements, the proponent (and the opponent) will need expert knowledge of the negotiation process, not just facts about the parties and issues of the day. Without understanding how the process works in general, our agents will be primed to step into pitfalls familiar to others, to overlook opportunities they would have found, or both. *The most general and most important improvement we could make would be to apply better negotiation analysis.*

Conflict resolution is a substantial part of good practice. We want our diplomats to avoid conflicts when they can do so without sacrificing important goals, and to reduce conflict costs when they can. But dispute settlement is not the only assignment of the typical government negotiator. Good practice in some situations may mean gaining at someone else's expense or defending against such attempts by others. A sound theory or analysis prepares the bargainer for both aspects of the process.

Undoubtedly some diplomats are doing an excellent job, playing their cards as well as we could expect given their constraints. We have no comprehensive "grade card" for them, for no one has produced data for evaluating negotiator performance uniformly and realistically. But we do know of particular outcomes that could have been better—for constituents, the world community, or both—and we ought to learn from them. The following ten practical guidelines are not mutually exclusive and go beyond the admonition to avoid cultural misunderstandings, a valid point that is made amply elsewhere.

---

[1] Chapter 9 begins with a summary of this book's main points up to that stage and identifies needs for further research.

1. DIAGNOSE THE SITUATION

The first step, when designing a strategy appropriate to principals' goals and the situation, is to determine which type of situation the negotiator is facing. The typical picture will seem hazy, because of deliberate misrepresentations as well as basic uncertainty. The sophisticated bargainer does not simply assume that every case will be a fight between pure opponents, nor that every conflict can be resolved for mutual benefit if parties try to understand each other. Uncovering the true situation takes some work. Basic questions introduced in chapter 2 can guide initial diagnosis.

- *What should be our top negotiating objectives and priorities, political as well as economic?* Which goals should be sacrificed in this case to achieve others, if necessary? *What will the others' priorities be?*
- What *outcome* is our aspiration—and what is most likely, according to the best information viewed in the cold light of day?
- *Who should be the parties?* Should we negotiate bilaterally, regionally, or globally? Should we try to exclude any?
- *What issues should be included and excluded* if possible? What linkages should be proposed or blocked?
- *Where is the possibility frontier?* What conceivable deals, if any, are excluded by technology or the parties' perceptions of their interests? Can anything be done to open new possibilities?
- *What is our best alternative to a negotiated agreement (our batna)* for achieving our top goal? What would we do if the talks ended in impasse, and how attractive or awful is that course of action? What does the other party believe is *its batna*, relative to its own top goals? Given these alternatives, what is each party's approximate *resistance point* (the worst terms the party would probably accept)? Does domestic politics raise or lower any of these resistance points? Which parties need a deal the most? Is the situation asymmetrical, and if so, in whose favor?
- *Does a positive zone of agreement[2] exist at this time, or can one be opened?* Are the parties' goals totally in conflict, largely consistent, or some mixture?
- What *strategy* is each other party likely to use?

Answering these questions is not a linear process. The objectives will vary with the issues and parties to be included. Which parties to invite will depend in part on which issues we want to lay on the table and what we want to accomplish. Later, finding the other's batna to be better in her view than we had realized at first glance might lead us to adjust our priorities. Considering these variables could reverse a preliminary decision to negotiate. Diagnosing the situation is an iterative process.

[2] The set of outcomes between the parties' resistance points.

Busy diplomats occasionally act without needed information that was available or without sufficient diagnosis, and suffer due to it. In 1985 U.S. bargainers launched a provocative negotiation with Brazil without having thought carefully about what they would do if the Brazilians refused to buckle. The administration evidently made its decisions without carefully testing how interested domestic firms would respond to its threatening strategy (chap. 6). A cogent negotiation analysis would pay more careful attention to both these key elements—not to mention making sure a threat does not fall on a friendly country's national day. In 1986 Brussels was caught by surprise when Washington reacted vehemently to the new EC enlargement treaty. Top levels in Washington may have been equally surprised by the treaty's implications for U.S. farmers. For both parties, relevant information was available and could have been considered earlier (chap. 6). A lesson: Task foreign ministry and intelligence networks to collect needed information before launching an economic negotiation[3] and factor it into a careful diagnosis. This chapter outlines types of information that will be needed.

Even after the best preparation, talks themselves often generate information that can make diagnosis more accurate. In chapter 7 agents of an engineers' union and management opened with conflicting positions regarding layoff rules, when in fact the parties' true, secret priorities allowed for some mutual gains. Neither negotiator knew the true situation completely at the outset, and probably neither could have known it without talking to the other. International negotiators made analogous discoveries in the international processes prior to Bretton Woods, on Brazilian instant coffee, and on Japanese beef. Sticking rigidly to a preconceived plan and failing to learn during the process could cost a negotiator missed opportunities.

2. AVOID SOME NEGOTIATIONS

Making a convincing case for bargaining means showing that the alternatives are worse. When Washington demands that Brazil tax its coffee exports and offers no concessions in return, the status quo is a better alternative for Brazil. The negotiator naturally will prefer not to bargain if the best alternative is better than the deal being considered by the other parties. In other cases it is more complicated to identify the value, political as well as economic, of the best alternative and of the likely outcome.

For economic negotiation, one popular alternative is to leave the matter to a market. *Waiting for the market to adjust* might or might not be the most efficient solution for a given economic problem and ought to be considered carefully. But delay can fail or even make matters worse when governments have political as well as efficiency objectives. In 1969, for example, one faction of the first Nixon administration advocated "benign neglect" of the U.S. payments deficit. Although

---

[3] I am grateful to Randall Henning for this suggestion.

the fixed dollar needed to decline relative to other currencies, this approach avoided official negotiations to bring it down. Instead the idea was that if Washington simply did nothing to restrain the outflows, markets would, in time, pressure surplus governments to upvalue their currencies against the dollar.[4] In that way President Nixon could avoid having to take the politically-dangerous initiative to devalue the dollar. The problem with this alternative was its assumption that other nations' politicians would accept the domestic political burden to solve Nixon's problem without any visible contribution from Nixon. Canada in 1970 and then West Germany in May 1971 did let their currencies float, but they were the only ones. Benign neglect failed in Tokyo, Paris, and other key capitals. (Only by devaluing the dollar himself did Nixon finally get agreement at the Smithsonian in 1971.) The seemingly apolitical alternative had to be abandoned and by then, delay during the calm of 1969–70 had shifted the official bargaining into a time when a gale was blowing. The world political economy went through a semi-chaotic two years of inflationary conflict among the most powerful governments that left the Bretton Woods institution much weakened. If the ship of state drifts with the wind, there is some risk of running aground.

Another alternative to bargaining is *new unilateral action*. During the 1980s Americans concerned about their yawning trade deficit sent trade negotiators abroad, with the goal, in some minds, of reducing that deficit. But the tools of the trade negotiator are too small to correct massive macroeconomic imbalances. For that goal, the United States had an alternative set of tools—especially domestic actions to shift the balance between national consumption and investment—that would have had a much stronger influence on the trade deficit. But these were not used very effectively in the 1980s.[5] Negotiating toward unrealistic goals is a recipe for disappointment. Those trade negotiations may still have been worthwhile as means toward more realistic goals.[6]

3. SELECT A STRATEGY THAT FITS THE SITUATION

Most generally, if bargaining is preferred but there is no positive zone of agreement, the situation indicates a strategy from the distributive side of the spectrum (chap. 2). If diagnosis finds a positive zone and partly consistent goals, a strategy from the integrative side probably offers the most efficient means.[7] If the situation

---

[4] Odell 1982a.

[5] Nau 1990.

[6] Bayard and Elliott 1994 and Schott 1994 assess some of them. For Paarlberg 1997, negotiating over agriculture via the Uruguay round did not prove superior to unilateral policy reform, and may have delayed reform in the United States. More generally, Paarlberg 1995.

[7] Chapter 2 defined a distributive or value-claiming strategy as a set of actions that promote the attainment of one party's goals when they are in conflict with those of the other party. An integrative or value-creating strategy is behavior that promotes the attainment of goals that are not in fundamental conflict, designed to expand the pie rather than split it. Purely integrative strategies are rarely observed in international relations.

is mixed or uncertain, then some intermediate, mixed strategy is indicated. For claiming value from others, chapters 6 and 7 are most directly relevant, and for partly-consistent objectives, chapters 5 and 7 focus the most directly. Other chapters address both types of situation.

The risk of hammering a square strategy into a round hole is especially great soon after having completed a successful negotiation. A diplomat should resist the temptation to apply the same strategy to a different country or in a different regime setting without bothering with a fresh diagnosis.

Market analysis (chap. 3) enters into strategy selection. For instance, consider using a mixed-integrative strategy toward economies or businesses that gain from market shifts when one's own country does, and a more distributive strategy toward those that gain when one's country loses.

The agent should estimate how the market at issue might change the negotiation process once it is underway, and if necessary, take that market into account in the strategy. Is this market relatively insensitive to official bargaining in the short run—like world monetary markets subject to controls during World War II, and like many goods markets during tariff negotiations since then? Or can official bargaining change this market's behavior quickly and thus entangle it and the negotiation process together—as with major foreign exchange markets in periods like 1969–73, 1985–87, and 1997–98? Will sensitive markets add any opportunity to claim value from another party or expose us to such claiming? When facing a short lag, what are the odds that making a proposal will stimulate markets to "overshoot," driving our government to choose a more extreme policy change than we prefer? Will a sensitive market tend to strangle an integrative scheme before advocates have had time to change initial skepticism? If so, can the official process be kept secret until a deal is set? Can policies be changed to lengthen the lag? Over the medium or long term, can companies be induced to enlarge the possibilities for integrative official deals, as the CFC talks suggested? Or will any foreseeable market trend extinguish any official deals that seem possible today, if governments do not move soon?

The negotiator should check each strategy option by estimating *the counterparts' most likely response to it* (chap. 4). If others will be skeptical of an effort to expand the common welfare as we see it and will exploit this strategy, caution is indicated whatever else might be said for it. If others will be open to such explorations, then a strict distributive strategy could destroy valuable opportunities for gain. While the other's response will probably have something to do with its position in the market, it will be risky to rely only on the facts about their market position as we frame them. Our agent needs information on the subjective level as well. Even if we regard our two countries' interests as compatible, do they? What do they see as their batna?

Any company, government, or international organization outside this prospective negotiation that may be affected by it could benefit by sketching a parallel negotiation analysis. Multinational investors have clear stakes in any official negotiations over rules on investment and trade in services. Poland watches while

European Union members bargain with one another over agricultural policy. European, Latin American, and Asian countries stand to be affected when Tokyo and Washington struggle over exchange rates and trade rules. A bargaining analysis that anticipated the primary parties' most likely strategies and outcomes could help third parties protect against future risks and take advantage of opportunities.

4. CUSTOMIZE A DISTRIBUTIVE STRATEGY

If diagnosis points to a strategy from the distributive side of the spectrum, our agent should customize the tactics to the particular situation, at the outset and as the process unfolds. For one thing, the initial situation might be altered by her own or others' bargaining moves, which could create either opportunities or risks. The initial situation is partly objective. Do not ignore objective no-deal alternatives or take them for granted. For claiming value, the agent should *consider ways to worsen the counterpart's alternative, improve our batna, or both*. In 1986 the American monetary negotiator "talked" the yen up, which may have squeezed greater macroeconomic policy concessions out of Tokyo. The agent also should imagine how others might do the same thing to her and plan to defend against such moves.

A more telling example of changing objective batnas "away from the table" arose during the 1960s in relations between U.S. multinational corporations, led by Kennecott and Anaconda, and the government of Chile concerning effective rights over copper properties. Kennecott anticipated the possibility of expropriation in the future and planned to defend against such claiming. Its managers put their new investments elsewhere; their Chilean mine accounted for only 13 percent of the firm's earnings in the mid-1960s.[8] When pressed by Santiago to expand production, Kennecott agreed to finance an expansion by selling 51 percent of their property to the Chilean government, and by taking out a loan from the U.S. government's Export-Import Bank. Thus expansion entailed no new financial risk for Kennecott. It also lined up other parties whose interests would be damaged if Chile nationalized the mine. In addition to the Ex-Im Bank, the U.S. Agency for International Development insured the new investment, making it obliged to pay Kennecott, in the case of expropriation without compensation, an amount larger than the entire value of its earlier Chilean operations. Besides engaging these two U.S. agencies, Kennecott sold future output from the mine to European and Asian customers, and sold collection rights on those contracts to two European and Japanese bank consortia. The aim of all these arrangements, in the words of a Kennecott executive, was "to insure that nobody expropriates Kennecott without upsetting relations to customers, creditors, and governments on three continents."[9]

---

[8] This paragraph relies on Moran 1973.

[9] Robert Haldeman, executive vice president of Kennecott's Chilean operations, interview in Santiago, 27 May 1970, quoted by Moran 1973, 279–80.

Anaconda, the other dominant multinational in Chilean copper, did not take such extensive steps to improve its own no-deal alternatives or worsen those of Santiago. It expanded its own capital investments in the country, such that 67 percent of the firm's total earnings came from Chile. Anaconda did not go to the same lengths to tie in other potential parties. After 1970 President Allende did expropriate both firms' mines without any compensation. Kennecott promptly sued in U.S. courts, and customers, bankers, and agencies on three continents brought pressures on Santiago exactly according to plan. The outcomes were a large compensation payment to Kennecott and none to Anaconda. Anaconda's board of directors fired its entire top management. A sound negotiation plan is not a mere luxury.

The initial situation is partly subjective, and *a counterpart's initial priorities and beliefs about batnas and possible agreements* may be altered or clarified without changes in objective facts. An overt threat of penalties is intended to lower the other's subjective resistance point without having to impose actual penalties on business. The U.S. threat in the EC enlargement episode (chap. 6) did sharply worsen European beliefs about the likely cost of no deal with Washington, compared with what they had assumed prior to Reagan's threat, and did so before any penalty duties had been collected. This threat would not have changed their behavior if it had not been credible. The EC-Brazil contrast identifies associated tactics that increase threat credibility—passing a supportive legislative resolution, naming the particular foreign industries to be hit, attaching a shorter fuse, making implementation less discretionary, and having carried out a threat in the past.[10]

Naturally the defending side will also want to tailor its tactics to the particular situation. Illustrations of defensive tactics in international negotiations appear in most of this book's episodes, including Brazil on instant coffee in 1966, Mexico and the United States on trade in the 1970s, and Japan on exchange rates and macroeconomics in the 1970s and 1980s and on beef in 1988.

A chief risk of a claiming strategy, including a defensive one, is that it will fail to discover gains for one's own side that could be realized only through joint value creation—opportunities which are sometimes invisible at first. An exclusively exploitative claimer will at least discourage creative, open exploration by the other side, and the harshest tactics risk provoking counterthreats and wider conflict. Even when parties' objectives are opposed for the most part, adding integrative tactics to the mix can, in some situations, gain more than adhering to strict claiming. Chapter 7 illustrated two such opportunities, one for an offensive claimer (Washington in the case of Japanese beef), and one for a defensive claimer (Brazil facing U.S. demands concerning instant coffee).[11]

---

[10] Even less powerful states have claimed some value by means of threats against more powerful ones, in rare cases. See Butler 1971 and Odell 1980.

[11] Additional distributive tactics are found in Lax and Sebenius 1986, chapter 6; Schelling 1960; Schelling 1966; Walton and McKersie 1965, chapter 3; Yoffie 1983.

Another consequence of strict claiming is that it may lead other parties to believe that in the future the actor will exploit an integrative strategy. If a party wants others to offer it such strategies, it should consider taking steps to reinforce the belief that it will respond favorably. Prior to the summer of 1971, Tokyo had given strong signals that it was not open to mutual-gains bargaining that would include a yen revaluation, and in 1971 this type of strategy was in fact not offered to Tokyo. Prior to the summer of 1985, Japan's government had not been sending the same uniformly negative signals, and Washington offered Tokyo a different, mostly value-creating strategy, despite a comparable market situation (chap. 4). To be sure, sending different signals today may be costly and one may have to make choices. In any case, today's actions, perhaps intended for a different purpose, may influence others' future strategy choices and thereby limit one's own.

5. CUSTOMIZE A MIXED-INTEGRATIVE STRATEGY

If, on the other hand, the situation points basically to a strategy from the integrative side of the spectrum, then the negotiator should customize its tactics for greater gain and protect it, too, from excessive narrowness, both at the outset and as the process unfolds.

Two broad scenarios for creating joint value through bargaining work from similarities and differences, respectively (chap. 7). In a world of distorted information, the most obvious tactics *explore for similar objectives or common problems* whose solution each would count as a gain. The Great Depression drove creation of the International Monetary Fund in 1944. European wars and economic incentives lead governments there to try unprecedented supranational integration by forming the European Coal and Steel Community in 1952. During exchange rate bargaining in 1985 (chap. 4), it turned out that finance ministers in both Japan and the United States were concerned about a common problem—rising protectionist pressure in the United States. In the ozone episode that yielded a 1987 agreement, governments initially disagreed over basic facts and whether any agreement could create a gain. But through negotiation and joint study many changed their initial positions and reached the conclusion that a worldwide reduction in use of chlorofluorocarbons would benefit them on balance, considering their environment as well as their economy. More recently, widespread dissatisfaction with weak enforcement of their trade claims under the GATT led member states of the World Trade Organization to agree in 1994 to strengthen their common institution for enforcing these rights established by their agreements.

The second broad approach is to *explore for differences in preference orders across issues, and for exchanges of concessions* that would make each party feel better off than without the exchange. Tactically this is accomplished either by finding concessions on existing agenda items to exchange, or by redefining the issues themselves. The parable in chapter 6 of two sisters who initially demanded the same orange, and the actual case of the engineers' union and the layoff rules, illustrated this form of exploration. A given agreement can include elements from each approach.

To implement either, *reduce initial uncertainty with research, either separate or joint*. One key question is always what will happen in markets, politics, and the environment if there is no new agreement. Additionally, at the outset of the Uruguay trade round, many governments were uncertain about exactly what would happen if barriers to trade in services were reduced. Not even Washington had studied precisely how various regulations affected these diverse industries within diverse countries. Governments did not know specifically what their national interests were. At the outset India attempted (unsuccessfully) to block the U.S. initiative to add this set of issues to the agenda. But later during the process, as India launched liberal reforms at home in 1991, New Delhi discovered that Indian service firms could reap substantial gains and changed its position.[12] For issues in dispute, joint research institutionalized through international organizations over a period of years might help open delegates' eyes to unsuspected opportunities for creating value via negotiation.[13]

To implement either scenario, the negotiator can consider *dividing the process into phases*. Especially with a highly complex problem, first propose that others agree on a broad *formula* that would specify the particular issues that need to be negotiated, giving diplomats a structure to organize the rest of their work. In 1942 Keynes and White each proposed a grand formula for reopening multilateral payments and avoiding currency conflicts after the war (chap. 9). The two formulas were not consistent in fundamental respects, and settling on one may involve distributive tactics in other cases as well. During the 1960s the governments that launched the Kennedy round initially vied over competing principles, finally agreeing on the formula that tariffs to be covered would be cut by half, but each government could propose items to be excluded and included. After the formula phase, subsequent talks get down to bargaining over the *details*.

When a negotiation involves multiple parties, *a complex strategy must identify a winning coalition and a tactical sequence for forming that coalition and breaking blocking coalitions*. A coalition is a means of claiming value as well as creating it. Elementary analysis will have identified the most affected parties and those that will be most influential, as either supporters or holdouts. One strategic question is how many parties should be included? Here bargainers often face a fundamental trade-off between the strength of the agreement and breadth of geographical coverage. Keeping the group small will reduce internal divisions and permit the like-minded to agree to more substantial commitments to each other. But then, more of the problem—currency instability, trade barriers, greenhouse gases, nuclear proliferation—will not be addressed, and in that sense the deal will probably create less value for the participants. The plan will need to make a choice regard-

---

[12] Paemen and Bensch 1995, 101.
[13] I am grateful to Robert Paarlberg for emphasizing this idea.

ing this dilemma as well. Given that decision, compare several alternative *tactical paths*: "easiest party first"; "most influential first"; "information first"; and "everybody first" (chap. 9).

When attempting to create joint value, how can the agent protect her side from exploitation? *The greatest risk of a pure integrative strategy* is that the other party will take advantage of one's relative openness. For instance, revealing one's true priorities creates an opportunity for the other to take a prime value hostage. After learning this information, the other could refuse to do anything to contribute to that value unless something substantial is relinquished on some other issue. Whenever parties have some genuine conflict of objectives, mixing at least some mild defensive tactics into the strategy, or holding some in reserve, will be a virtual necessity.[14]

6. TAKE ADVANTAGE OF MARKET CHANGES

After the process begins, the diplomat, whether primarily claiming or creating value, should monitor market conditions for changes that could open new opportunities or risks. *Some changes will aid the value claimer on one side of the market at the expense of the other side.* During the 1960s the rising world coffee price improved coffee exporters' alternatives to the International Coffee Agreement, creating a new claiming opportunity for them. During the same era, other developing countries gradually improved their technical skills in management of natural resources extraction, and many, not only Chile, demanded more favorable terms from multinational firms. Many company leaders were surprised by this "obsolescing" of their earlier bargains.[15] During the 1970s, however, some negotiators in developing countries overgeneralized from the stunning success of oil exporters to the conclusion that conditions were favorable for dramatic claiming over many other international commodity markets. Proponents of the New International Economic Order were exaggerating their chances, illustrating again the consequences of flawed negotiation analysis.[16]

Meanwhile, during the 1970s and 1980s, increases in scale economies in industries such as commercial aircraft and semiconductors increased incentives for the European Community, Japan, and the United States to attempt to claim value from each other through struggles to dominate these industries (chap. 3). As a final example, a sudden capital flight from country A to B, like those from East Asia and Russia in 1997 and 1998, will create a claiming opportunity for B and a vulnerability for A in macroeconomics, foreign aid and perhaps trade as well. Government A will need to be ready with defensive tactics.

In other ways, changing markets expand opportunities for governments to cre-

---

[14] Additional tactical ideas for creating value can be found in Walton and McKersie 1965 and Fisher and Ury 1981.
[15] Vernon 1971; Moran 1974, chapter 6.
[16] Krasner 1974, Smith 1977.

ate value. The prospect that companies would create a commercial substitute for chlorofluorocarbons probably moved the possibility frontier outward for governments negotiating over the ozone problem during the late 1980s and early 1990s. Governments could encourage firms to take such steps.

The prudent planner will estimate other negotiators' *beliefs* about how markets would respond both to possible deals and to stalemate. If others believe that a stalemate would lead to damaging market consequences, for example, they might initiate moves that would surprise us. Likewise they might reject a proposal that seems favorable for their country if they believe it would provoke a market reaction they wish to avoid.

7. COMPENSATE FOR JUDGMENT BIASES

Negotiating is partly an art, requiring cognitive judgments of the situation. Social psychologists have documented biases affecting the judgments of negotiators, including those with professional experience (chap. 5). A busy diplomat with incomplete information will be tempted to anchor estimates of important values—such as her no-deal alternative, the value of the other's proposal, and batnas of others—on handy available reference points, rather than canvassing comprehensively and making elaborate calculations. If the initial course of action generates negative consequences, she will be tempted, like Robert Campeau and Jorge Díaz Serrano, to remain committed or even increase the stakes rather than publicly acknowledge having made an error.

The best science indicates that the average negotiator will be biased toward distributive and away from integrative tactics. Partisans for one side tend to exaggerate the incompatibility of the two sides' goals, failing to see opportunities for mutual gain that neutral observers perceive. Without compensatory mechanisms, the partisan overestimates the value of her batna, which can cause both partisans to miss a genuine positive agreement zone between them. The partisan tends to use a self-serving concept of fairness, believes it to be impartial, and sees conflicting behavior by the other side as an effort to grab an unfair share. A mixed strategy can fail because of overly optimistic claiming, as in the 1977 case of Mexican gas exports.

What can be done? *When a minister seeks approval to negotiate, have her speak privately to a group meeting that includes "devil's advocates"* at the same or higher level, who are expected to ask questions that would uncover biases. A similar group could make interim assessments of the negotiation and help force mid-course corrections, should they be needed, before it is too late.

Even when the chief negotiator has had experience and special education in negotiation, *consider creating a team with at least one member assigned exclusively to monitor and report on other parties' beliefs.* Hearing these reports could function as a mechanism for correcting biases as well as providing useful tactical information. Reward these specialists according to the thoroughness and eventual accuracy of their estimates, however unwelcome the information may be to the chief negotiator. Rotate different individuals through this role, so that each team member develops the corresponding skills.

The diplomat may consider *hiring neutral consultants* to investigate, evaluate, and propose courses of action. Consultants from other countries may also supply more accurate information about the other side's beliefs, as in the Mexican vegetable trade case. Foreign technicians and well-connected lobbyists are not the only way to correct judgment biases, however, nor are they guaranteed to do so. Nationals might be better suited than foreigners in a given situation. Mexico has long stood out as a leader in developing its own internal expertise regarding U.S. institutions.[17]

Check also for any bias *against* claiming. For example, if a seller allows a buyer's low initial bid to anchor her aspiration for the outcome, she will use less demanding claiming tactics and gain less from that buyer than was possible if she had analyzed the other's resistance point more carefully. Loss aversion framing can work either way. If a negotiator thinks of a stalemate as foregoing a possible gain, rather than taking a loss of the same magnitude, she is likely to use less intense tactics to avoid that stalemate. This implies a greater chance of agreement but a smaller share of the gain than if she was fighting to avoid losing something she already had. Either a gain frame or a loss frame could be a bias if not understood in light of possible alternatives. The team should attack bias from both directions.

Consider assigning chief responsibility to different agents in different phases of the process. Some negotiators excel in defending the status quo, intimidating, and claiming value, while others' greatest talents lie in listening, relaxed interchange of information, discovering logrolls, and imagining new arrangements. One way to finesse the tension between claiming and creating value is first to send an integrative specialist to a secret intergovernmental "working group" to see what can be discovered, without making any commitment to accept the results. If a formula is agreed on and some attractive provisional deals come into view, consider sending a different, perhaps higher-ranking negotiator to a later phase, with instructions to protect the gains created provisionally but to claim as large a share as possible.

Take steps to offset or take advantage of other parties' biases as well. When claiming, the negotiator may identify the other's reference points for what counts as fair, and advance a different standard of fairness that is defensible internationally as well as being more favorable to her own side. Even if the others do not accept it, making the argument may at least undermine the tendency to attribute her behavior to unreasonable motives and conspiracies. When attempting to create joint gains, she may divert attention from partisan hostilities by exploring true preferences directly and relatively openly, for example by asking which issues rank the highest and which not quite so high for them. Or design a hypothetical

[17] Odell 1980.

package deal for the purpose of eliciting relative preferences more accurately, and ask whether the other would view it as a gain.

8. BUILD DOMESTIC POLITICS INTO THE NEGOTIATION PLAN

This implication jumps out from many chapters. It suggests powerful ways to customize a strategy for either creating mutual gains or claiming them. Many politicians have the idea that successful experience in business is good preparation for managing a government department and conducting international negotiations, at least on economic issues. But neither business experience nor the study of economics is sufficient preparation for what happens when the parties are national governments. Negotiators' moves can change the politics both at home and abroad.

If negotiators take the domestic political landscape for granted, they can step on a land mine. In the first Reagan administration, Treasury Secretary Donald Regan dismissed requests from abroad to negotiate agreements to manage exchange rates, claiming the Reagan administration would handle the economy unilaterally. But they failed to get Congress to agree to measures that would have kept the dollar from rocketing upward in the currency markets. Three years later after a huge import surge, Regan and Reagan faced an overflowing of demands for greater protection at home—surely not what they had intended to generate. This ideological free trader in fact granted more new protection than any President since Herbert Hoover.[18] It was after seeing their own politics backfire that the second Reagan administration decided in 1985 to change currency strategy (chap. 4), as well as to shift to offensive claiming over trade (chaps. 3 and 6).

In any future episode, estimating each country's national interest will not be enough. Sophisticated preparation means disaggregating—identifying which segments within each society will lose and which will benefit from the collapse of the Russian ruble, a trade sanction, or adoption of a new global warming regime. An agent also needs a sense of which domestic segments will weigh the heaviest in decisions on that issue.

When claiming value

An offensive claimer should beware the pitfall of making a threat that lacks sufficient support from the supposed beneficiary at home. Avoid offensive claiming when home opposition to implementing the threat will substantially undermine its credibility (chap. 6). If the strategy is chosen nonetheless, add domestic tactics to reduce this opposition and increase home support for hard claiming, ranging from public speeches to private side deals.

For a threatening strategy, relatively open domestic political institutions raise

---

[18] Magee and Young 1987.

an interesting longer-term dilemma. The most sophisticated governments maintain their own networks of contacts with American suppliers, customers, and bankers, and urge them to speak out politically in such cases. A U.S. government decision to issue a threat could itself worsen the government's credibility in subsequent episodes, if internal counterpressures in this one prove sufficient to tie the hands of the threatener, as they did for many months in the case of Brazil informatics. Negotiators should take this risk of embarrassment into account before launching the strategy.

When threat credibility is high, on the other hand, the risk is that the threat will stimulate greater conflict than its negotiator can control, because of domestic politics. From the U.S. standpoint, the EC episode (chap. 6) illustrates how to gain with this strategy. The EC yielded desired concessions, and hard claiming did not provoke an actual trade war or sour European political attitudes sufficiently to spoil a WTO deal or security cooperation. But in other cases threats always will carry the risk that after successfully stirring the home folks into hostility and raising expectations, the faction for conflict will block concessions needed for settlement or take the matter out of the negotiator's hands altogether. Our representatives should *monitor home politics for any emerging signs of such a loss of control, and if signs appear, consider tactics to deflate the hard line segment or settle abroad before it is too late.*

A claiming plan should *add tactics designed to persuade and rally potential supporters abroad, and if possible avoid tactics likely to energize opponents, or consider ways to buy them out or help their negotiator do so.*[19] When comparing strategy options, estimate the domestic scenarios each will most likely stimulate inside key countries, and factor these scenarios into decisions. In 1986 the same strategy generated greater U.S. gains from the more powerful party in part because the internal process moved more favorably in the EC than in Brazil. Interestingly, Brazilians later fell victim to analogous unintended consequences. Because of a success by the nationalist faction to codify the market reserve for software in 1986, the U.S. industry closed ranks behind Washington's hard line for the first time, compelling Brazilian diplomats to yield a significant concession—hardly what the nationalist faction had intended.

The claimer defending against a threat should likewise seek tactical opportunities in domestic politics abroad. Even a developing country facing a large industrial country or the IMF is not without defenses. The defender too should attempt to stimulate potential domestic supporters abroad to call for accommodation. When México's vegetable exporters faced a crippling antidumping duty in Washington in 1979, they illustrated not only these moves but also a different class of tactics that might be called technocratic. One masters the technical details of the relevant business and related laws, precedents, and institutions of the other country. Use this mastery to craft proposals that will better fit their institutional requirements, and thus persuade technical-level officials to accept arguments more

---

[19] The 1988 Japan beef case (chap. 6) illustrates one way to do so.

favorable to one's side.[20] Mobilizing influential allies at the political level to twist arms may prove less effective or insufficient, and the two tactics are not mutually exclusive.[21] Local subsidiaries of multinational corporations based in one's own country can become allies in such tactical efforts. But anticipating companies' political behavior requires as careful a diagnosis as that of governments, judging from the informatics case. Which way a company goes will be a function of the political bargaining process, not just market conditions and purely commercial calculations.

When creating value

The negotiator using a mixed-integrative strategy should scan actively for risks and opportunities in domestic politics abroad and at home. International Monetary Fund negotiators use mixed strategies with borrowing governments, offering loans in return for policy reforms. Fund diplomats often make implicit bets on how domestic politics in those countries will react. During spring 1998, the Fund offered balance-of-payments loans to Indonesia's government, insisting that Jakarta quickly end subsidies for food and fuel, reportedly without fully understanding how much pain these concessions would cause poor Indonesians and how much rioting would result. Having stepped on a mine, Fund negotiators quickly became more flexible with the government.[22] Evidently the IMF position would have been more flexible earlier had it been able to anticipate domestic politics more accurately.

Domestic politics gives the integrative negotiator a well-known incentive to *keep the process secret*. The founders of the European Community, for example, conducted their historic 1950 negotiation in secret, insulating their agents from minority pressures that might have vetoed particular concessions before a package deal was reached. Secrecy may well disturb some citizens who, as environmentalists or employees of particular industries, prefer to have full information and the chance to stop any step that would be contrary to their preferences. But with unqualified transparency, the government negotiator will have a more difficult time negotiating gains for the country as a whole. Citizens on each side of the domestic aisle might use interim information to kill trades of concessions that would benefit the whole. *An institutionalized ratification phase* is the time for full transparency and participation. When negotiators must anticipate it, an open ratification process should provide a formidable safeguard against abuse.

The negotiator trying to claim as well as create value must manage the same two-level tactical dilemma in which Mexico's petroleum negotiator found himself in 1977. He made a public commitment to a given sale price, which can be expected to increase its credibility abroad but also to raise domestic expectations. If

---

[20] See Odell 1980 for additional examples of technocratic tactics, which were associated more closely with success in trade disputes than almost any other approach.

[21] Odell 1985 and Odell and Lang 1992 illustrate defensive tactics used by Korea on trade issues.

[22] *New York Times*, 2 October 1998, 1; 30 October 1998, C1.

a negotiator miscalculates and fails to get agreement at such a price, then constituents may punish her politically if she settles for less, even if the lesser deal is better than the country's best alternative. Yet if she does not rally constituents during the process, she may have less leverage abroad. The lesson of that particular case is to *either avoid making such a public commitment before the home audience, make it more ambiguous, or make certain the proposed deal is not outside the zone of agreement.*

Domestic institutions

If domestic institutions hamper effective negotiations, institutional change may be in order. If ratification failures are a problem, tightening the slack between the agent and principals during the talks should keep the two closer together (chap. 8), though it may mean fewer international agreements will be reached. Additionally, if one negotiator has greater autonomy at home while other agents' domestic institutions keep them on short tethers, the latter may be able to claim from the former a larger share of whatever gain is created internationally.[23]

9. SELECT OR MODIFY AN INTERNATIONAL ORGANIZATION?

This book concentrates on bilateral negotiation—for analytical reasons, because they have been neglected, and because no book can treat everything equally. But of course multilateral rules and institutions cover many issues in today's world economy, and negotiators face frequent decisions about using them.

One practical decision is whether to negotiate outside an organization or under its umbrella. When more than one organization has jurisdiction, a second question is which forum to select. These institutions vary enormously as to which nations belong, the precision of their rules, the strength of enforcement, and how much authority governments delegate to joint bodies and secretariats. Should a developing country with a sudden monetary deficit seek credit from private banks, friendly governments, the IMF, or some combination? For dealing globally with the threat of periodic financial crises, which forum is best—the G7 leading financial powers, a new Asian organization, or the IMF? Should governments of Thailand and Malaysia negotiate new trade agreements bilaterally, or under the ASEAN umbrella, or through Asia-Pacific Economic Cooperation which includes more states but has no enforcement authority, or through the World Trade Organization, which has much stronger enforcement authority but does not include some trading states? Should the European Union try to negotiate new codes of conduct on foreign investments bilaterally, or under the OECD which does not cover developing countries, or in the WTO, which does?

[23] Regarding international monetary policy, Henning 1994 offers suggestions for institutional changes for Germany, Japan, and the United States.

One option is to propose changes in international rules or creation of a new organization. In this book the negotiations at Bretton Woods, in Havana in 1948, and in the Uruguay round were of this type. One reason for strengthening the WTO dispute settlement mechanism during the Uruguay round was to divert governments away from claiming bilaterally and toward using this quieter forum instead. Chapter 6 speculated that this may be happening. Might changes in monetary or other international organizations have similar effects on negotiators' strategy choices?

At the same time, we saw that ongoing multilateral talks may not always constrain aggressive national policies in the short term. This intuition—that keeping the bicycle rolling is a good way to keep it from falling over—is widespread, and it may be valid on average. Ongoing negotiations that are believed to have some chance of creating joint gains ought to give all parties a special incentive not to thwart the prospective deal, and give executives an argument to use at home to delay new protection measures. Yet in the Uruguay round the presence of a coalition blocking the new U.S. demands may have made one of those bilateral threats *more* likely. Regime bargaining sometimes may amplify conflict along the way, straining relationships, even if the end result is a collective improvement. We need deeper applied research to support negotiator decisions about bargaining with and within international organizations (chap. 9).

10. EDUCATE ALL NEGOTIATORS IN NEGOTIATION ANALYSIS

Surely the most efficient way to acquire expertise in this process is not to learn exclusively by doing—not to walk into the first meeting without prior study that could have transmitted the findings of earlier bargainers and researchers. Yet this is exactly how it happens often, especially in the United States, famous for its "government of strangers."[24] Many governments, including the United States, do provide dedicated negotiation training to their career diplomats. But U.S. Foreign Service Officers are not the chief negotiators for many of their country's economic negotiations. Typically these tasks are assigned to political appointees for short terms in the White House, the Departments of the Treasury, Agriculture, Energy, Commerce, and Transportation, the Environmental Protection Agency, Federal Communications Commission, U.S. Trade Representative's office, and even in the Department of State itself—often without any special education in two-level international bargaining. Nor do the immediate principals—Congress members and staff—necessarily have such education. Some incumbents may have studied the subject in law or graduate schools years earlier, but this is not a general requirement. Nor typically will the new U.S. economic negotiator, looking through her file cabinets, find internal records of even that office's own negotia-

[24] Heclo 1977.

tions more than two or three years old, let alone lessons from analogous episodes that occurred outside that office's purview.

Undoubtedly on-the-job learning is valuable, and perhaps more so than any other form, for developing practical expertise. Still, there is no guarantee that any individual's experiences will have generated a comprehensive mental road map equivalent to the findings of research designed for that purpose. Our countries should not be represented by anyone who is insensitive to pitfalls and opportunities that any reader of a book like this would know. Any negotiator should have participated at least briefly in executive education designed to sharpen this form of expertise, to show how to design and supervise complex negotiations. This short course should be open to legislators or their staffs.

Naturally no theory or amount of training will guarantee perfect results. As in playing cards or managing a sports team on the field, any bargainer plays the odds. But knowing the process is a potent advantage. To reduce conflict among nations and gain more from our partnerships, it will not be enough to have the best intentions and command of the economics. Only by applying astute negotiation analysis will our governments excel when negotiating the world economy.

Partly Subjective Theory

A partly subjective theory sometimes provokes questions: How can we ever get evidence adequate for identifying what negotiators truly believe? What can be done if little or no direct evidence is available? How can such a theory avoid becoming circular, or so complex and particular as to lose its claim to be theory at all?

First and most important, if we think actors' expectations, beliefs, and values truly are part of the causal chain, then the best theory should represent what we think as accurately as possible, without regard to anticipated data problems. Why would it be better to substitute other concepts and lead ourselves in the wrong direction? Omitting subjective concepts altogether may seem a convenient way to draw attention away from the need to gather evidence for them, but such thinking is short-sighted. It reduces the theory's value for guiding both research and practice. I believe the academic habit of sweeping this problem under the rug is one reason why so few international politics practitioners respect and use political science theories.

Second, we should seek the most direct evidence we can get about beliefs, and the weaker the evidence the more cautious we should be, as with any other claim. Suppose the belief in question is attitudes toward a proposal to liberalize trade in services on the part of negotiators for various governments. One analyst might use trade data as a rough proxy for attitudes: assume that negotiators for countries with a services export surplus will favor the proposal and those representing importing countries will oppose. Even evidence this remote, if offered explicitly as an indicator for a subjective theoretical variable, will move us toward valid theory faster than research that misstates the theory in the first place. More direct, more nuanced, and more convincing would be public statements by the negotiators expressing their attitudes. In turn, such statements are less convincing alone than public statements plus confidential interviews with negotiators and with others who have been present while they have spoken in private, and so forth. At the end of the day, of course no inference from evidence in social science is free from all uncertainty. All empirical methods have inherent drawbacks, and these are matters of degree. We should aim, over time, to improve on the evidence that has been collected before.

Third, no theory is worthy of the label if it becomes infinitely complex. Mine is limited by simplifying assumptions, and it highlights certain beliefs and biases, not all conceivable ones. Beyond some point, however, even experts differ regarding the ideal trade-off between simplicity and empirical validity, and they probably always will.

Operational Definitions of Negotiating Strategies

VALUE-CLAIMING STRATEGY

Code a party's strategy as pure claiming if any of the following actions are observed and no more than a small minority of the behavior fits the definition of value creating.

Both defensive and offensive variants

The negotiator

- criticizes the other party's actions or arrangements, blames it for the problem under discussion;
- attempts to exclude from the agenda issues on which her side would probably have to make concessions;
- rejects or ignores demands for concessions or delays their consideration;
- avoids saying her side is partly responsible for the problem under discussion, avoids expressing concern for the other's objectives or a desire for a mutual-gain outcome, avoids making a proposal characterized a beneficial to the other parties or the world as a whole;
- manipulates information for her own advantage: avoids revealing information about her own genuine objectives and priorities; makes arguments whose effect is to support her demands or refusal to concede and does not present information or arguments that are inconsistent with that position; e.g., argues that the other's alternative to agreement is worse for them than they realize, that her alternative is better than they realize, or that the other's forecasts showing future improvement for her (in absence of agreement) are not convincing, or that she simply does not have the capacity to deliver what is demanded; or that the other's proposal would harm her side or others;
- establishes a commitment to a particular outcome, by means of some public action tied to that outcome such that accepting less would be costly to the negotiator or her country;
- denies that she believes the other's commitments.

Offensive variant

The negotiator also

- demands concessions for the benefit of her own side;
- files a formal complaint against the other under global or regional rules;
- takes steps to worsen the other's alternative to agreement and improve her own—e.g., unilateral actions or negotiations with third parties that would help compensate her country for a breakdown in relations with the other or provide itself with a superior alternative, or raise the cost of a breakdown for the other; actions could include introducing draft legislation for official consideration at home or "talking the national currency down";
- threatens to take action harmful to others unless they yield the desired concessions;
- actually imposes such penalties and implements her alternative to agreement.

Defensive variant

The negotiator also

- brings a countercomplaint against the other under international rules;
- threatens or imposes countersanctions.

VALUE-CREATING STRATEGY

Code a party's strategy as pure value creating if the following actions or tactics are observed and if no more than a small minority of the behavior fits value claiming. The negotiator

- states that the two (or more) parties have an interest in common or expresses concern for an objective held by the other;
- proposes negotiations designed to benefit both sides, usually aiming to agree on a joint approach to a common problem or an exchange of concessions;
- praises the other and avoids public statements criticizing the other country or blaming it for the problem or issue under discussion;
- invites the other to state frankly its genuine concerns and objectives and their priority order, as distinguished from its demands and proposals;
- proposes and implements a series of meetings whose only or main purpose is to engage the parties in joint study of problems and objectives they have in common;
- uses and refers to information about the issue or problem without shaping it to her side's advantage; engages in an even-handed discussion of all the facts whether favorable or unfavorable to her side;

- proposes an exchange of concessions for mutual benefit;
- argues that a different conception of other's interests or a redefinition of the issues could lead to an agreement that would benefit both parties;
- proposes an agreement described as helpful to other parties as well.

MIXED OR COMBINED STRATEGY

Code a party's behavior in a conflict or negotiation as a mixed strategy if claiming and creating tactics are mixed in some proportion, either simultaneously, or in a sequence dominated by claiming in one phase and creating in another.

References

Aaronson, Susan Ariel. 1993. "For the People, but not by the People: A History of the International Trade Organization (ITO)." Ph.D. diss., Johns Hopkins University.

———. 1996. *Trade and the American Dream: A Social History of Postwar Trade Policy.* Lexington, Ky.: University Press of Kentucky.

Adler, Emanuel. 1986. "Ideological 'Guerrillas' and the Quest for Technological Autonomy: Brazil's Domestic Computer Industry." *International Organization* 40: 673–706.

Adler, Robert S., Benson Rosen, and Elliot M. Silverstein. 1998. "Emotions in Negotiation: How to Manage Fear and Anger." *Negotiation Journal* 14: 161–79.

Aggarwal, Vinod K. 1985. *Liberal Protectionism: The International Politics of Organized Textile Trade.* Berkeley: University of California Press.

———. 1996. *Debt Games: Strategic Interaction in International Debt Rescheduling.* Cambridge: Cambridge University Press.

Alker, Hayward R. 1988. "The Dialectical Logic of Thucydides' Melian Dialogue." *American Political Science Review* 82: 805–20.

The American Chamber of Commerce in Japan. 1997. *Making Trade Talks Work: Lessons from Recent History.* Tokyo: ACCJ.

Angel, Robert C. 1991. *Explaining Economic Policy Failure: Japan in the 1969–1971 International Monetary Crisis.* New York: Columbia University Press.

Axelrod, Robert. 1978. "Argumentation in Foreign Policy Settings: Britain in 1918, Munich in 1938, and Japan in 1970." In *The Negotiation Process: Theories and Applications,* ed. I. William Zartman, 175–92. Beverly Hills: Sage.

Babcock, Linda, and George Loewenstein. 1997. "Explaining Bargaining Impasse: The Role of Self-Serving Biases." *The Journal of Economic Perspectives* 11: 109–26.

Bailey, John J., and Gustavo Vega Canovas. 1989. *The Mexico-U.S. Natural Gas Negotiations of 1977–1979.* Pew Case Studies in International Affairs, 146. Washington, D.C.: Institute for the Study of Diplomacy, School of Foreign Service, Georgetown University.

Baldwin, David A. 1985. *Economic Statecraft.* Princeton: Princeton University Press.

Baldwin, Robert E. 1985. *The Political Economy of U.S. Import Policy.* Cambridge, Mass.: MIT Press.

———. 1986. "Trade Policies in Developed Countries." In *International Trade: Surveys of Theory and Policy,* ed. Ronald Jones. Amsterdam: North-Holland.

Bartlett, David, and Anna Seleny. 1998. "The Political Enforcement of Liberalism: Bargaining, Institutions, and Auto Multinationals in Hungary." *International Studies Quarterly* 42: 319–38.

Bartos, Otomar J. 1978. "Simple Model of Negotiation: A Sociological Point of View." In *The Negotiation Process: Theories and Applications,* ed. I. William Zartman, 13–27. Beverly Hills: Sage.

Bastos, Maria-Ines. 1994. *Winning the Battle to Lose the War: Brazilian Electronics Policy under US Threat of Sanctions.* Essex, England: Frank Cass and Company.

Bates, Robert H. 1997. *Open-Economy Politics: The Political Economy of the World Coffee Trade.* Princeton: Princeton University Press.

Bayard, Thomas O., and Kimberly Ann Elliott. 1994. *Reciprocity and Retaliation in US Trade Policy*. Washington, D.C.: Institute for International Economics.

Bazerman, Max H., and Margaret A. Neale. 1992. *Negotiating Rationally*. New York: Free Press.

Berejekian, Jeffrey. 1997. "The Gains Debate: Framing State Choice." *American Political Science Review* 91: 789–805.

Bendor, Jonathan. 1995. "A Model of Muddling Through." *American Political Science Review* 89: 819–40.

Benedick, Richard Elliot. 1991. *Ozone Diplomacy: New Directions in Safeguarding the Planet*. Cambridge, Mass.: Harvard University Press.

——. 1993. "Perspectives of a Negotiation Practitioner." In *International Environmental Negotiation,* ed. Gunnar Sjöstedt, 219–43. Newbury Park, Calif.: Sage Publications.

Bennett, D. Scott. 1996. "Security, Bargaining, and the End of Interstate Rivalry." *International Studies Quarterly* 40: 157–84.

Berejekian, Jeffrey. 1997. "The Gains Debate: Framing State Choice." *American Political Science Review* 91: 789–805.

Bergsten, C. Fred, and C. Randall Henning. 1996. *Global Economic Leadership and the Group of Seven*. Washington, D.C.: Institute for International Economics.

Berton, Peter, Hiroshi Kimura, and I. William Zartman, eds. 1999. *International Negotiation: Actors, Structure/Process, End Values*. New York: St. Martin's Press.

Beyers, Jan, and Guido Dierickx. 1997. "Nationality and European Negotiations: The Working Groups of the Council of Ministers." *European Journal of International Relations* 3: 435–71.

Blair, David J. 1993. *Trade Negotiations in the OECD: Structures, Institutions and States*. New York: Kegan Paul International.

Bloomfield, Richard J. 1972. *Who Makes American Foreign Policy? Some Latin American Case Studies*. Cambridge, Mass.: Center for International Affairs, Harvard University.

Bonham, G. Matthew, Victor M. Sergeev, and Pavel B. Parshin. 1997. "The Limited Test-Ban Agreement: Emergence of New Knowledge Structures in International Negotiations." *International Studies Quarterly* 41: 215–40.

Brett, Jeanne M., Wendi Adair, Alain Lempereur, Tetsushi Okumura, Peter Shikhirev, Catherine Tinsley, and Ann Lytle. 1998. "Culture and Joint Gains in Negotiation." *Negotiation Journal* 14: 61–87.

Bueno de Mesquita, Bruce. 1990. "Multilateral Negotiations: a Spatial Analysis of the Arab-Israeli Dispute." *International Organization* 44: 317–40.

Bueno de Mesquita, Bruce, James D. Morrow, and Ethan R. Zorick. 1997. "Capabilities, Perception, and Escalation." *American Political Science Review* 91: 15–27.

Bunn, George. 1992. *Arms Control by Committee: Managing Negotiations with the Russians*. Stanford, Calif.: Stanford University Press.

Butler, Robert W., Jr. 1971. "Trade Conflict: The Mexican-Canadian Yarn War of 1969–1970." *Inter-American Economic Affairs* 25: 21–30.

Calvert, Randall L., Mathew D. McCubbins, and Barry R. Weingast. 1989. "A Theory of Political Control and Agency Discretion." *American Journal of Political Science* 33: 588–611.

Cameron, Maxwell A. 1997. "North American Free Trade Negotiations: Liberalization Games Between Asymmetric Players." *European Journal of International Relations* 3: 105–39.

Campbell, John C. 1949. *The United States in World Affairs 1948–1949*. New York: Harper & Brothers.

Chang, Jaw-ling Joanne. 1991. "Negotiation of the 17 August 1982 U.S.-PRC Arms Communiqué: Beijing's Negotiating Tactics." *The China Quarterly* 125: 33–54.

Chang, Roberto. 1995. "Bargaining a Monetary Union." *Journal of Economic Theory* 66: 89–112.

Clarke, Stephen V. O. 1973. *The Reconstruction of the International Monetary System: The Attempts of 1922 and 1933*. Princeton Studies in International Finance, No. 33. Princeton, N.J.: International Finance Section, Department of Economics, Princeton University.

Cohen, Andy. 1996. "Getting to Yes, Chinese Style (Negotiations in China)." *Sales and Marketing Management* 148: 44–46.

Cohen, Benjamin J. 1990. "The Political Economy of International Trade." *International Organization* 44: 261–81.

Cohen, Raymond. 1991. *Negotiating Across Cultures: Communication Obstacles in International Diplomacy*. Washington, D.C.: U.S. Institute of Peace.

Cohn, T. 1978–1980. "The 1978–79 Negotiations for an International Wheat Agreement: An Opportunity Lost?" *International Journal* 35: 132–49.

Conlisk, John. 1996. "Why Bounded Rationality?" *Journal of Economic Literature* 34: 669–700.

Conybeare, John A. C. 1987. *Trade Wars: The Theory and Practice of International Commercial Rivalry*. New York: Columbia University Press.

Cordell, Arthur J. 1969. "The Brazilian Soluble Coffee Problem: A Review." *Quarterly Review of Economics and Business* 9: 29–38.

Cottam, Martha L. 1985. "The Impact of Psychological Images on International Bargaining: the Case of Mexican Natural Gas." *Political Psychology* 6: 413–40.

Cowhey, Peter F. 1993. "Domestic Institutions and the Credibility of International Commitments: Japan and the United States." *International Organization* 47: 299–326.

Cowhey, Peter F., and Jonathan D. Aronson. 1993. *Managing the World Economy: The Consequences of Corporate Alliances*. New York: Council on Foreign Relations Press.

Cross, John G. 1978. "Negotiation as a Learning Process" In *The Negotiation Process: Theories and Applications*, ed. I. William Zartman, 29–54. Beverly Hills: Sage Publications.

Curran, Timothy J. 1983. "The Politics of Trade Liberalization." *Journal of International Affairs* 37: 49–66.

Dabringhausen, Michaela. 1997. "The End of International Pegged Exchange Rates? How Industries Influence Governments' Ability to Maintain a Political Exchange Rate Regime." Ph.D. diss., University of Chicago.

De Rivera, Joseph. 1968. *The Psychological Dimension of Foreign Policy*. Columbus, Ohio: Merrill.

Destler, I. M. 1995. *American Trade Politics*, 3d ed. Washington, D.C. and New York: Institute for International Economics and the Twentieth Century Fund.

Destler, I. M., and C. Randall Henning. 1989. *Dollar Politics: Exchange Rate Policymaking in the United States*. Washington, D.C.: Institute for International Economics.

Destler, I. M., Haruhiro Fukui, and Hideo Sato. 1979. *The Textile Wrangle: Conflict in Japanese-American Relations, 1969–1971*. Ithaca: Cornell University Press.

Destler, I. M., and John S. Odell. 1987. *Anti-Protection: Changing Forces in U.S. Trade Politics*. Washington, D.C.: Institute for International Economics.

Diebold, William, Jr. 1952. *The End of the ITO*. Essays in International Finance, No. 16. Princeton, N.J.: International Finance Section, Department of Economics, Princeton University.

Dornbusch, Rudiger, and Jeffrey A. Frankel. 1987. "Macroeconomics and Protection." In

U.S. Trade Policies in a Changing World Economy, ed. Robert M. Stern, 77–130. Cambridge, Mass.: MIT Press.

Downs, George W. 1989. "The Rational Deterrence Debate." *World Politics* 41: 225–37.

Downs, George W., and David M. Rocke. 1990. *Tacit Bargaining, Arms Races, and Arms Control*. Ann Arbor: The University of Michigan Press.

Dryden, Steve. 1995. *Trade Warriors: USTR and the American Crusade for Free Trade*. New York: Oxford University Press.

Duffy, Gavan, Brian K. Frederking, and Seth A. Tucker. 1998. "Language Games: Dialogical Analysis of INF Negotiations." *International Studies Quarterly* 42: 271–94.

Eckes, Alfred E., Jr. 1975. *A Search for Solvency*. Austin: University of Texas Press.

Eichengreen, Barry. 1989. "Hegemonic Stability Theories of the International Monetary System." In *Can Nations Agree?* Richard N. Cooper, Barry Eichengreen, C. Randall Henning, Gerald Holtham, and Robert D. Putnam. Washington, D.C.: Brookings.

Eisenberg, Theodore. 1994. "Differing Perceptions of Attorney Fees in Bankruptcy Cases." *Washington University Law Quarterly* 72: 979–95.

Elliott, Kimberly Ann. 1998. "The Sanctions Glass: Half Full or Completely Empty?" *International Security* 23: 50–65.

Encarnation, Dennis, and Louis T. Wells, Jr. 1985. "Sovereignty en Garde: Negotiating with Foreign Investors." *International Organization* 39: 47–78.

Epstein, David, and Sharyn O'Halloran. 1994. "Administrative Procedures, Information, and Agency Discretion." *American Journal of Political Science* 38: 697–722.

Evans, Peter. 1986. "State, Capital, and the Transformation of Dependence: The Brazilian Computer Case." *World Development* 14: 791–808.

———. 1989. "Declining Hegemony and Assertive Industrialization: U.S.-Brazil Conflicts in the Computer Industry." *International Organization* 43: 207–38.

———. 1993. "Building an Integrative Approach to International and Domestic Politics: Reflections and Projections." In *Double-Edged Diplomacy: International Bargaining and Domestic Politics*, ed. Peter B. Evans, Harold K. Jacobson, and Robert D. Putnam, 397–430. Berkeley: University of California Press.

Evans, Peter, Harold K. Jacobson, and Robert D. Putnam, eds. 1993. *Double-Edged Diplomacy: International Bargaining and Domestic Politics*. Berkeley: University of California Press.

Fagen, Richard R., and Henry R. Nau. 1979. "Mexican Gas: The Northern Connection." In *Capitalism and the State in U.S.-Latin American Relations*, ed. Richard R. Fagen, 382–424. Stanford: Stanford University Press.

Faure, Guy Olivier, and Jeffrey Z. Rubin, eds. 1993. *Culture and Negotiation*. Newbury Park, Calif.: Sage Publications.

Fearon, James D. 1991. "Counterfactuals and Hypothesis Testing in Political Science." *World Politics* 43: 169–95.

———. 1994. "Domestic Political Audiences and the Escalation of International Disputes." *American Political Science Review* 88: 577–92.

———. 1998. "Bargaining, Enforcement, and International Cooperation." *International Organization* 52: 269–308.

Feis, Herbert. 1966. *Characters in Crisis*. Boston, Little, Brown.

Felder, Ellene A., and Andrew Hurrell. 1988. *The U.S.-Brazilian Informatics Dispute*. Pew Case Studies in International Affairs, 122. Washington, D.C.: The Foreign Policy Institute, Johns Hopkins University.

Finnemore, Martha. 1996. *National Interests in International Society*. Ithaca: Cornell University Press.

Finnemore, Martha, and Kathryn Sikkink. 1998. "International Norm Dynamics and Political Change." *International Organization* 52: 887–918.

Fisher, Bart S. 1972. *The International Coffee Agreement: A Study in Coffee Diplomacy.* New York: Praeger.

Fisher, Roger, and William Ury. 1981. *Getting to Yes: Negotiating Agreement without Giving In.* Boston: Houghton Mifflin.

Frankel, Jeffrey. 1996. *Regional Trading Blocs.* Washington, D.C.: Institute for International Economics.

Frieden, Jeffry A. 1988a. "Capital Politics: Creditors and the International Political Economy." *Journal of Public Policy* 8: 265–86.

——. 1988b. "Sectoral Conflict and U.S. Foreign Economic Policy, 1914–1940." *International Organization* 42: 59–90.

——. 1991. "Invested Interests: The Politics of National Economic Policies in a World of Global Finance." *International Organization* 45: 425–52.

Friedheim, Robert L. 1993. *Negotiating the New Ocean Regime.* Columbia, South Carolina: University of South Carolina Press.

Friman, H. Richard. 1993. "Side Payments versus Security Cards: Domestic Bargaining Tactics in International Economic Negotiations." *International Organization* 47: 387–410.

Funabashi, Yoichi. 1988. *Managing the Dollar: From the Plaza to the Louvre.* Washington, D.C.: Institute for International Economics.

Ganitsky, Joseph, and Elizabeth A. Burnham. 1971. *Maxwell House Division of General Foods: The International Coffee Agreement.* Case 4–371–479. Boston: Harvard Business School.

Gardner, Richard N. 1956. *Sterling-Dollar Diplomacy: Anglo-American Collaboration in the Reconstruction of Multilateral Trade.* Oxford: Clarendon Press.

Garrett, Geoffrey. 1992. "International Cooperation and Institutional Choice: the European Community's Internal Market." *International Organization* 46: 533–60.

Garrett, Geoffrey, and Barry R. Weingast. 1993. "Ideas, Interests and Institutions: Constructing the E.C.'s Internal Market." In *Ideas and Foreign Policy: Beliefs, Institutions, and Political Change*, ed. Judith Goldstein and Robert O. Keohane, 173–106. Ithaca: Cornell University Press.

George, Alexander L. 1969. "The 'Operational Code': A Neglected Approach to the Study of Political Leaders and Decision-Making." *International Studies Quarterly* 13: 190–222.

George, Alexander L., and Juliette George. 1964. *Woodrow Wilson and Colonel House.* New York: Dover Publications.

George, Alexander L., and William E. Simons, eds. 1994. *The Limits of Coercive Diplomacy.* 2d ed. Boulder: Westview Press.

Gilmer, Robert W. 1980. "Federal Regulation and the National Market for Natural Gas." *Texas Business Review* 54: 138–43.

Gilpin, Robert. 1975. *U.S. Power and the Multinational Corporation: The Political Economy of Foreign Direct Investment.* New York: Basic Books.

Glenny, M. V. 1970. "The Anglo-Soviet Trade Agreement, March 1921." *Journal of Contemporary History* 5: 63–82.

Goldstein, Joshua S., and Jon C. Pevehouse. 1997. "Reciprocity, Bullying and International Cooperation: Time-Series Analysis of the Bosnia Conflict." *American Political Science Review* 91: 515–29.

Goldstein, Judith. 1993. *Ideas, Interests, and American Trade Policy.* Ithaca: Cornell University Press.

——. 1996. "International Law and Domestic Institutions: Reconciling North American 'Unfair' Trade Laws." *International Organization* 50: 541–65.

Goldstein, Judith, and Robert O. Keohane, eds. 1993. *Ideas and Foreign Policy: Beliefs, Institutions and Political Change.* Ithaca: Cornell University Press.

Goodman, John B. 1992. *Monetary Sovereignty: The Politics of Central Banking in Western Europe*. Ithaca: Cornell University Press.

Goodman, John B., Debora L. Spar, and David B. Yoffie. 1996. "Foreign Direct Investment and the Demand for Protection in the United States." *International Organization* 50: 565–92.

Gourevitch, Peter. 1986. *Politics in Hard Times*. Ithaca: Cornell University Press.

Gowa, Joanne. 1984. "Hegemons, IOs, and Markets: The Case of the Substitution Account." *International Organization* 38: 661–83.

——. 1994. *Allies, Adversaries, and International Trade*. Princeton: Princeton University Press.

Graham, John L. 1993. "The Japanese Negotiation Style: Characteristics of a Distinct Approach." *Negotiation Journal* 9: 123–40.

Grayson, George W. 1980. *The Politics of Mexican Oil*. Pittsburgh: University of Pittsburgh Press.

Grieco, Joseph. 1990. *Cooperation among Nations: Europe, America, and Non-tariff Barriers to Trade*. Ithaca: Cornell University Press.

Haas, Ernst B. 1958. *The Uniting of Europe: Political, Social and Economic Forces 1950–1957*. Stanford: Stanford University Press.

——. 1980. "Why Collaborate? Issue-Linkage and International Regimes." *World Politics* 32: 357–405.

Haas, Peter M. 1992. "Banning Chlorofluorocarbons: Epistemic Community Efforts to Protect Stratospheric Ozone." *International Organization* 46: 187–224.

Haggard, Stephan, and Beth A. Simmons. 1987. "Theories of International Regimes." *International Organization* 41: 491–517.

Hall, Peter A. 1986. *Governing the Economy: The Politics of State Intervention in Britain and France*. New York: Oxford University Press.

Hampson, Fen Osler, and Michael Hart. 1994. *Multilateral Negotiations: Lessons from Arms Control, Trade and the Environment*. Baltimore: Johns Hopkins University Press.

Hart, Michael, Bill Dymond, and Colin Robertson. 1994. *Decision at Midnight: Inside the Canada-US Free-Trade Negotiations*. Vancouver: UBC Press.

Hasenclever, Andreas, Peter Mayer, and Volker Rittberger. 1997. *Theories of International Regimes*. Cambridge: Cambridge University Press.

Heclo, H. Hugh. 1977. *A Government of Strangers*. Washington, D.C.: Brookings.

Heilperin, Michael. 1949. "How the US Lost the ITO Conferences." *Fortune* 40: 80–82.

Helleiner, Eric. 1994. *States and the Reemergence of Global Finance: From Bretton Woods to the 1990s*. Ithaca: Cornell University Press.

Henning, C. Randall. 1994. *Currencies and Politics in the United States, Germany and Japan*. Washington, D.C.: Institute for International Economics.

Hoekman, Bernard M., and Michel M. Kostecki. 1995. *The Political Economy of the World Trading System: From GATT to WTO*. Oxford: Oxford University Press.

Hoffmann, Stanley. 1960. "Problems of Scope, Method and Purpose." In *Contemporary Theory in International Politics*, ed. Stanley Hoffman, 4–12. Englewood Cliffs: Prentice Hall.

Holsti, Ole R. 1972. *Crisis, Escalation, War*. Montreal and London: McGill-Queen's University Press.

Hopmann, P. Terrence. 1974. "Bargaining in Arms Control Negotiations: The Sea Beds Denuclearization Treaty." *International Organization* 28: 313–443.

——. 1996. *The Negotiation Process and the Resolution of International Conflicts*. Columbia, South Carolina: University of South Carolina Press.

Hopmann, P. Terrence, and Theresa C. Smith. 1978. "An Application of a Richardson Process Model: Soviet-American Interactions in the Test Ban Negotiations 1962–1963." In *The Negotiation Process: Theories and Applications*, ed. I. William Zartman, 149–74. Beverly Hills: Sage Publications.

Horsefield, J. K. 1969. *The International Monetary Fund 1945–1965*. Washington, D.C.: International Monetary Fund.

Hudec, Robert E. 1993. *Enforcing International Trade Law: GATT Dispute Settlement in the 1980s*. Salem, New Hampshire: Butterworth Legal Publishers.

Hudson, Valerie, ed. 1991. *Artificial Intelligence and International Politics*. Boulder: Westview Press.

Hufbauer, Gary C., Jeffrey J. Schott, and Kimberly Ann Elliott. 1990. *Economic Sanctions Reconsidered: History and Current Policy*, 2d ed. Washington, D.C.: Institute for International Economics.

Iida, Keisuke. 1993. "Analytic Uncertainty and International Cooperation: Theory and Application to International Economic Policy Coordination." *International Studies Quarterly* 37: 431–57.

———. 1995. "International Cooperation in Exchange Rate Management: Coordination of U.S. and Japanese Intervention, 1977–1990." *International Interactions* 20: 279–96.

———. 1996. "Involuntary Defection in 2-Level Games." *Public Choice* 89: 283–303.

Iklé, Fred Charles. 1964. *How Nations Negotiate*. New York: Harper & Row.

Irwin, Douglas A. 1995. "The GATT's Contribution to Economic Recovery in Post-War Western Europe." In *Europe's Post-War Recovery*, ed. Barry Eichengreen. Cambridge: Cambridge University Press.

Jackson, John H. 1990. *Restructuring the GATT System*. New York: Council on Foreign Relations Press.

———. 1996. "The WTO Dispute Settlement Procedures: A Preliminary Appraisal." In *The World Trading System: Challenges Ahead*, ed. Jeffrey J. Schott, 153–66. Washington, D.C.: Institute for International Economics.

Janis, Irving. 1972. *Victims of Groupthink: A Psychological Study of Foreign Policy Decisions and Fiascoes*. Boston: Houghton Mifflin.

Jervis, Robert. 1976. *Perception and Misperception in International Politics*. Princeton: Princeton University Press.

Jervis, Robert, and Janice Gross Stein. 1985. *Psychology and Deterrence*. Baltimore: Johns Hopkins University Press.

Johnson, Chalmers. 1982. *MITI and the Japanese Miracle: The Growth of Industrial Policy, 1925–1975*. Stanford: Stanford University Press.

Jönsson, Christer. 1987. *International Aviation and the Politics of Regime Change*. New York: St. Martin's Press.

———. 1990. *Communication in International Bargaining*. London: Pinter Publishers.

Jönsson, Christer, and Jonas Tallberg. 1998. "Compliance and Post-Agreement Bargaining." *European Journal of International Relations* 4: 371–408.

Kahler, Miles. 1993. "Multilateralism with Small and Large Numbers." *International Organization* 46: 68–708.

Kahneman, Daniel, Jack L. Knetsch, and Richard H. Thaler. 1990. "Experimental Tests of the Endowment Effect and Coase Theorem." *Journal of Political Economy* 98: 1325–48.

Kapstein, Ethan B. 1989. "Resolving the Regulator's Dilemma: International Coordination of Banking Regulation." *International Organization* 43: 323–47.

———. 1994. *Governing the Global Economy: International Finance and the State*. Cambridge, Mass.: Harvard University Press.

Katzenstein, Peter, ed. 1978. *Between Power and Plenty*. Madison: University of Wisconsin Press.

——. 1996. *The Culture of National Security: Norms and Identity in World Politics*. New York: Columbia University Press.

Keeley, James F. 1983. "Cast in Concrete for all Time? The Negotiation of the Auto Pact." *Canadian Journal of Political Science* 16: 281–98.

Kemp, K. E., and Smith W. P. 1994. "Information Exchange, Toughness, and Integrative Bargaining—The Roles of Explicit Cues and Perspective-Taking." *International Journal of Conflict Management* 5: 5–21.

Keohane, Robert O. 1984. *After Hegemony: Cooperation and Discord in the World Political Economy*. Princeton: Princeton University Press.

Keohane, Robert O., and Helen V. Milner, eds. 1996. *Internationalization and Domestic Politics*. Cambridge: Cambridge University Press.

Keohane, Robert O., and Joseph S. Nye. 1977. *Power and Interdependence: World Politics in Transition*. Boston: Little, Brown.

Kindleberger, Charles. 1973. *The World in Depression, 1929–1939*. Berkeley: University of California Press.

——. 1981. "Dominance and Leadership in the International Economy: Exploitation, Public Goods, and Free Rides." *International Studies Quarterly* 25: 242–54.

Kirkbride, Paul S., and Sara F. Y. Tang. 1990. "Negotiation: Lessons from Behind the Bamboo Curtain (China)." *Journal of General Management* 16: 1–12.

Kirshner, Jonathan. 1995. *Currency and Coercion: The Political Economy of International Monetary Power*. Princeton: Princeton University Press.

Kobrin, Stephen J. 1987. "Testing the Bargaining Hypothesis in the Manufacturing Sector in Developing Countries." *International Organization* 41: 609–38.

Kolb, Deborah M., and Guy-Olivier Faure. 1994. "Organization Theory: The Interface of Structure, Culture, Procedures, and Negotiation Processes." In *International Multilateral Negotiation: Approaches to the Management of Complexity*, ed. I. William Zartman, 113–31. San Francisco: Jossey-Bass Publishers.

Kowert, Paul A., and Margaret G. Hermann. 1997. "Who Takes Risks? Daring and Caution in Foreign Policy Making." *Journal of Conflict Resolution* 41: 611–37.

Krasner, Stephen D. 1971. "The Politics of Primary Commodities: A Study of Coffee 1900–1970." Ph.D. diss., Harvard University.

——. 1974. "Oil is the Exception." *Foreign Policy* 14: 68–83.

——. 1976. "State Power and the Structure of International Trade." *World Politics* 28: 317–47.

——. 1985. *Structural Conflict: The Third World Against Global Liberalism*. Berkeley: University of California Press.

——. 1991. "Global Communications and National Power: Life on the Pareto Frontier." *World Politics* 43: 336–66.

——. 1993. "Sovereignty, Regimes, and Human Rights." In *Regime Theory and International Relations*, ed. Volker Rittberger, 139–67. Oxford: Clarendon Press.

Krauss, Ellis S. 1993. "U.S.-Japan Negotiations on Construction and Semiconductors, 1985–88." In *Double-Edged Diplomacy: International Bargaining and Domestic Politics*, ed. Peter B. Evans, Harold K. Jacobson, and Robert D. Putnam, 265–99. Berkeley: University of California Press.

Krauss, Ellis S., and Simon Reich. 1992. "Ideology, Interests, and the American Executive: Toward a Theory of Foreign Competition and Manufacturing Trade Policy." *International Organization* 46: 857–97.

Kusano, Atsushi. 1983. *Nichibei Orenji Kosho (The Japan-US Orange Negotiations)*. Tokyo: Nihon Keizai Shimbunsha.

Kuznets, Simon. 1966. *Modern Economic Growth*. New Haven: Yale University Press.

Lake, David A. 1988. *Power, Protection, and Free Trade: International Sources of U.S. Commercial Strategy, 1887–1939*. Ithaca: Cornell University Press.

——. 1993. "Leadership, Hegemony, and the International Economy: Naked Emperor or Tattered Monarch with Potential?" *International Studies Quarterly* 37: 459–89.

Larson, Deborah. 1985. *Origins of Containment: A Psychological Explanation*. Princeton: Princeton University Press.

Lawrence, Robert Z. 1996. "Regionalism and the WTO: Should the Rules Be Changed?" In *The World Trading System: Challenges Ahead*, ed. Jeffrey J. Schott, 41–56. Washington, D.C.: Institute for International Economics.

Lax, David A., and James K. Sebenius. 1986. *The Manager as Negotiator: Bargaining for Cooperation and Competitive Gain*. New York: Free Press.

——. 1991. "Thinking Coalitionally: Party Arithmetic, Process Opportunism, and Strategic Sequencing." In *Negotiation Analysis*, ed. H. Peyton Young, 153–93. Ann Arbor: University of Michigan Press.

League of Nations. 1945. *Industrialization and Foreign Trade*. Princeton: Princeton University Press.

Legro, Jeffrey W. 1996. "Culture and Preferences in the International Cooperation Two-Step." *American Political Science Review* 90: 118–37.

Leng, Russell J. 1993. "Reciprocating Influence Strategies in Interstate Crisis Bargaining." *Journal of Conflict Resolution* 37: 3–41.

Levy, Jack S. 1992. "Prospect Theory and International Relations: Theoretical Applications and Analytical Problems." *Political Psychology* 13: 283–310.

——. 1994. "Learning and Foreign Policy: Sweeping a Conceptual Minefield." *International Organization* 48: 279–312.

——. 1997. "Prospect Theory, Rational Choice, and International Relations." *International Studies Quarterly* 41: 87–112.

Lewicki, Roy J. 1997. "Teaching Negotiation and Dispute Resolution in Colleges of Business: The State of the Practice." *Negotiation Journal* 13: 253–70.

Li, Chien-pin. 1993. "The Effectiveness of Sanction Linkages: Issues and Actors." *International Studies Quarterly* 37: 349–70.

Lieber, Robert J. 1970. *British Politics and European Unity: Parties, Elites and Pressure Groups*. Berkeley: University of California Press.

Liebert, Robert M., William P. Smith, J. H. Hill, and Miriam Keiffer. 1968. "The Effects of Information and Magnitude of Initial Offer on Interpersonal Negotiation." *Journal of Experimental Social Psychology* 4: 431–41.

Lipson, Charles H. 1976. "Corporate Preferences and Public Policies: Foreign Aid Sanctions and Investment Protection." *World Politics* 28: 396–421.

Magee, Stephen, and Leslie Young. 1987. "Endogenous Protection in the United States, 1900–1984." In *U.S. Trade Policies in a Changing World Economy*, ed. by Robert M. Stern. Cambridge, Mass.: MIT Press.

Mannix, Elizabeth A., Catherine H. Tinsley, and Max H. Bazerman. 1995. "Negotiating over Time: Impediments to Integrative Solutions." *Organizational Behavior and Human Decision Processes* 62: 241–51.

Mares, David R. 1987. *Penetrating the International Market: Theoretical Considerations and a Mexican Case Study*. New York: Columbia University Press.

Martin, Lisa L. 1992. *Coercive Cooperation: Explaining Multilateral Economic Sanctions*. Princeton: Princeton University Press.

——. 2000. *Democratic Commitments: Legislatures and International Cooperation*. Princeton: Princeton University Press.

Martin, Lisa L., and Beth A. Simmons. 1998. "Theories and Empirical Studies of International Institutions." *International Organization* 52: 729–58.

Mayer, Frederick W. 1998. *Interpreting NAFTA: The Science and Art of Political Analysis.* New York: Columbia University Press.

McDonough, Mark G. 1979. *Panama Canal Treaty Negotiations,* Part A and Part B. Kennedy School of Government Cases C14–79–223 and C14–79–224. Cambridge, Mass.: Kennedy School of Government, Harvard University.

McKeown, Timothy J. 1983. "Hegemonic Stability Theory and 19th Century Tariff Levels in Europe." *International Organization* 37: 73–91.

Merton, Robert K. 1968. *Social Theory and Social Structure,* enlarged ed. New York: Free Press.

Messerlin, Patrick A. 1996. "France and Trade Policy: Is the 'French Exception' *Passée*?" *International Affairs* 72: 298–310.

Meyer, John W., David John Frank, Ann Hironaka, Evan Schofer, and Nancy Brandon Tuma. 1997. "The Structuring of a World Environmental Regime, 1870–1990." *International Organization* 51: 623–51.

Mill, John Stuart. 1843. "System of Logic." *Philosophy of Scientific Method*, ed. Ernest Nagel. London: Longmans.

Milner, Helen V. 1988. *Resisting Protectionism: Global Industries and the Politics of International Trade.* Princeton: Princeton University Press.

———. 1992. "International Theories of Cooperation among Nations: Strengths and Weaknesses." *World Politics* 44: 466–96.

———. 1997. *Interests, Institutions, and Information: Domestic Politics and International Relations.* Princeton: Princeton University Press.

Milner, Helen V., and B. Peter Rosendorff. 1997. "Democratic Politics and International Trade Negotiations: Elections and Divided Government as Constraints on Trade Liberalization." *Journal of Conflict Resolution* 41: 117–46.

Milner, Helen V., and David B. Yoffie. 1989. "Between Free Trade and Protectionism: Strategic Trade Policy and a Theory of Corporate Trade Demands." *International Organization* 43: 239–72.

Mingst, Karen A., and Craig P. Warkentin. 1996. "What Difference Does Culture Make in Multilateral Negotiations?" *Global Governance* 2: 169–88.

Mo, Jongryn. 1994. "The Logic of Two-Level Games with Endogenous Domestic Coalitions." *Journal of Conflict Resolution* 38: 402–22.

Moler, Elizabeth, and James Bruce. 1979. *Mexico: The Promise and Problems of Petroleum.* Washington: U. S. Senate Committee on Energy and Natural Resources.

Moran, Theodore H. 1973. "Transnational Strategies of Protection and Defense by Multinational Corporations: Spreading the Risk and Raising the Cost for Nationalization in Natural Resources." *International Organization* 27: 273–301.

———. 1974. *Multinational Corporations and the Politics of Dependence: Copper in Chile.* Princeton: Princeton University Press.

Moravcsik, Andrew. 1997. "Taking Preferences Seriously: A Liberal Theory of International Politics." *International Organization* 51: 513–53.

———. 1998. *The Choice for Europe: Social Purpose & State Power from Messina to Maastricht.* Ithaca: Cornell University Press.

———. 1999. "A New Statecraft? Supranational Entrepreneurs and International Cooperation." *International Organization* 53: 267–306.

Morgan, T. Clifton, and Valerie L. Schwebach. 1997. "Fools Suffer Gladly: The Use of Economic Sanctions in International Crises." *International Studies Quarterly* 41: 27–50.

Mosely, Paul. 1987. *Conditionality as a Bargaining Process: Structural Adjustment Lend-*

ing, 1980–1986. Essays in International Finance, No. 168. Princeton, N.J.: International Finance Section, Department of Economics, Princeton University.

Nau, Henry. 1990. *The Myth of America's Decline: Leading the World Economy into the 1990s*. New York: Oxford University Press.

Neale, Margaret A., and Max H. Bazerman. 1991. *Cognition and Rationality in Negotiation*. New York: Free Press.

Neustadt, Richard E. 1980. *Presidential Power: The Politics of Leadership*. New York: Wiley Press.

Noland, Marcus. 1997. "Chasing Phantoms: The Political Economy of USTR." *International Organization* 51: 365–88.

North, Douglass C., and Barry R. Weingast. 1989. "Constitution and Commitment: The Evaluation of Institutions Governing Public Choice in Seventeenth-century England." *Journal of Economic History* 49: 803–32.

Northcraft, Gregory B., and Margaret A. Neale. 1987. "Amateurs, Experts, and Real Estate: An Anchoring-and-Adjustment Perspective on Property Pricing Decisions." *Organizational Behavior and Human Decision Processes* 39: 84–97.

Oatley, Thomas, and Robert Nabors. 1998. "Redistributive Cooperation: Market Failure, Wealth Transfers, and the Basle Accord." *International Organization* 52: 35–55.

Odell, John S. 1979. "The Politics of Debt Relief: Official Creditors and Brazil, Ghana and Chile." In *Debt and the Less Developed Countries*, ed. Jonathan D. Aronson, 253–81. Boulder: Westview Press.

——. 1980. "Latin American Trade Negotiations with the United States." *International Organization* 34: 207–28.

——. 1982a. "Bretton Woods and International Political Disintegration: Implications for Monetary Diplomacy." In *The Political Economy of Domestic and International Monetary Relations*, eds. Raymond Lombra and William Witte, 39–58. Ames, Iowa: Iowa State University Press.

——. 1982b. *U.S. International Monetary Policy: Markets, Power, and Ideas as Sources of Change*. Princeton: Princeton University Press.

——. 1985. "The Outcomes of International Trade Conflicts: The U.S. and South Korea, 1960–1981." *International Studies Quarterly* 29: 263–86.

——. 1988. "From London to Bretton Woods: Sources of Change in Bargaining Strategies and Outcomes." *Journal of Public Policy* 8: 287–316.

——. 1990. "Understanding International Trade Policies: An Emerging Synthesis." *World Politics* 43: 139–67.

Odell, John S., and Anne Dibble. 1992. *Brazilian Informatics and the United States: Defending Infant Industry Versus Opening Foreign Markets*. Pew Case Studies in International Affairs, 128, Parts A and B. Washington, D.C.: Institute for the Study of Diplomacy, School of Foreign Service, Georgetown University.

Odell, John S., and Barry Eichengreen. 1998. "The United States, the ITO, and the WTO: Exit Options, Agent Slack, and Presidential Leadership." In *The WTO as an International Organization*, ed. Anne O. Krueger, 181–209. Chicago: University of Chicago Press.

Odell, John S., and David Lang. 1992. *Korean Joggers*. Pew Case Studies in International Affairs, 129. Washington, D.C.: Institute for the Study of Diplomacy, School of Foreign Service, Georgetown University.

Odell, John S., and Margit Matzinger-Tchakerian. 1991. *European Community Enlargement and the United States*. Pew Case Studies in International Affairs, 130, Parts A and B. Washington, D.C.: Institute for the Study of Diplomacy, School of Foreign Service, Georgetown University.

O'Halloran, Sharyn. 1994. *Politics, Process and American Trade Policy*. Ann Arbor: University of Michigan Press.

Oxley, Alan. 1990. *The Challenge of Free Trade*. New York: St. Martin's Press.

Oye, Kenneth A., ed. 1986. *Cooperation Under Anarchy*. Princeton: Princeton University Press.

———. 1992. *Economic Discrimination and Political Exchange: World Political Economy in the 1930s and 1980s*. Princeton: Princeton University Press.

Paarlberg, Robert L. 1995. *Leadership Abroad Begins at Home: U.S. Foreign Economic Policy after the Cold War*. Washington, D.C.: Brookings.

———. 1997. "Agricultural Policy Reform and the Uruguay Round: Synergistic Linkage in a Two-Level Game?" *International Organization* 51: 413–44.

Paemen, Hugo, and Alexandra Bensch. 1995. *From the GATT to the WTO: The European Community in the Uruguay Round*. Leuven: Leuven University Press.

Pape, Robert A. 1997. "Why Economic Sanctions Do Not Work." *International Security* 22: 90–136.

Parson, Edward A. 1997. "International Environmental Negotiations: The Current State of Empirical and Analytic Study." *Negotiation Journal* 13: 161–84.

Pen, Jan. 1952. "A General Theory of Bargaining." *American Economic Review* 42: 24–42.

Peterson, Susan. 1996. *Crisis Bargaining and the State: The Domestic Politics of International Conflict*. Ann Arbor: University of Michigan Press.

Porges, Amelia. 1994. "Japan: Beef and Citrus." In *Reciprocity and Retaliation in U.S. Trade Policy*, ed. Thomas O. Bayard and Kimberly Ann Elliott, 233–66. Washington, D.C. Institute for International Economics.

Powell, Robert. 1988. "Nuclear Brinkmanship with Two-Sided Incomplete Information." *American Political Science Review* 82: 155–78.

Preeg, Ernest H. 1970. *Traders and Diplomats: An Analysis of the Kennedy Round of Negotiations Under the GATT*. Washington, D.C.: Brookings.

———. 1995. "The Post-Uruguay Round Free Trade Debate." *The Washington Quarterly* 19: 223–38.

Prestowitz, Clyde V., Jr. 1988. *Trading Places: How We Allowed Japan to Take the Lead*. New York: Basic Books.

Pruitt, Dean G., and Jeffrey Z. Rubin. 1986. *Social Conflict: Escalation, Stalemate and Settlement*. New York: Random House.

Putnam, Robert D. 1988. "Diplomacy and Domestic Politics: The Logic of Two-Level Games." *International Organization* 42: 427–60.

Putnam, Robert D., and Nicholas Bayne. 1987. *Hanging Together: Cooperation and Conflict in the Seven-Power Summits*. London: Sage Publications.

Rabin, Matthew. 1998. "Psychology and Economics." *Journal of Economic Literature* 36: 11–46.

Raiffa, Howard. 1982. *The Art and Science of Negotiation*. Cambridge, Mass.: Harvard University Press.

Raustiala, Kal. 1997. "Domestic Institutions and International Regulatory Cooperation: Comparative Responses to the Convention on Biological Diversity." *World Politics* 49: 482–509.

Ravenhill, John. 1979–1980. "Asymmetrical Interdependence: Renegotiating the Lomé Convention." *International Journal* 25: 150–69

Reich, Michael, Yoshio Endo, and Peter Timmer. 1986. "Agriculture: The Political Economy of Structural Change." In *America versus Japan*, ed. Thomas McCraw, 151–92. Cambridge, Mass.: Harvard University Press.

Remmer, Karen L. 1998. "Does Democracy Promote Interstate Cooperation? Lessons from the Mercosur Region." *International Studies Quarterly* 42: 25–52.

Rhodes, Carolyn. 1993. *Reciprocity, US Trade Policy, and the GATT Regime*. Ithaca: Cornell University Press.

Rightor-Thornton, Anne H. 1975. "An Analysis of the Office of the Special Representative for Trade Negotiations: The Evolving Role 1962–1974." In *Report. Volume 3. Appendix H*. U.S. Commission on the Organization of the Government for the Conduct of Foreign Policy, 88–104.

Rogowski, Ronald. 1989. *Commerce and Coalitions: How Trade Affects Political Alignments*. Princeton: Princeton University Press.

Rooth, T. J. T. 1984. "Limits of Leverage: The Anglo-Danish Trade Agreement of 1933." *Economic History Review* 37: 211–28.

Ross, Robert S. 1995. *Negotiating Cooperation: The United States and China, 1969–1989*. Stanford: Stanford University Press.

Rothstein, Robert L. 1979. *Global Bargaining: UNCTAD and the Quest for a New International Economic Order*. Princeton: Princeton University Press.

Ryan, Michael P. 1991. "Strategy and Compliance with Bilateral Trade Dispute Settlement Agreements: USTR's Section 301 Experience in the Pacific Basin." *Michigan Journal of International Law* 12: 799–827.

——. 1995. "USTR's Implementation of 301 Policy in the Pacific." *International Studies Quarterly* 39: 333–50.

Safire, William. 1975. *Before the Fall: An Inside View of the Pre-Watergate White House*. Garden City: Doubleday.

Sandholtz, Wayne, and John Zysman. 1989. "1992: Recasting the European Bargain." *World Politics* 42: 95–128.

Sato, Hideo, and Timothy J. Curran. 1982. "Agricultural Trade: The Case of Beef and Citrus." In *Coping with U. S. - Japanese Economic Conflicts*, ed. I. M. Destler and Hideo Sato, 121–84. Lexington, Mass.: Lexington Books.

Schelling, Thomas C. 1960. *The Strategy of Conflict*. Cambridge, Mass.: Harvard University Press.

——. 1966. *Arms and Influence*. New Haven: Yale University Press.

Schoppa, Leonard J. 1999. "The Social Context in Coercive International Bargaining." *International Organization* 53: 307–42.

Schott, Jeffrey J., ed. 1989. *Free Trade Areas and U.S. Trade Policy*. Washington, D.C.: Institute for International Economics.

——. 1994. *The Uruguay Round: An Assessment*. Washington, D.C.: Institute for International Economics.

Schultz, Kenneth A. 1998. "Domestic Opposition and Signaling in International Crises." *American Political Science Review* 92: 829–44.

Schuman, Robert. 1953. "Origines et Elaboration du Plan Schuman." *Cahiers De Bruges*: 13–18.

Sebenius, James K. 1983. "Negotiating Arithmetic: Adding and Subtracting Issues and Parties." *International Organization* 37: 281–316.

——. 1984. *Negotiating the Law of the Sea: Lessons in the Art and Science of Reaching Agreement*. Cambridge, Mass.: Harvard University Press.

——. 1991. "The Negotiation Analytic Approach." In *International Negotiation: Problems and New Approaches*, ed. Victor Kremenyuk, 203–15. San Francisco: Jossey-Bass.

——. 1992a. "Challenging Conventional Explanations of International Cooperation: Negotiation Analysis and the Case of Epistemic Communities." *International Organization* 46: 323–66.

——. 1992b. "Formal Individual Mediation and the Negotiators' Dilemma: Tommy Koh at the Law of the Sea Conference." In *Mediation in International Relations: Multiple Approaches to Conflict Management*, ed. Jacob Bercovitch and Jeffrey Z. Rubin. London: Macmillan.

——. 1992c. "Negotiation Analysis: A Characterization and Review." *Management Science* 38: 19–38.

——. 1996. "Sequencing to Build Coalitions: With Whom Should I Talk First?" In *Wise Choices: Decisions, Games, and Negotiations*, ed. Richard J. Zeckhauser and others, 324–48. Boston: Harvard Business School Press.

Shenkar, Oded, and Simcha Ronen. 1987. "The Cultural Context of Negotiations: The Implications of Chinese Interpersonal Norms." *Journal of Applied Behavioral Science* 23: 263–75.

Simmons, Beth A. 1994. *Who Adjusts? Domestic Sources of Foreign Economic Policy During the Interwar Years*. Princeton: Princeton University Press.

Simon, Herbert A. 1982. *Models of Bounded Rationality. Volume 1. Economic Analysis and Public Policy. Volume 2. Behavioral Economics and Business Organization*. Cambridge, Mass.: MIT Press.

——. 1997. *Models of Bounded Rationality. Volume 3. Empirically Grounded Economic Reason*. Cambridge, Mass.: MIT Press.

Sissons, D. C. S. 1981. "Private Diplomacy in the 1936 Trade Dispute with Japan." *Australian Journal of Politics and History* 27: 143–59.

Sjöstedt, Gunnar, ed. 1993. *International Environmental Negotiation*. Beverly Hills: Sage.

Skalnes, Lars S. 1998. "Grand Strategy and Foreign Economic Policy: British Grand Strategy in the 1930s." *World Politics* 50: 582–616.

Smith, David N., and Louis T. Wells, Jr. 1975. *Negotiating Third World Mineral Agreements: Promises as Prologue*. Cambridge, Mass.: Ballinger.

Smith, Tony. 1977. "Changing Configurations of Power in North-South Relations Since 1945." *International Organization* 31: 1–28.

Snidal, Duncan. 1985. "The Limits of Hegemonic Stability Theory." *International Organization* 39: 579–614.

——. 1991. "Relative Gains and the Patterns of International Cooperation." *American Political Science Review* 85: 701–26.

Snyder, Glenn, and Paul Diesing. 1977. *Conflict among Nations: Bargaining, Decision Making, and System Structure in International Crises*. Princeton: Princeton University Press.

Spar, Debora L. 1992. "Co-developing the FSX Fighter: The Domestic Calculus of International Co-operation." *International Journal* 47: 265–92.

Staw, Barry M. 1976. "Knee-Deep in the Big Muddy: A Study in Escalating Commitment to a Chosen Course of Action." *Organizational Behavior and Human Performance* 16: 27–44.

Stein, Janice Gross, ed. 1989. *Getting to the Table: The Processes of International Prenegotiation*. Baltimore: Johns Hopkins University Press.

——. 1993. "The Political Economy of Security Agreements: The Linked Costs of Failure at Camp David." In *Double-Edged Diplomacy: International Bargaining and Domestic Politics*, ed. Peter B. Evans, Harold K. Jacobson, and Robert D. Putnam, 77–103. Berkeley: University of California Press.

Stein, Janice Gross, and Louis W. Pauly, eds. 1992. *Choosing to Cooperate: How States Avoid Loss*. Baltimore: Johns Hopkins University Press.

Stewart, Terence. 1994. *The GATT Uruguay Round: A Negotiating History*. Deventer: Kluwer.

Stoever, William. 1981. *Renegotiations in International Business Transactions: The Pro-*

cess of Dispute Resolution Between Multinational Investors and Host Societies. Lexington, Mass.: Lexington Books.

Susskind, Lawrence E. 1994. *Environmental Diplomacy: Negotiating More Effective Global Agreements*. New York: Oxford University Press.

Suzuki, Motoshi. 1994. "Economic Interdependence, Relative Gains, and International Cooperation: The Case of Monetary Policy Coordination." *International Studies Quarterly* 38: 475–99.

Taylor, Paul. 1983. *The Limits of European Integration*. New York: Columbia University Press.

Tetlock, Philip E., and Aaron Belkin. 1996. *Counterfactual Thought Experiments in World Politics: Logical, Methodological, and Psychological Perspectives*. Princeton: Princeton University Press.

Thompson, Leigh. 1990. "Negotiation Behavior and Outcomes: Empirical Evidence and Theoretical Issues." *Psychological Bulletin* 108: 515–32.

——. 1995. "They Saw a Negotiation: Partisanship and Non-Partisan Perspectives." *Journal of Personality and Social Psychology* 68: 839–53.

Thompson, Leigh, and G. Loewenstein. 1992. "Egocentric Interpretations of Fairness and Negotiation." *Organizational Behavior and Human Decision Processes* 51: 176–97.

Thompson, W. Scott. 1975. *Unequal Partners: Philippine and Thai Relations with the United States, 1965–1975*. Lexington, Mass.: Lexington Books.

Tollison, Robert, and Thomas D. Willett. 1979. "An Economic Theory of Mutually Advantageous Issue Linkages in International Negotiations." *International Organization* 33: 425–450.

Triffin, Robert. 1957. *Europe and the Money Muddle*. New Haven: Yale University Press.

Tse, David K., June Francis, and Jan Walls. 1994. "Cultural Differences in Conducting Intra- and Intercultural Negotiations: A Sino-Canadian Comparison." *Journal of International Business Studies* 25: 537–55.

Tucker, Jonathan B. 1991. "Partners and Rivals: A Model of International Collaboration in Advanced Technology." *International Organization* 45: 83–120.

Tung, Rosalie L. 1982. "U.S.-China Trade Negotiations: Practices, Procedures and Outcomes." *Journal of International Business Studies* 13: 25–37.

Tyson, Laura D'Andrea. 1992. *Who's Bashing Whom? Trade Conflict in High-Technology Industries*. Washington D.C.: Institute for International Economics.

U.S. Advisory Committee for Trade Policy and Negotiations. 1994. *A Report to the President, the Congress, and the United States Trade Representative concerning the Uruguay Round of Negotiations on the General Agreement on Tariffs and Trade*.

U.S. President. 1994. *Economic Report of the President*.

U.S. President. 1995. *Economic Report of the President*.

Urban, Laszlo K. 1983. "Once More with Hindsight: German-Polish Interwar Trade Negotiations." *East European Quarterly* 17: 89–108.

Van Dormael, Armand. 1978. *Bretton Woods: Birth of a Monetary System*. New York: Holmes and Meier.

Varg, Paul A. 1976. "The Economic Side of the Good Neighbor Policy: The Reciprocal Trade Program and South America." *Pacific History Review* 45: 47–71.

Verdier, Daniel. 1994. *Democracy and International Trade: Britain, France, and the United States, 1860–1990*. Princeton: Princeton University Press.

Vernon, Raymond. 1971. *Sovereignty at Bay: The Multinational Spread of U. S. Enterprise*. New York: Basic Books.

——. 1995. "The World Trade Organization: A New Stage in International Trade and Development." *Harvard International Law Journal* 36: 329–40.

Vietor, Richard H. K. 1982. *Mexican Natural Gas*. Case 9–382–048. Boston: Harvard Business School.

Volcker, Paul, and Toyoo Gyohten. 1992. *Changing Fortunes: The World's Money and the Threat to American Leadership*. New York: Times Books.

von Furstenberg, George M. 1991. "Policy Undertakings by the Seven 'Summit' Countries: Ascertaining the Degree of Compliance." In *Carnegie-Rochester Conference Series on Public Policy*, ed. Allan H. Meltzer and Charles I. Plosser, 267–308. Amsterdam: North-Holland.

von Furstenberg, George M., and Joseph P. Daniels. 1992. *Economic Summit Declarations, 1975–1989: Examining the Written Record of International Cooperation*. Princeton Studies in International Finance. Princeton, N.J.: International Finance Section, Department of Economics, Princeton University.

Walter, Barbara F. 1997. "The Critical Barrier to Civil War Settlement" *International Organization* 51: 335–64.

Walton, Richard E., Joel E. Cutcher-Gershenfeld, and Robert B. McKersie. 1994. *Strategic Negotiations: A Theory of Change in Labor-Management Relations*. Boston: Harvard Business School Press.

Walton, Richard E., and Robert B. McKersie. 1965. *A Behavioral Theory of Labor Negotiations: An Analysis of a Social Interaction System*. New York: McGraw-Hill.

Ward, Hugh. 1990. "Three Men in a Boat, Two Must Row: An Analysis of a Three-Person Chicken Pregame." *Journal of Conflict Resolution* 34: 371–400.

Webb, Michael C. 1991. "International Economic Structures, Government Interests, and International Coordination of Macroeconomic Adjustment Policies." *International Organization* 45: 309–42.

Weber, Steve. 1991. *Cooperation and Discord in U.S.-Soviet Arms Control*. Princeton: Princeton University Press.

———. 1994. "The Origins of the European Bank for Reconstruction and Development." *International Organization* 48: 1–38.

Weiner, Jarrod. 1995. *Making Rules in the Uruguay Round of the GATT*. Aldershot: Dartmouth.

Wilcox, Clair. 1949. *A Charter for World Trade*. New York: Macmillan.

Winham, Gilbert R. 1977. "Negotiation as a Management Process." *World Politics* 30: 87–114.

———. 1979. "The Mediation of Multilateral Negotiations." *Journal of World Trade Law* 13: 193–208.

———. 1980. "Robert Strauss, the MTN, and the Control of Faction." *Journal of World Trade Law* 14: 377–397.

———. 1986. *International Trade and the Tokyo Round Negotiation*. Princeton: Princeton University Press.

Wolf, Dieter, and Bernhard Zangl. 1996. "The European Economic and Monetary Union: 'Two-Level Games' and the Formation of International Institutions." *European Journal of International Relations* 2: 355–93.

Wriggins, W. Howard. 1976. "Up for Auction: Malta Bargains with Great Britain, 1971." In *The 50% Solution*, ed. I. William Zartman, 208–34. Garden City: Anchor Press/Doubleday.

Yannopoulos, G. N. 1988. *Customs Unions and Trade Conflicts: The Enlargement of the European Community*. London: Routledge.

Yarbrough, Beth V., and Robert M. Yarbrough. 1992. *Cooperation and Governance in International Trade: the Strategic Organizational Approach*. Princeton: Princeton University Press.

Yoffie, David B. 1983. *Power and Protectionism: Strategies of the Newly Industrializing Countries*. New York: Columbia University Press.

Young, Michael D., and Mark Schafer. 1998. "Is There Method in our Madness? Ways of Assessing Cognition in International Relations." *Mershon International Studies Review* 42: 63–96.

Young, Oran R. 1989. *International Cooperation: Building Regimes for Natural Resources and the Environment*. Ithaca: Cornell University Press.

———. 1991. "Political Leadership and Regime Formation: On the Development of Institutions in International Society." *International Organization* 45: 281–308.

———. 1994. *International Governance: Protecting the Environment in a Stateless Society*. Ithaca: Cornell University Press.

Zartman, I. William. 1971. *The Politics of Trade Negotiations Between Africa and the European Economic Community: the Weak Confront the Strong*. Princeton: Princeton University Press.

———, ed. 1987. *Positive Sum: Improving North-South Negotiations*. New Brunswick: Transaction Books.

———. 1989. "Prenegotiation: Phases and Functions." In *Getting to the Table: The Processes of International Prenegotiation*, ed. by Janice Gross Stein, 1–17. Baltimore: Johns Hopkins University Press.

———, ed. 1994. *International Multilateral Negotiation: Approaches to the Management of Complexity*. San Francisco: Jossey-Bass.

———, ed. 1995. *Elusive Peace: Negotiating an End to Civil Wars*. Washington, D.C.: Brookings Institution.

Zartman, I. William, and Antonella Bassani. 1988. *The Algerian Gas Negotiations*. Pew Case Studies in International Affairs, No. 103. Washington, D.C.: Foreign Policy Institute, Johns Hopkins University.

Zartman, I. William, and Maureen R. Berman. 1982. *The Practical Negotiator*. New Haven: Yale University Press.

Zeuthen, Frederick. 1930. *Problems of Monopoly and Economic Warfare*. London: Routledge.

Index

Cornell Studies in Political Economy

A Series Edited by

Peter J. Katzenstein